WRITING ETHNOGRAPHIC FIELDNOTES

SECOND EDITION

Chicago Guides
to *Writing*, **Editing**,
and Publishing

WRITING ETHNOGRAPHIC FIELDNOTES

SECOND EDITION

Robert M. Emerson

Rachel I. Fretz

Linda L. Shaw

THE UNIVERSITY OF CHICAGO PRESS • CHICAGO AND LONDON

ROBERT M. EMERSON is professor emeritus in the Department of Sociology at the University of California, Los Angeles. He is the author of *Contemporary Field Research: Perspectives and Formulations*, now in its second edition. RACHEL I. FRETZ is a lecturer in the Writing Programs unit at UCLA. LINDA L. SHAW is professor in and chair of the sociology department at California State University, San Marcos.

The University of Chicago Press, Chicago 60637
The University of Chicago Press, Ltd., London
© 1995, 2011 by The University of Chicago
All rights reserved. Published 2011.
Printed in the United States of America

20 19 18 17 16 15   4 5 6 7 8 9

ISBN-13: 978-0-226-20683-7 (paper)
ISBN-10: 0-226-20683-1 (paper)

Library of Congress Cataloging-in-Publication Data

Emerson, Robert M.
    Writing ethnographic fieldnotes / Robert M. Emerson, Rachel I. Fretz,
Linda L. Shaw. — 2nd ed.
        p. cm. — (Chicago guides to writing, editing, and publishing)
    ISBN-13: 978-0-226-20683-7 (pbk.: alk. paper)
    ISBN-10: 0-226-20683-1 (pbk.: alk. paper)
    1. Ethnology—Authorship. 2. Ethnology—Fieldwork. 3. Ethnology—
Research. 4. Academic writing. I. Fretz, Rachel I. II. Shaw, Linda L. III. Title.
GN307.7.E44 2011
808'.066305—dc22

                                                          2011016145

♾ This paper meets the requirements of ANSI/NISO Z39.48-1992
(Permanence of Paper).

To our friend and colleague,
Mel Pollner (1940–2007)

Contents

Preface to the Second Edition

Over the past twenty-five years or so, ethnography has become a widely recognized and generally accepted approach to qualitative social research. But ironically, in the years since the publication of the first edition of *Writing Ethnographic Fieldnotes* in 1995, the surge of interest in ethnographic writing we noted at that time seemingly has receded. Sociologists and anthropologists no longer take up the complexities of representation in ethnography as frequently as they did in the 1980s and 1990s; they offer fewer considerations of the nature and effects of writing in ethnographic research than in those decades, although these issues seem to remain lively concerns in community studies and writing programs. But the earlier concern with the processes of writing fieldnotes, as opposed to polished ethnographic articles and monographs, does appear to have made significant marks on the practice of ethnography: Some ethnographers now publish articles on key issues and processes in writing fieldnotes, including Warren (2000) and Wolfinger (2002). In addition, and probably more significantly, some ethnographic anthologies (e.g., Atkinson, Coffey, Delamont, Lofland, and Lofland's *Handbook of Ethnography*) and qualitative research guides (e.g., Lofland, Snow, Anderson, and Lofland, *Analyzing Social Settings*, fourth edition; Warren and Karner, *Discovering Qualitative Methods: Field Research, Interviews, and Analysis*, second edition) now provide extended discussions of how to produce and work with fieldnotes. These developments provide some indication that addressing policies and practices for writing fieldnotes is increasingly part of ethnographic training for many social scientists.

These developments provide part of the motivation for a second edition of *Writing Ethnographic Fieldnotes*. But our own experiences teaching ethnographic fieldwork to another generation of students played a much larger role in this decision. As we continued to work with both undergraduate and graduate students in fieldwork courses, we were struck again and again by the pivotal role that writing fieldnotes plays in introducing ethnography and in molding and deepening students' research experiences. And we remain intrigued by the varieties of writing issues that students have to grapple with and try to resolve in order to create lively, detailed, and accurate fieldnote depictions of the social worlds they are trying to comprehend.

Teaching in large part from *Writing Ethnographic Fieldnotes* had another effect: As the result of continuing student questions and confusion, we saw at close hand some of the limitations in parts of the book. These student reactions led us to make changes at a number of points in the text, although we have tried to retain as much continuity as possible with the first edition. In particular, we have substantially reorganized chapters 3 and 4 on strategies and tactics for writing fieldnotes to more closely mirror the sequencing of stages through which beginning ethnographers pass in learning to write fieldnotes. In these chapters, we deepened our discussion of point of view, in particular, focusing on the shifts between first and third person as well as showing the benefits of writing in focused third person. We also clarified the many ways that fieldnote writing is a kind of narrating, both in creating a loosely structured day's entry and in composing more cohesive fieldnote tales within those entries. We have made fewer and less drastic changes in the other chapters, although we have provided a fuller discussion of the issues of race, class, and gender as well as the relationship of fieldnotes and ethnography to broader social patterns and structures. Throughout, we have updated our references to reflect contributions to ethnographic practice since the publication of the first edition and included new student fieldnote excerpts that exemplify our concerns and recommendations.

In terms of the actual substance of these changes, in our teaching we now place strong emphasis on beginning analysis as early as possible. Developing theory from fieldnote and interview data is not an easy or straightforward process and should be started early enough to allow the fieldworker to look for, find, and write up observations that will advance such analysis. The new edition reflects these concerns: We now urge writing brief asides and more elaborate commentaries from day one in the field, one-paragraph summary commentaries at the end of each set of fieldnotes, and lengthier in-process memos within a matter of weeks. We continue to distinguish these forms of in-process analysis and analytic writing from the full-bore processes of coding and memo writing that best occur after a substantial amount of field data has been collected.

We want to acknowledge the help and support of a number of students from our courses who have contributed feedback on the first edition and/or fieldnotes that we have incorporated in this second edition. These students include Diego Avalos, Caitlin Bedsworth, Stefani Delli Quadri, Marie Eksian, Katie Falk, Christy Garcia, Graciella Gutierrez, Blaire Hammer, Brian Harris, Heidi Joya, Eric Kim, Jaeeun Kim, Norma Larios, Grace Lee, Nicole Lozano, Miles Scoggins, Sara Soell, and Jennifer Tabler.

We would also like to thank the following family, friends, and colleagues for their intellectual and personal support in this project: Bruce Beiderwell, Sharon Cullity, Amy Denissen, Sharon Elise, Shelley Feldman, Bob Garot, Jack Katz, Leslie Paik, Mary Roche, Garry Rolison, Bob Tajima, Erin von Hofe, and Carol Warren.

Preface to the First Edition

In recent years many ethnographers have emphasized the central place of *writing* in their craft. Geertz's (1973) characterization of "inscription" as the core of ethnographic "thick description" and Gusfield's (1976) dissection of the rhetorical underpinnings of science provided seminal statements in the 1970s. Subsequently, Clifford and Marcus's edited collection, *Writing Culture: The Poetics and Politics of Ethnography* (1986), Van Maanen's *Tales of the Field* (1988), and Atkinson's *The Ethnographic Imagination* (1990) have advanced consideration of ethnographic writing.

Yet examinations of ethnographic writing remain partial in scope: All begin with *already written* fieldnotes and move on to examine matters such as the rhetorical character of these fieldnotes or the more general structure of the whole, finished ethnographies built up from them. In so doing, they neglect a primal occasion of ethnographic writing—*writing fieldnotes*. Thus, they ignore a key issue in the making of ethnographies—understanding how an observer/researcher sits down and turns a piece of her lived experience into a bit of written text in the first place.

Indeed, most analyses of the "poetics of ethnography" (Clifford and Marcus 1986) take as their subject matter the polished accounts of social life provided in published monographs. But such finished texts incorporate and are built up out of these smaller, less coherent bits and pieces of writings—out of fieldnotes, many composed long before any comprehensive ethnographic overview has been developed. Moreover, fieldnotes in finished ethnographies are reordered and rewritten, selected and molded to some analytic purpose. They thus appear in very different forms and carry very different implications than the original corpus of fieldnotes that the ethnographer produced in the field. In these respects, writing fieldnotes, not writing polished ethnographies, lies at the core of constructing ethnographic texts.

On the practical methodological level, field researchers have similarly neglected issues of how to write fieldnotes. "How to do it" manuals of fieldwork provide reams of advice on how to manage access and relations with unknown others in different cultures and settings. But they offer only occasional, ad hoc commentary on how to take fieldnotes, what to take notes on, and so on.[1] Field researchers, in general, have not given close, systematic attention to how fieldnotes are written in particular projects. Nor have they considered how to effectively train fieldwork novices to write more sensitive, useful, and stimulating fieldnotes. Instead, fieldwork manuals direct practical advice toward how to work with existing fieldnotes in order to organize and write finished ethnographies. For example, Strauss (1987) and his coworkers (Strauss and Corbin 1990) provide detailed treatments of how to code notes and how to work with codings to produce finished ethnographies. But this focus on coding assumes that the ethnographer has completed writing a set of fieldnotes and now faces the task of analyzing, organizing, and making sense of them. These guides say nothing about how ethnographers wrote these fieldnotes in the first place or about how they might have written notes differently. Similarly, three practical guides to field research—Fetterman (1989), Richardson (1990), and Wolcott (1990)—devote primary attention to developing and writing finished ethnographic analyses in ways that presuppose the existence of a set of fieldnotes.

In the past few years, however, some ethnographers have begun to redress this problem, giving serious attention to the nature and uses of fieldnotes. In 1990, Sanjek's edited volume, *Fieldnotes: The Making of Anthropology*, brought together a collection of papers written in response to a symposium call "to examine what anthropologists do with fieldnotes, how they live with them, and how attitudes toward the construction and use of fieldnotes may change through individual professional careers" (Sanjek 1990b:xii). The collection includes an extended history of "fieldnote practice" in Western anthropology (Sanjek 1990d), as well as analyses of the research and personal uses and meanings of fieldnotes to anthropologists (Jackson 1990b; Sanjek 1990c; Ottenberg 1990), of fieldnotes as means of describing and representing cultures (Clifford 1990; Lederman 1990), and of reading and using others' fieldnotes (Lutkehaus 1990).

At the same time, Atkinson's *The Ethnographic Imagination* (1990) began to examine the textual properties of classic and contemporary sociological ethnography. Although he focuses on the rhetorical structure of completed ethnographies, Atkinson does call attention to the importance of analyzing fieldnotes. Emphasizing that at the moment "field notes remain private documents" unavailable for analysis, he urges the future importance of close study of "the stylistic features of field notes from particular authors or sociological schools" (1990:57) and takes an initial step in this direction by analyzing two fieldnote extracts originally published in Junker's *Field Work: An Introduction to the Social Sciences* (1960).

Several factors underlie this long-term, if perhaps now dissipating, neglect of ethnographic fieldnotes. To begin with, ethnographers are often uneasy or embarrassed about fieldnotes. Many seem to regard fieldnotes as a kind of backstage scribbling—a little bit dirty, a little bit suspect, not something to talk about too openly and specifically. Fieldnotes seem too revealingly personal, too messy and unfinished to be shown to any audience. For these and other reasons, scholars do not have ready access to original, unedited fieldnotes but only to completed ethnographies with the selected, reordered fieldnotes they contain. As a result, how ethnographers write fieldnotes remains largely hidden and mysterious.

In contrast, later stages of ethnographic writing, centered around producing finished ethnographic monographs, are more theoretically driven and less obviously personal. With a body of fieldnotes assembled, the ethnographer withdraws from the field to try to weave some of these strands into an ethnographic story. At this point, the ethnographer handles fieldnotes more impersonally as data—as objects to be studied, consulted, and reordered in developing a tale for other audiences. The issues and procedures that mark this phase of ethnographic writing—coding, developing an analytic focus, and so on—are closer to the finished, published product and, thus, more amenable to presentation to others.

Furthermore, field researchers show no consensus on what kinds of writing to term "fieldnotes," when and how fieldnotes should be written, and their value for ethnographic research. These diverse, and at times discordant views of the nature and value of fieldnotes, have stymied self-conscious consideration of how to write fieldnotes.

In the first place, field researchers may have a variety of different forms of written records in mind when they refer to "fieldnotes." A recent inventory (Sanjek 1990c) found that ethnographers talked about all of the following: "headnotes," "scratch notes," "fieldnotes proper," "fieldnote records," "texts," "journals and diaries," and "letters, reports, papers." Hence, there is wide variation in what ethnographers characterize as fieldnotes. Some field researchers, for example, consider fieldnotes to be writings that record both what they learn and observe about the activities of others and their own actions, questions, and reflections. Others insist on a sharp distinction between records of what others said and did—the "data" of fieldwork—and those notes incorporating their own thoughts and reactions. Yet deep differences also exist between those who emphasize this distinction between writings about others and writings about oneself: Some view only the former as fieldnotes and consider the latter as personal "journals" or "diaries"; others "*contrast* fieldnotes with data, speaking of fieldnotes as a record of one's reactions, a cryptic list of items to concentrate on, a preliminary stab at analysis, and so on" (Jackson 1990b:7).

Second, field researchers may write fieldnotes in very different ways. Many compose fieldnotes only as "a running log written at the end of each day" (Jackson 1990b:6). But others contrast such "fieldnotes proper" with "fieldnote records" that involve "information organized in sets separate from the sequential fieldwork notes" (Sanjek 1990c:101). Furthermore, some field researchers try to write elaborate notes as soon after witnessing relevant events as possible, typically sitting down to type up complete, detailed observations every evening. Others initially produce less detailed records, filling notebooks with handwritten notes to be elaborated and "finished" upon leaving the field. And still others postpone the bulk of writing until they have left the field and begun to grapple with writing a coherent ethnographic account.

Finally, ethnographers disagree about whether fieldnotes are a resource or barrier to understanding. While some see them as the core of the research enterprise, others suggest that they provide little more than crutches to help the field researcher deal with the stresses and anxieties of living in another world while trying to understand it from the outside. Indeed, some contend that fieldnotes stymie deeper understanding. As one anthropologist quoted by Jackson noted (1990b:13): "[Without notes there is] more chance to schematize, to order conceptually . . . free of niggling exceptions, grayish half-truths you find in your own data."

In sum, ethnographers have failed to closely examine the processes of writing fieldnotes. While this failure arises in part from differing views of what fieldnotes are, it also results from disagreements about the skills needed for ethnographic observation and writing and about how necessary skills can be acquired. At one extreme, many field researchers assume that almost any literate, adventurous person can simply go to the field and do fieldwork; technical skills, if any, can be learned on the spot in a "sink or swim" vein. At another extreme, others contend that ethnographic research, particularly writing fieldnotes, involves God-given talents and sensitivities that simply cannot be taught. Some argue, for example, that only those with the special abilities of an Erving Goffman can become insightful field researchers. Training is not an issue to those so innately skilled.

Still others seem to concede that aspects of field research should and can be learned, but they exclude writing fieldnotes from these teachable skills. They view fieldnotes as so deeply idiosyncratic and personal as to preclude formal instruction. Both what the fieldworker does with those under study and how she understands and recounts these events will vary from one person to another. Thus, different researchers write very different notes depending upon disciplinary orientation, theoretical interests, personality, mood, and stylistic commitments. Writing fieldnotes supposedly resists formal instruction because the sense and meanings of whatever ethnographers write draw upon "tacit knowledge" and direct experiences that are not explicitly included in the notes.

We reject both the "sink or swim" method of training ethnographers and the attitude that ethnography involves no special skills or no skills beyond those that a college-educated person possesses. We take the position that writing fieldnotes is not simply the product of innate sensibilities and insights but also involves skills learned and sharpened over time. Indeed, we maintain that ethnographers *need* to hone these skills and that the quality of ethnography will improve with self-conscious attention to how to write fieldnotes.

Furthermore, we contend that ethnographers can move beyond the impasse created by differing conceptions of fieldnotes by making explicit the assumptions and commitments they hold about the nature of ethnography as a set of practical research and writing activities. Such assumptions and commitments have direct implications for how to understand and write fieldnotes. If, for example, one sees ethnography as collecting information that can be "found" or "discovered" in much the same way by any researcher, one can reasonably separate the "findings" from the processes of making them and "data" from "personal reactions." Similarly, the sense that fieldnotes get in the way of intuitive understanding and deeper analytic insight reflects a theoretical commitment to grasping the "big picture" and to identifying broad patterns of activity rather than to tracking day-to-day routines and processes. This view, in turn, assumes that achieving these qualities can get lost beneath "too many facts" or "too much detail."

Thus, while universal guidelines for writing fieldnotes are quixotic, one can develop specific guidelines appropriate to a particular understanding of ethnographic research. In this book, we assume and draw upon an interactionist, interpretive understanding of ethnography that derives from the traditions of symbolic interaction and ethnomethodology in order to elaborate one approach to fieldnotes and to the processes of writing them. Clearly, we offer only one among many possible approaches; field researchers starting with more positivist commitments or informed by other traditions within ethnography would approach many of the issues and procedures we discuss very differently. Nonetheless, we expect that much of what we recommend will be useful and suggestive for anyone beginning to do field research and to write fieldnotes.

We pursue a further goal in this book: to demystify writing fieldnotes, giving explicit attention to the processes of transforming observation and experience into inspectable texts. To do so, it is critical to look at actual working, "unfinished" fieldnotes rather than at published, polished fieldnotes and to consider how such notes are composed, rewritten, and worked into finished texts. Thus, we focus on writing fieldnotes in its own right, considering a variety of technical, interactional, personal, and theoretical issues that arise with such writing. We also examine the processes and the practicalities of working with fieldnotes to write analytic memos and final ethnographic accounts for wider audiences.

Our goal is not only practical. We also want to bridge the gap that divides reflections on ethnographic texts from the actual practice of ethnography. By examining the practices actually used to write fieldnotes, we hope to advance understanding of the nature of ethnography in calling attention to the fundamental processes entailed in turning talk, observations, and experiences into written texts. It is misleading to try to grasp the transformation of experience into text by looking only at finished ethnographies and the fieldnotes they rely on. The problems and processes of writing initial, unpolished accounts of observations and experiences differ significantly from those involved in reviewing, selecting from, editing, and revising fieldnotes in order to produce a finished ethnography. Published fieldnotes are not only polished; they are also highly selected because they have to be tied to the specific themes used to construct the ethnography as a whole. In contrast, unfinished fieldnotes, written more or less contemporaneously with the events depicted, are not theoretically focused or integrated, not consistent in voice or purpose, or even always clear or stylistically compelling.

Our attention to issues of writing fieldnotes grew out of our own experiences in teaching field research to undergraduate and graduate students. In the early 1980s two of us—Robert Emerson and Linda Shaw—began teaching a UCLA undergraduate course on field research methods. Organized as a practicum focused on fieldnotes and the field experiences they depicted, the course insisted that all students go to a field setting and immediately begin to write fieldnotes about what they saw and heard. In addition to intensive small group discussions of students' notes, we devoted class time to examining a xeroxed page or two of students' "notes of the week"—excerpts selected to illustrate key issues in field relations, writing strategies, or theoretical focusing. Throughout the course, students posed endless questions about writing fieldnotes, beginning with such matters as "What do I write about?" and concluding with problems of "How do I write it all up in a final paper?" Emerson and Shaw increasingly sought the experience of faculty in the Writing Programs at UCLA for advice in these matters. They met with Rachel Fretz, a folklorist with extensive field experience in Africa. These consultations led to the decision to coordinate a course on writing ethnographic fieldnotes with the existing field research methods course.

This manuscript began to take shape while team teaching these courses as part of an Immersion Quarter program at UCLA in the mid-1980s. Students in this program participated in internships while enrolled in a cluster of three courses—field research methods, ethnographic writing, and a variable topic substantive course (mental illness; control of crime; gender, race, and ethnicity in schools). The field methods and writing courses were tightly integrated, with coordinated topic, readings, and field assignments. As instructors, we met regularly to discuss the problems and successes of our students. We pooled our experiences and problem-solved, giving one another ideas for better ways to work with students as they learned to subject real world experience to sociological analysis. The ideas that comprise the core of the manuscript developed early on as a result of these meetings and their collective processes.

Junker's *Field Work: An Introduction to the Social Sciences* (1960) provided a model for assembling and presenting our materials. *Field Work* resulted from a collection of materials, "Cases on Field Work," created at the University of Chicago in a project organized by Everett C. Hughes to conduct "field work on field work" (Hughes 1960:v). This project involved "putting together what we had learned from [having taught methods to] several hundred students about the learning and doing of field work" (vii). Similarly, in order to illustrate useful practices and alternate possibilities for writing fieldnotes, we saturate the chapters that follow with "raw" fieldnotes.

We rely heavily upon fieldnotes and ethnographic extracts written by both undergraduate and graduate students who have taken our courses on field research and ethnographic writing at UCLA, California State University, San Marcos, and Cornell University. Some might object to the use of student fieldnotes on the grounds that these are not the writings of professionally trained researchers. In part, our preference for student notes reflects the way we began to develop this book—by reading and commenting upon such writings, clarifying and articulating what impressed us as effective, exciting notes, and collecting examples of particular issues for teaching purposes. But in addition, we desire to demystify fieldnotes, an end better achieved by showing what can be done by students like those who will read and use this book. And finally, every quarter we found ourselves impressed by the quality, excitement, and freshness of the fieldnote accounts our students provided on ordinary and exceptional events in a variety of social settings.

In addition to student fieldnotes, we also draw examples from our own unpublished fieldnotes, which were compiled during a number of different research projects. These projects include Robert Emerson's study of litigants applying for domestic violence restraining orders, carried out in the late 1980s and early 1990s;[2] Rachel Fretz's ethnographic fieldwork on storytelling among the Chokwe in Zaire in 1976, 1977, 1982, and 1983 and in Zambia in 1992–93;[3] and field research carried out in a psychiatric facility for ex-mental patients by Linda Shaw in the early 1980s.

We address issues of writing fieldnotes for two general audiences. One audience includes those concerned with ethnography and field research primarily for academic research purposes. Here, we seek to develop practical guidelines for writing fieldnotes that will prove helpful to both undergraduate and graduate students in several academic disciplines. These disciplines include sociology, anthropology, folklore, oral history, education, and ethnomusicology, in which field research and ethnographic methods have a prominent place; and disciplines such as political science, business administration, communication, composition studies, social welfare, and public health, in which ethnography and field research may be offered as secondary methodological options.

But in this book, we also address audiences who commonly recognize few links with ethnography—those committed to experiential education and service learning. In promoting learning through doing, experiential education places students in community service settings or in internships in some institutional setting. In these placements, students confront practical challenges in carrying out real world activities; the task is then to relate these experiences to traditional academic concerns.

To this point, the key to this integration has been the critical incident journal (Batchelder and Warner 1977). But service learning journals encourage writing about the students' perceptions and feelings more than about what others are doing and saying. Such journals often do not encourage students to write at length or in real detail about their observations. They tend to be "crisis focused," attending to the dramatic and remarkable rather than to the everyday and routine; therefore, they lead to very general accounts or to decontextualized accounts of "critical incidents" that inhibit reflection and in-depth understanding of daily processes.

We maintain that writing ethnographic fieldnotes, rather than journal entries, promises to strengthen and deepen the integration of experience with classroom knowledge. Writing fieldnotes would encourage experiential education students to observe more finely and systematically, to consider both the mundane and the dramatic, and to attend to others' activities and concerns as closely as their own. Furthermore, systematic, contemporaneously written fieldnotes provide a means for capturing the distinct phases or stages of an intern's adaptation to a particular setting. Such fieldnotes allow close documentation of the explicit and implicit instruction given to interns about what things are important and how things should be done. Such instructions are a major mechanism by which newcomers are socialized to any particular setting; instructions reveal both the working skills and knowledge and also the actual priorities, assumptions, and commitments of those in the setting.

Obviously, points of strain will remain between the practice of ethnographic field research and experiential education. For example, writing extensive fieldnotes might require more commitment to research than is common to many experiential education students who are often motivated—at least initially—by a desire to serve others or to assess the attractions of a particular career. Yet, a persuasive case can be made to those who hold such priorities that ethnography can contribute a deeper understanding of the personal, work, and organizational processes likely to be encountered. Thus, the approach to ethnographic participation and writing developed here opens up much common ground between two traditions that have long gone their separate ways; it does so by providing a means to convert experiences into textual forms that can be brought back into the classroom and closely examined for their bearing on broader issues of social and intellectual life (cf. Bleich 1993).

We have set ourselves a very specific task in this book: to examine the different processes of writing involved in producing and using ethnographic fieldnotes. Hence, we do not intend this book to stand on its own as an introduction to the practice of ethnographic field research. In particular, we do not treat in any detail either the deeper theoretical groundings of ethnography or the intricacies and dilemmas of actually carrying out a fieldwork project. Rather, we complement existing overviews of the premises and procedures of ethnographic inquiry[4] by looking specifically at key practical issues involved in writing and using fieldnotes. We do consider, moreover, how writing fieldnotes is inextricably intertwined with methodological and theoretical commitments.

The chapters that follow are organized in ways that reflect our dual concerns with learning to write ethnographic fieldnotes and with understanding the relevance of these practices for ethnographic research more broadly. We use as our point of departure the experience and practice of students actually learning to write fieldnotes rather than an idealized or prescriptive version of how fieldnotes "ought to be written." After an overview of the nature and place of fieldnotes in ethnographic research, successive chapters address step-by-step processes and practices for writing and working with fieldnotes. Each chapter concludes with "Reflections" on the implications of the practices and processes we have been examining for more general issues of ethnographic theory and method.

Substantively, we begin in chapter 1 by considering the centrality of writing fieldnotes to ethnographic research and by specifying the assumptions and commitments that underlie our approach. Chapter 2 examines the distinctive stance of the ethnographer—that of participating in and observing the ongoing life of a natural setting in order to produce written accounts of events observed there; it then considers issues of jotting phrases or notes while in the setting. Chapter 3 explores procedures for writing up fieldnotes, either from memory or from previous jottings. Chapter 4 discusses various writing strategies for envisioning scenes on a page, for describing observed events, for organizing extended descriptions, and for writing in-process analytic ideas about these scenes. In chapter 5, we address ways of writing notes and developing analyses that effectively capture and convey what events mean to participants. Chapter 6 turns to working with lengthy sets of "completed" fieldnotes, considering how to read, sort, and code notes and how to begin analysis. Chapter 7 considers the ethnographer's choices about how to organize and write more polished, coherent ethnographies for wider audiences. Finally, in chapter 8, we reflect on the need in ethnographic writing to balance often contradictory requirements and concerns—loyalties to those studied with obligations to future readers, self-conscious reflection with getting accounts written down on paper, and sensitivity to indigenous meanings with analytic relevance.

We wish to acknowledge our gratitude to the Field Studies Program at UCLA for encouraging and supporting the Immersion Quarter program from which this book emerged. We owe special thanks in this regard to Jane Permaul, Rob Shumer, and Parvin Kassaie. We also wish to thank the following colleagues for comments and suggestions on this manuscript: Timothy Diamond, Dianne Dugaw, Shelley Feldman, Jan Frodesen, George Gadda, Dwight Giles, Claudia Ingram, Michael O. Jones, Jack Katz, Susan McCoin, Anita McCormick, Melvin Pollner, Anita Pomerantz, Amanda Powell, Judith Richlin-Klonsky, Mike Rose, Ruth M. Stone, Carol Warren, Randy Woodland, and two anonymous reviewers for the University of Chicago Press. And we wish to thank our copyeditor, Richard Allen, who promised he would "give us a hard time" and who did so in ways that pushed us to clarify our concerns and specify our arguments.

Finally, we wish the thank the following students from our field research courses who have generously given us permission to use their fieldnote and ethnographic writings as exemplars and illustrations: Karin Abell, Teri Anderson, Jim Angell, Erin Artigiani, Ben Beit-Zuri, Nancy S. Blum, Paul Brownfield, Jennifer Cheroske, Rebecca Clements, Cabonia Crawford, John Cross, Maria Estrada, Julie Finney, Robert Garot, Mauricio A. Gormaz, Heather W. Guthrie, David Hillyard, Suzanne Hirsch, Ronald X. Kovach, Shawn Lemone, Wendy Lin, Storm Lydon, Francisco "Chuck" Martinez, Martha Moyes, Deanna Nitta, Phil Okamoto, Blair Paley, Kristin Rains, Lisa Ravitch, Joanna Saporito, Kristin D. Schaefer, Joe Scheuermann, Cliff Spangler, Lakshmi Srinivas, Martha Stokes, Kathryn L. Tatar, Laura Miles Vahle, Linda Van Leuven, Karina Walters, David Whelan, Nicholas H. Wolfinger, and Terri Young. We especially thank Lisa Holmes and Martha Millison, not only for allowing us to use excerpts from their fieldnotes, but also for providing a "student response" after reading an earlier draft of the manuscript.

1

Fieldnotes in Ethnographic Research

Ethnographic field research involves the study of groups and people as they go about their everyday lives. Carrying out such research involves two distinct activities. First, the ethnographer enters into a social setting and gets to know the people involved in it; usually, the setting is not previously known in an intimate way. The ethnographer participates in the daily routines of this setting, develops ongoing relations with the people in it, and observes all the while what is going on. Indeed, the term "participant observation" is often used to characterize this basic research approach. But, second, the ethnographer writes down in regular, systematic ways what she observes and learns while participating in the daily rounds of the lives of others. In so doing, the researcher creates an accumulating written record of these observations and experiences. These two interconnected activities comprise the core of ethnographic research: firsthand participation in some initially unfamiliar social world and the production of written accounts of that world that draw upon such participation.

However, ethnographers differ in how they see the primary benefits of participant observation and in how they go about representing in written form what they have seen and experienced in the field. How we understand and present processes of writing and analyzing ethnographic fieldnotes in this and subsequent chapters reflects our distinctive theoretical orientations to these differences. Here, we want to present briefly our core theoretical assumptions and commitments; we will further specify and elaborate these assumptions and commitments as we address the processes of writing and analyzing fieldnotes in subsequent chapters.

We approach ethnography as a way to understand and describe social worlds, drawing upon the theoretical traditions of symbolic interaction and ethnomethodology. Common to both these traditions is the view that social worlds are interpreted worlds: "Social reality is an interpreted world, not a literal world, always under symbolic construction" (Altheide and Johnson 1994:489). These social worlds also are created and sustained in and through interaction with others, when interpretations of meanings are central processes. Symbolic interaction, insisting "that human action takes place always in a situation that confronts the actor and that the actor acts on the basis of *defining this situation* that confronts him" (Blumer 1997:4), focuses on "the activities of people in face-to-face relations" as these affect and relate to definitions of the situation (Rock 2001:26). The result is a distinctive concern with *process*, with sequences of interaction and interpretation that render meanings and outcomes both unpredictable and emergent. Ethnomethodology, inspired, in part, by Schutz's (1962, 1964) analyses of the taken-for-granted meanings and assumptions that make interaction possible, can be understood as proposing, in effect, "that society consists of the ceaseless, ever-unfolding transactions through which members engage one another and the objects, topics, and concerns that they find relevant" (Pollner and Emerson 2001:120). Such transactions depend and draw upon a number of "generic processes and practices," including unarticulated "background understandings," a variety of distinctive "interpretive practices," and members' processes of "practical reasoning" (Pollner and Emerson 2001:122). These general emphases on interpretation and interaction, on the social construction and understandings of meaning in different groups and situations, underlie our approaches to ethnographic participation, description and inscription, and the specific implications we draw from these processes for writing fieldnotes.[1]

ETHNOGRAPHIC PARTICIPATION

Ethnographers are committed to going out and getting close to the activities and everyday experiences of other people. "Getting close" minimally requires physical and social proximity to the daily rounds of people's lives and activities; the field researcher must be able to take up positions in the midst of the key sites and scenes of others' lives in order to observe and understand them. But given our emphasis on interpretation, getting close has another, far more significant, component: The ethnographer seeks a deeper *immersion* in others' worlds in order to grasp what they experience as meaningful and important. With immersion, the field researcher sees from the inside how people lead their lives, how they carry out their daily rounds of activities, what they find meaningful, and how they do so. In this way, immersion gives the fieldworker access to the fluidity of others' lives and enhances his sensitivity to interaction and process.

Furthermore, immersion enables the fieldworker to directly and forcibly experience for herself both the ordinary routines and conditions under which people conduct their lives and the constraints and pressures to which such living is subject. Goffman (1989:125), in particular, insists that field research involves "subjecting yourself, your own body and your own personality, and your own social situation, to the set of contingencies that play upon a set of individuals, so that you can physically and ecologically penetrate their circle of response to their social situation, or their work situation, or their ethnic situation." Immersion in ethnographic research, then, involves both being with other people to see how they respond to events as they happen and experiencing for oneself these events and the circumstances that give rise to them.

Clearly, ethnographic immersion precludes conducting field research as a detached, passive observer; the field researcher can only get close to the lives of those studied by actively participating in their day-to-day affairs. Such participation, moreover, inevitably entails some degree of *resocialization*. Sharing everyday life with a group of people, the field researcher comes "to enter into the matrix of meanings of the researched, to participate in their system of organized activities, and to feel subject to their code of moral regulation" (Wax 1980:272–73). In participating as fully and humanly as possible in another way of life, the ethnographer learns what is required to become a member of that world and to experience events and meanings in ways that approximate *members' experiences*.[2] Indeed, some ethnographers seek to do field research by doing and becoming—to the extent possible—whatever it is they are interested in learning about. Ethnographers, for example, have become skilled at activities they are seeking to understand (Diamond 1992; Lynch 1985; Wacquant 2004) or, in good faith, have joined churches or religious groups (Jules-Rosette 1975; Rochford 1985) on the grounds that by becoming members, they gain fuller insight and understanding into these groups and their activities. Or, villagers might assign an ethnographer a role, such as sister or mother, in an extended family, which obligates her to participate and resocialize herself to meet local expectations.

In learning about others through active participation in their lives and activities, the fieldworker cannot and should not attempt to be a fly on the wall.[3] No field researcher can be a completely neutral, detached observer who is outside and independent of the observed phenomena (Emerson and Pollner 2001). Rather, as the ethnographer engages in the lives and concerns of those studied, his perspective "is intertwined with the phenomenon which does not have objective characteristics independent of the observer's perspective and methods" (Mishler 1979:10). But, the ethnographer cannot take in everything; rather, he will, in conjunction with those in the setting, develop certain perspectives by engaging in some activities and relationships rather than others. Moreover, often relationships with those under study follow political fault lines in the setting, exposing the ethnographer selectively to varying priorities and points of view. As a result, the task of the ethnographer is not to determine "the truth" but to reveal the multiple truths apparent in others' lives.[4]

Furthermore, the ethnographer's presence in a setting inevitably has implications and consequences for what is taking place, since the fieldworker must necessarily interact with and, hence, have some impact on those studied.[5] But "consequential presence," often linked to *reactive effects* (that is, the effects of the ethnographer's participation on how members may talk and behave), should not be seen as "contaminating" what is observed and learned. Rather, these effects might provide the very source of that learning and observation (Clarke 1975:99). Relationships between the field researcher and people in the setting do not so much disrupt or alter ongoing patterns of social interaction as they reveal the terms and bases on which people form social ties in the first place. For example, in a village where social relations depend heavily on kinship ties, people might adopt a fieldworker into a family and assign her a kinship term that then designates her rights and responsibilities toward others. Hence, rather than detracting from what the fieldworker can learn, firsthand relations with those studied might provide clues to understanding the more subtle, implicit underlying assumptions that are often not readily accessible through observation or interview methods alone.[6] Consequently, rather than viewing reactivity as a defect to be carefully controlled or eliminated, the ethnographer needs to become sensitive to, and perceptive about, how she is seen and treated by others.

To appreciate the unavoidable consequences of one's own presence strips any special merit from the highly detached, "unobtrusive," and marginal observer roles that have long held sway as the implicit ideal in field research. Many contemporary ethnographers assume highly participatory roles (Adler and Adler 1987) in which the researcher actually performs the activities that are central to the lives of those studied. In this view, assuming real responsibility for actually carrying out core functions and tasks, as in service learning internships, provides special opportunities to get close to, participate in, and experience life in previously unknown settings. The intern with real work responsibilities or the researcher participating in village life actively engages in local activities and is socialized to, and acquires empathy for, local ways of acting and feeling.

Close, continuing participation in the lives of others encourages appreciation of social life as constituted by ongoing, fluid processes of interaction and interpretation. Through participation, the field researcher sees firsthand and up close how people grapple with uncertainty and ambiguity, how meanings emerge through talk and collective action, how understandings and interpretations change over time, and how these changes shape subsequent actions. In all these ways, the fieldworker's closeness to others' daily lives and activities heightens sensitivity to social life as process.

Yet, even with intensive participation, the ethnographer never becomes a member in the same sense that those who are "naturally" in the setting are members. The fieldworker plans on leaving the setting after a relatively brief stay, and his experience of local life is colored by this transience. As a result, "the participation that the fieldworker gives is neither as committed nor as constrained as the native's" (Karp and Kendall 1982:257). Furthermore, the fieldworker orients to many local events, not as "real life" but, rather, as objects of possible research interest and as events that he may choose to write down and preserve in fieldnotes. In these ways, research and writing commitments qualify ethnographic immersion, making the field researcher at least something of an outsider and, at an extreme, a cultural alien.[7]

THE COMPLEXITIES OF DESCRIPTION

In writing about one's experiences and observations deriving from intense and involved participation, the ethnographer creates *descriptive* fieldnotes. But writing descriptive accounts of experiences and observations is not simply a process of accurately capturing as closely as possible observed reality, of "putting into words" overheard talk and witnessed activities. To view the writing of descriptions as essentially a matter of producing texts that *correspond* accurately to what has been observed is to assume that there is but one "best" description of any particular event. But, in fact, there is no one "natural" or "correct" way to write about what one observes. Rather, because descriptions involve issues of perception and interpretation, different descriptions of similar or even the same situations and events are both possible and valuable.

Consider, for example, the following descriptions of express checkout lines in three Los Angeles supermarkets, each written by a different student researcher. These descriptions share a number of common features: all describe events from the point of view of shoppers/observers moving through express checkout lines; all provide physical descriptions of the checkout counter and players in the lines—checkers, baggers, other shoppers—and of at least some of the grocery items being handled; and all attend closely to some minute details of behavior in express lines. Yet, each of these descriptions is written from a different point of view; each shapes and presents what happens on the express line in different ways. In part, differences arise because the researchers observed different people and occasions; but differences also reflect both distinctive orientations and positionings taken by the observers, different ways of presenting the observer's self in "writing the other" (Warren 2000), and different writing choices in creating and framing different kinds of "stories" in representing what they observed happening.

Mayfair Market Express Line

There were four people in line with their purchases separated by an approx. 18" rectangular black rubber bar. I put my frozen bags down on the "lazy susan linoleum conveyor belt," and I reached on top of the cash register to retrieve one of the black bars to separate my items. The cashier was in her mid thirties, approx., about 5'2" dark skinned woman with curly dark brown hair. I couldn't hear what she as saying but recognized some accent in her speech. She was in a white blouse, short sleeved, with a maroon shoulder to mid thigh apron. She had a loose maroon bow tie, not like a man's bow tie, more hangie and fluffy. Her name tag on her left chest side had red writing that said "Candy" on it.

[Describes the woman and three men in front of her in line.] . . . Candy spent very little time with each person, she gave all a hello and then told them the amount, money was offered, and change was handed back onto a shelf that was in front of the customer whose turn it was. Before Candy had given the dark-haired woman her change back, I noticed that the man in the pink shirt had moved into her spatial "customer" territory, probably within a foot of her, and in the position that the others had taken when it was their turn in front of the "check writing" shelf (I thought it was interesting that the people seemed more concerned about the proper separation of their food from another's than they did about body location).

This account gives a central place to the cashier, first providing a description of her physical appearance and apparel, then offering a summary of her procedure for handling customers. It also focuses on the close sequencing of purchase encounters, noting that the pink-shirted man has moved into position to be the "next served"—within a foot of the woman in front of him—even before she had received her change. Indeed, this description highlights *spatial* aspects of the grocery line, contrasting in an aside the care taken to separate grocery items and the seeming disregard of personal space as one shopper moves in to succeed an about-to-depart one.

In contrast, in the following excerpt, the observer focuses on her own position and experience in line, highlighting her own social and interactional concerns in relating to those immediately in front of and behind her.

Ralph's Express Line, Easter Morning

I headed east to the checkout stands with my romaine lettuce to garnish the rice salad I was bringing to brunch and my bottle of Gewürztraminer, my new favorite wine, which I had to chill in the next half hour. As I approached the stands, I realized that the 10-items-or-less-cash-only line would be my best choice. I noticed that Boland was behind the counter at the register—he's always very friendly to me—"Hey, how you doing?"

I got behind the woman who was already [in the ten-items-or-less line]. She had left one of the rubber separator bars behind the things she was going to buy, one of the few personal friendly moves one can make in this highly routinized queue. I appreciated this, and would have thanked her (by smiling, probably), but she was already looking ahead, I suppose, in anticipation of checking out. I put my wine and lettuce down. There was already someone behind me. I wanted to show them the courtesy of putting down a rubber separator bar for them too. I waited until the food in front of mine was moved up enough for me to take the bar, which was at the front of the place where the bars are (is there a word for that? bar bin?), so that I wouldn't have to make a large, expansive move across the items that weren't mine, drawing attention to myself. I waited, and then, finally, the bar was in sight. I took it and then put it behind my items, looking at the woman behind me and smiling at her as I did so. She looked pleased and a bit surprised, and I was glad to have been able to do this small favor. She was a pretty blonde woman, and was buying a bottle of champagne (maybe also for Easter brunch?). She was wearing what looked like an Easter dress—it was cotton and pretty and flowery. She looked youngish, maybe about my age. She was quite tall for a woman, maybe 5'10" or so.

This observer describes on a moment-by-moment basis placing her groceries on the checkout counter and signaling their separation from those of the person in front of her and then from those of the person behind her. This style of description highlights her own thoughts and feelings as she engages in these routine activities; thus, while she treats space as an issue, she does so by noting its implications for self and feelings (e.g., avoiding "a large expansive move across the items that weren't mine").

In the third excerpt, the writer shifts focus from self to others, highlighting the actions of one particularly outgoing character that transforms the express line into a minicommunity:

Boy's Market Express Line

. . . I picked a long line. Even though the store was quiet, the express line was long. A lot of people had made small purchases today. I was behind a man with just a loaf of bread. There was a cart to the side of him, just sitting there, and I thought someone abandoned it (it had a few items in it). A minute later a man came up and "claimed" it by taking hold of it. He didn't really try to assert that he was back in line—apparently he'd stepped away to get something he'd forgotten—but he wasn't getting behind me either. I felt the need to ask him if he was on line, so I wouldn't cut him off. He said yes, and I tried to move behind him—we were sort of side by side—and he said, "That's okay. I know where you are."

At this point the guy who I'd spoken to earlier, the guy who was right in front of me, showed a look of surprise and moved past me, over to an abandoned cart at the end of the aisle. He was looking at what was in it, picking up the few items with interest and then put them back. I thought he'd seen something else he wanted or had forgotten. He came back over to his cart, but then a supermarket employee walked by, and he called out to the man, walking over to the cart and pointing at it, "Do you get many items like this left behind?" The employee hesitated, not seeming to understand the question, and said no. The guy on line said, "See what's here? This is formula (cans of baby formula). That's poor people's food. And see this (a copper pot scrubber)? They use that to smoke crack." The employee looked surprised. The guy says, "I was just wondering. That's very indicative of this area." The employee: "I live here, and I didn't know that." The guy: "Didn't you watch Channel 28 last night?" Employee: "No." Guy: "They had a report about inner-city problems." Employee, walking away as he talks: "I only watch National Geographic, the MacNeil-Lehrer Hour, and NPR." He continues away. . . .

Meanwhile the man with the bread has paid. As he waits momentarily for his change, the "guy" says, "Long wait for a loaf of bread." Man says, "Yeah," and then adds, jokingly (and looking at the cashier as he says it, as if to gauge his reaction), "these cashiers are slow." The cashier does not appear to hear this. Man with bread leaves, guy in front of me is being checked out now. He says to the cashier, "What's the matter, end of your shift? No sense of humor left?" Cashier says, "No. I'm tired." Guy: "I hear you." Guy then says to the bagger: "Can I have paper and plastic please, Jacob" (he emphasizes the use of the bagger's name)? Jacob complies, but shows no other sign that he's heard the man. Guy is waiting for transaction to be completed. He's sitting on the railing, and he is singing the words to the Muzak tune that's playing, something by Peabo Bryson. Guy's transaction is done. He says thank you to the bagger, and the bagger tells him to have a good day.

In these notes, the observer picks up on and accents the informal talk among customers waiting in the line. He spotlights one particularly outgoing character who comments to a store employee on the meaning of an abandoned shopping cart, expresses sympathy to the man in front of him for having to wait so long just to buy a loaf of bread (a move that this customer, in turn, uses to make a direct but careful criticism of the cashier's speed), and then chats with the cashier. He represents this express line as a place of ongoing exchanges between those in line, which draw in a passing store employee and culminate in interactions between this character and the checker and the bagger.

Writing fieldnote descriptions, then, is not a matter of passively copying down "facts" about "what happened." Rather, these descriptive accounts select and emphasize different features and actions while ignoring and marginalizing others. Some fieldworkers habitually attend to aspects of people and situations that others do not, closely describing dress, or hair, or demeanor, or speech hesitations that others ignore or recount in less detail. In this way, descriptions differ in what their creators note and write down as "significant," and, more implicitly, in what they note but ignore as "not significant" and in what other possibly significant things they may have missed altogether. But differences between fieldnote descriptions result not simply from different ways of selecting or filtering observed and experienced events; different fieldnote accounts also invoke and rely on different *lenses* to interpret, frame, and represent these matters. Descriptive fieldnotes, in this sense, are products of active processes of interpretation and sense-making that frame or structure not only what is written but also how it is written. Description, then, relies on interpretive/constructive processes that can give different fieldnotes distinctive shapes and feel.

Inevitably, then, *fieldnote descriptions of even the "same event," let alone the same kind of event, will differ, depending upon the choices, positioning, personal sensitivities, and interactional concerns of the* observers. By way of example, consider the following fieldnote accounts of initial portions of an intake interview with a client named Emily, a Ugandan woman with a seven-year-old child, who sought a restraining order against her husband, written by two student interns who were working together in a domestic violence legal aid clinic helping people fill out applications for temporary restraining orders.[8] In this interview, the first intern elicited and entered on a computer form a court-required narrative "declaration" detailing a recent "specific incident of abuse"; the second acted as a novice/observer sitting beside and providing emotional support to the client.

CB's Account

[Paul, a more experienced staff member, tells Emily:] You indicated on your intake form that the most recent abuse was on April 1. Why don't you tell Caitlin what happened on that day? Emily says, He says I owe him money for our marriage, that my family never paid the dowry. Paul presses, but what happened on this day? He called me "bitch," she says, and "whore." I type these two words. She continues, he had a bottle in his hand and was trying to hit me, but my brother and his friend grabbed his arm and took the bottle from him. As she says this, she raises her arm up as if there is a bottle in it, and then acts out the part of her husband by raising her arms up and flailing them. I ask, a glass bottle or a plastic bottle? Emily stutters, "G-g-glass." (It seems like she has to think back to the incident to remember more clearly.) I write, "RP [respondent] was trying to strike me with a glass bottle, but my brother grabbed hold of his arm and took the bottle away."

Emily continues, they took him away in a car and locked me in the house. Paul asks, what provoked this incident? Emily says, I told him I don't want marriage anymore, and he go berserk. Paul clarifies, so you told him you did not want the marriage to continue, and that made him angry? Emily agrees. She says that she went to the police two days later, and they gave her an emergency protective order, which Paul asks to see. He looks at it with squinted eyes (the paper does not look like what we usually see), and all of a sudden, they open up again. You were in Uganda at this time? he asks. Yes, Emily replies. Our families were together to try to make good our marriage.

NL's Account

We are ready for the declaration. Caitlin asks E how long she has been married to RP. We were together for 9 years, she says in a low voice, but married for 4. Caitlin then asks her to tell us about her most recent incident of abuse which according to the paperwork she filled out occurred on April 1st. He tried to hit me she said. Paul then says, right with a bottle like you told me outside. What happened? Her voice gets loud again as she says that her family thought that she and RP should talk about their marriage at their house (at this point I am thinking that she is talking about her house in California). Paul asks, whose family and friends were there? Were they yours, his, or both? She quickly responds, His friends. Paul asks, so your friends weren't there. She pauses for a brief second and says my friends. Paul asks, so both your friends were there? She nods. Looking at Caitlin, then back at Paul, she tells us that RP got angry when she asked for a divorce. He tried to hit her with a glass bottle. She grabs my arm and looks straight at me as she tells me that "brothers" grab his arms, hold him down, and take him away in his car. "Whose brother?" asks Paul. She says that it was her brother and his friend. They locked me in the house so that RP wouldn't hurt me, she says as she gently grabs my hand once more.

She pulls out a form from her pile of papers, and looks at it, saying that the police gave it to her two days later. What is it? Paul asks. She looks at it for a few seconds, and I look at it from over her shoulder. I look back at Paul and ask him if it is an emergency protective order. She looks up and says, Yes that's what it is! A—A—She motions her hand in my direction as she tries to find the word that I had said. Paul looks at it and says that it is like a Ugandan equivalent to an emergency protective order (now I understand that this incident occurred in Uganda).

These excerpts include many common features. Both accounts make clear that the incident arose from family differences over the client's marriage, that she reported her husband as trying to hit her with a glass bottle, that her brother and a friend restrained him from doing so, and that she went to the police and obtained an emergency protective order. In addition, both accounts reveal that staff had initially assumed that these events took place in California but changed their interpretation upon realizing the police restraining order had been issued in Uganda.

But the descriptions also differ on a number of counts. First, there are differences in the substance of what gets included in each account. For example, CB reports Emily's complaint that "he called me 'bitch' and 'whore'" and that this incident was provoked when "I told him I don't want marriage anymore, and he go berserk." While NL mentions neither of these incidents, she reports that the husband was restrained and taken away by both her brother and his friend and that she was locked in the house to protect her from her enraged husband. Second, there are differences in detail and meaning in what is reported about specific topics. For example, CB indirectly quotes Emily as saying, "He says I owe him money for our marriage, that my family never paid the dowry"; NL does not indicate this specific complaint but, rather, indirectly quotes Emily as saying, "Her family thought that she and RP should talk about their marriage at their house." Third, the accounts reflect different decisions about whether to simply report what was determined to be a "fact" or a specific "outcome" or to detail the processes of questioning and answering through which that "fact" or "outcome" was decided. CB, for example, highlights the specific moment of understanding by reporting Paul's question about the emergency protection order, "You were in Uganda at the time?" NL, in contrast, recounts this process in detail, describing the client and her own initial uncertainty about just what this piece of paper is, a similar query from Paul ("what is it?"), his conclusion that "it is like a Ugandan equivalent to an emergency protective order," and her own realization that this whole incident "occurred in Uganda."

While many descriptive writing choices are conscious and deliberate, others reflect more subtle, implicit processes of researcher involvement in, and orientation to, ongoing scenes and interaction. Here, CB was responsible for turning the client's words into a legally adequate account for purposes of the declaration; her descriptions show an orientation toward content and narrative coherence, and she notes at several points her decisions about what to enter on the computer ("bitch," "whore"; "RP was trying to strike me with a glass bottle, but my brother grabbed hold of his arm and took the bottle away"). NL, in contrast, had no formal responsibilities for conducting the interview and becomes involved as a sympathetic supporter; her notes seem attuned the client's emotions ("low voice") and bodily movements (handling the emergency protection paper), and she reports two particularly stressful moments in the interaction when the client "gently grabs" her arm or hand. While both researchers were present at the "same event," each participated in a different fashion, and these different modes of involvement lead to subtle, but significant, differences in how they wrote about what occurred.

INSCRIBING EXPERIENCED/OBSERVED REALITIES

Descriptive fieldnotes, then, involve *inscriptions* of social life and social discourse. Such inscriptions inevitably *reduce* the welter and confusion of the social world to written words that can be reviewed, studied, and thought about time and time again. As Geertz (1973:19) has characterized this core ethnographic process: "The ethnographer 'inscribes' social discourse; *he writes it down*. In so doing, he turns it from a passing event, which exists only in its own moment of occurrence, into an account, which exists in its inscriptions and can be reconsulted."

As inscriptions, fieldnotes are products of, and reflect conventions for, *transforming* witnessed events, persons, and places into words on paper.

In part, this transformation involves inevitable processes of *selection;* the ethnographer writes about certain things and thereby necessarily "leaves out" others. But more significantly, descriptive fieldnotes also inevitably *present or frame* events in particular ways, "missing" other ways that such events might have been presented or framed. And these presentations reflect and incorporate sensitivities, meanings, and understandings the field researcher has gleaned from having been close to and participated in the described events.

There are other ways of reducing social discourse to written form. Survey questionnaires, for example, record "responses" to prefixed questions, often reducing these lived experiences to numbers, sometimes preserving something of the respondents' own words. Audio and video recordings, which seemingly catch and preserve almost everything occurring within an interaction, actually capture but a slice of ongoing social life. This means that what is recorded in the first place depends upon when, where, and how the equipment is positioned and activated, what it can pick up mechanically, and how those who are recorded react to its presence.

Further reduction occurs with the representation of a recorded slice of audio and/or video discourse as sequential lines of text in a "transcript." For while talk in social settings is a "multichanneled event," writing "is linear in nature, and can handle only one channel at a time, so must pick and choose among the cues available for representation" (Walker 1986:211). A transcript thus selects particular dimensions and contents of discourse for inclusion while ignoring others, for example, nonverbal cues to local meanings such as eye gaze, gesture, and posture. Researchers studying oral performances spend considerable effort in developing a notational system to document the verbal and at least some of the nonverbal communication; the quality of the transcribed "folklore text" is critical as it "represents the performance in another medium" (Fine 1984:3). Yet the transcript is never a "verbatim" rendering of discourse because it "represents . . . an analytic interpretation and selection" (Psathas and Anderson 1990:75) of speech and action. That is, a transcript is the product of a transcriber's ongoing interpretive and analytic decisions about a variety of problematic matters: how to transform naturally occurring speech into specific words (in the face of natural speech elisions); how to determine when to punctuate to indicate a completed phrase or sentence (given the common lack of clear-cut endings in ordinary speech); deciding whether or not to try to represent such matters as spaces and silences, overlapped speech and sounds, pace stresses and volume, and inaudible or incomprehensible sounds or words.[9] In sum, even those means of recording that researchers claim as being closest to realizing an "objective mirroring" necessarily make reductions in the lived complexity of social life similar, in principle, to those made in writing fieldnotes.[10]

Given the reductionism of any method of inscription, choice of method reflects researchers' deeper assumptions about social life and how to understand it. Fieldwork and ultimately fieldnotes are predicated on a view of social life as continuously created through people's efforts to find and confer meaning on their own and others' actions. Within this perspective, the interview and the recording have their uses. To the extent that participants are willing and able to describe these features of social life, an interview may prove a valuable tool or even the only access. Similarly, a video recording provides a valuable record of words actually uttered and gestures actually made. But the ethos of fieldwork holds that in order to fully understand and appreciate action from the perspective of participants, one must get close to and participate in a wide cross-section of their everyday activities over an extended period of time. Ethnography, as Van Maanen (1988:ix) insists, is "the peculiar practice of representing the social reality of others through the analysis of one's own experience in the world of these others." Fieldnotes are distinctively a method for capturing and preserving the insights and understandings stimulated by these close and long-term experiences. Thus, fieldnotes inscribe the sometimes inchoate understandings and insights the fieldworker acquires by intimately immersing herself in another world, by observing in the midst of mundane activities and jarring crises, and by directly running up against the contingencies and constraints of the everyday life of another people. Indeed, it is exactly this deep immersion—and the sense of place that such immersion assumes and strengthens—that enables the ethnographer to inscribe the detailed, context-sensitive, and locally informed fieldnotes that Geertz (1973) terms "thick description."[11]

This experiential character of fieldnotes is also reflected in changes in their content and concerns over time. Fieldnotes grow through gradual accretion, adding one day's writing to the next. The ethnographer writes particular fieldnotes in ways that are not predetermined or prespecified; hence, fieldnotes are not collections or samples decided in advance according to set criteria. Choosing what to write down is not a process of sampling according to some fixed-in-advance principle. Rather, it is both intuitive, reflecting the ethnographer's changing sense of what might possibly be made interesting or important to future readers, and empathetic, reflecting the ethnographer's sense of what is interesting or important to the people he is observing.

IMPLICATIONS FOR WRITING FIELDNOTES

We draw four implications from our interpretive-interactionist understanding of ethnography as the inscription of participatory experience: (1) what is observed and ultimately treated as "data" or "findings" is inseparable from the observational processes; (2) in writing fieldnotes, the field researcher should give special attention to the indigenous meanings and concerns of the people studied; (3) contemporaneously written fieldnotes are an essential grounding and resource for writing broader, more coherent accounts of others' lives and concerns; and (4) such fieldnotes should detail the social and interactional processes that make up people's everyday lives and activities.

Connecting "Methods" and "Findings"

Modes of participating in and finding out about the daily lives of others make up key parts of ethnographic methods. These "methods" determine what the field researcher sees, experiences, and learns. But if substance ("data," "findings," "facts") are products of the methods used, substance cannot be considered independently of the interactions and relations with others that comprise these methods; *what* the ethnographer finds out is inherently connected with *how* she finds it out (Gubrium and Holstein 1997). As a result, these methods should not be ignored; rather, they should comprise an important part of written fieldnotes. It thus becomes critical for the ethnographer to document her own activities, circumstances, and emotional responses as these factors shape the process of observing and recording others' lives.[12]

From this point of view, the very distinction between fieldnote "data" and "personal reactions," between "fieldnote records" and "diaries" or "journals" (Sanjek 1990c), is deeply misleading. Of course, the ethnographer can separate what he says and does from what he observes others saying and doing, treating the latter as if it were unaffected by the former.[13] But such a separation distorts processes of inquiry and the meaning of field "data" in several significant ways. First, this separation treats data as "objective information" that has a fixed meaning independent of *how* that information was elicited or established and by whom. In this way, the ethnographer's own actions, including his "personal" feelings and reactions, are viewed as independent of, and unrelated to, the events and happenings involving others that constitute "findings" or "observations" when written down in fieldnotes. Second, this separation assumes that "subjective" reactions and perceptions can and should be controlled by being segregated from "objective," impersonal records. And finally, such control is thought to be essential because personal and emotional experiences are devalued, comprising "contaminants" of objective data rather than avenues of insight into significant processes in the setting.

Linking method and substance in fieldnotes has a number of advantages: It encourages recognizing "findings," not as absolute and invariant, but, rather, as contingent upon the circumstances of their "discovery" by the ethnographer. Moreover, the ethnographer is prevented, or at least discouraged, from too readily taking one person's version of what happened or what is important as the "complete" or "correct" version of these matters. Rather, "what happened" is one account made by a particular person to a specific other at a particular time and place for particular purposes. In all these ways, linking method and substance builds sensitivity to the multiple, situational realities of those studied into the core of fieldwork practice.

The Pursuit of Indigenous Meanings

In contrast to styles of field research that focus on others' behavior without systematic regard for what such behavior means to those engaged in it, we see ethnographic fieldnotes as a distinctive method for uncovering and depicting local interpretations or indigenous meanings. Ultimately, the participating ethnographer seeks to get close to those studied in order to understand and write about what their experiences and activities *mean to them*.[14]

Ethnographers should attempt to write fieldnotes in ways that capture and preserve indigenous meanings. To do so, they must learn to recognize and limit reliance upon preconceptions about members' lives and activities. They must become responsive to what others are concerned about in their own terms. But while fieldnotes are about others, their concerns, and doings gleaned through empathetic immersion, they necessarily reflect and convey the ethnographer's understanding of these concerns and doings. Thus, fieldnotes are written accounts that filter members' experiences and concerns through the person and perspectives of the ethnographer; fieldnotes provide the ethnographer's, not the members', accounts of the latter's experiences, meanings, and concerns.

It might initially appear that forms of ethnography concerned with "polyvocality" (Clifford and Marcus 1986:15), or oral histories and feminist ethnographies (Stacey 1998) that seek to let members "speak in their own voices," can avoid researcher mediation in its entirety. But even in these instances, researchers continue to select what to observe, to pose questions, or to frame the nature and purpose of the interview more generally, in ways that cannot avoid mediating effects (see Mills 1990).

Writing Fieldnotes Contemporaneously

In contrast to views holding that fieldnotes are crutches, at best, and blinders, at worst, we see fieldnotes as providing the primary means for deeper appreciation of how field researchers come to grasp and interpret the actions and concerns of others. In this respect, fieldnotes offer subtle and complex understandings of these others' lives, routines, and meanings.

As argued earlier, the field researcher comes to understand others' ways by becoming part of their lives and by learning to interpret and experience events much as they do. It is critical to document closely these subtle processes of learning and resocialization *as they occur.* In part, such documentation limits distortions of memory loss in recalling more distant events. But furthermore, continuing time in the field tends to dilute the insights generated by initial perceptions that arise in adapting to and discovering what is significant to others; it blunts early sensitivities to subtle patterns and underlying tensions. In short, the field researcher does not learn about the concerns and meanings of others all at once but, rather, in a constant, continuing process in which she builds new insight and understanding upon prior insights and understandings. Researchers should document how these emergent processes and stages unfold rather than attempt to reconstruct them at a later point in light of some final, ultimate interpretation of their meaning and import. Fieldnotes provide a distinctive resource for preserving experience close to the moment of occurrence and, hence, for deepening reflection upon and understanding of those experiences.

Similar considerations hold when examining the ethnographer's "findings" about those studied and their routine activities. Producing a record of these activities, as close to their occurrence as possible, preserves their idiosyncratic, contingent character in the face of the homogenizing tendencies of retrospective recall. In immediately written fieldnotes, distinctive qualities and features are sharply drawn and will elicit vivid memories and luminous images (Katz 2001c, 2002) when the ethnographer rereads notes for coding and analysis. Furthermore, the distinctive and unique features of such fieldnotes, brought forward into the final analysis, create texture and variation, avoiding the flatness that comes from generality.

The Importance of Interactional Detail

Field researchers seek to get close to others in order to understand their ways of life. To preserve and convey that closeness, they must describe situations and events of interest in detail. Of course, there can never be absolute standards for determining when there is "enough detail." How closely one should look and describe depends upon what is "of interest," and this varies by situation and by the researcher's personality, discipline, and theoretical concerns. Nonetheless, most ethnographers attend to observed events in an intimate or "microscopic" manner (Geertz 1973:20–23) and in writing fieldnotes seek to recount "what happened" in fine detail.

Beyond this general "microscopic" commitment, however, our specifically interactionist approach leads us to urge writers to value close, detailed reports of interaction. First, interactional detail helps one become sensitive to, trace, and analyze the interconnections between methods and substance. Since the fieldworker discovers things about others by interacting with them, it is important to observe and minutely record the sequences and conditions marking such interactions. Second, in preserving the details of interaction, the researcher is better able to identify and follow *processes* in witnessed events and, hence, to develop and sustain processual interpretations of happenings in the field (Emerson 2009). Field research, we maintain, is particularly suited to documenting social life as process, as emergent meanings established in and through social interaction (Blumer 1969). Attending to the details of interaction enhances the possibilities for the researcher to see beyond fixed, static entities, to grasp the active "doing" of social life. Writing fieldnotes as soon and as fully as possible after events of interest have occurred also encourages detailed descriptions of the processes of interaction through which members of social settings create and sustain specific, local social realities.

REFLECTIONS: WRITING FIELDNOTES
AND ETHNOGRAPHIC PRACTICE

Ethnography is an active enterprise, and its activity incorporates dual impulses. On the one hand, the ethnographer must make her way into new worlds and new relationships. On the other hand, she must learn how to represent in written form what she sees and understands as the result of these experiences.

It is easy to draw a sharp contrast between these activities, between doing fieldwork and writing fieldnotes. After all, while in the field, ethnographers must frequently choose between "join(ing) conversations in unfamiliar places" (Lederman 1990:72) and withdrawing to some more private place to write about these conversations and witnessed events. By locating "real ethnography" in the time spent talking with and listening to those studied, many ethnographers not only polarize participating and writing but also discount the latter as a central component of fieldwork. "Doing" and "writing" should not be seen as separate and distinct activities, but, rather, as dialectically related, interdependent, and mutually constituitive activities. Writing accounts of what happened during face-to-face encounters with others in the field is very much part of the doing of ethnography; as Geertz emphasizes, "the ethnographer 'inscribes' social discourse; he writes it down" (1973:19). This process of inscribing, of writing fieldnotes, helps the field researcher to understand what he has been observing in the first place and, thus, enables him to participate in new ways, to hear with greater acuteness, and to observe with a new lens.

While ethnographers increasingly recognize the centrality of writing to their craft, they frequently differ about how to characterize that writing and its relationship to ethnographic research. Some anthropologists have criticized Geertz's notion of "inscription" as too mechanical and simplistic, as ignoring that the ethnographer writes not about a "passing event" but, rather, about "already formulated, fixed discourse or lore"; hence, inscription should more aptly be termed "transcription" (Clifford 1990:57). "Inscription" has also been criticized as being too enmeshed in the assumptions of "salvage ethnography," which date back to Franz Boas's efforts to "write down" oral cultures before they and their languages and customs disappeared (Clifford 1986:113). Indeed, ethnographers have suggested a number of alternative ways of characterizing ethnographic writing. Anthropologists frequently use "translation" (or "cultural translation") to conceptualize writing a version of one culture that will make it comprehensible to readers living in another. Richardson (1990), Richardson and St. Pierre (2005), and other sociologists describe the core of ethnographic writing as "narrating." And Clifford (1986) and Marcus (1986) use the more abstract term "textualization" to refer to the generic processes whereby ethnography "translates experience into text" (Clifford 1986:115).

In general, however, these approaches conflate writing final ethnographies with writing ethnographic fieldnotes; thus, they fail to adequately illuminate the key processes and features of producing fieldnotes. Yet, each approach has implications for such contemporaneous writing about events witnessed in the field. First *translation* entails reconfiguring one set of concepts and terms into another; that is, the ethnographer searches for comparable concepts and analogous terms. In a sense, while writing fieldnotes, an ethnographer is always interpreting and translating into text what she sees, even when writing notes for herself. Of course, in composing the final ethnography, the writer not only translates concepts but also a whole way of life for a future audience who may not be familiar with the world she describes. Second, *narrating* often aptly characterizes the process of writing a day's experiences into a fieldnote entry. However, not all life experiences are well represented as cohesive stories: A narrative could push open-ended or disjointed interactions into a coherent, interconnected sequence that distorts the actual experience of the interaction. Thus, while many fieldnotes tell about the day in a storytelling mode, recounting what happened in a chronological order, most entries lack any overall structure that ties the day's events into a story line with a point. As a result, the storytelling of fieldnotes is generally fragmented and episodic. Finally, *textualization* clearly focuses on the broader transformation of experience into text, not only in final ethnographies, but especially so in writing fieldnotes. Indeed, such transformation first occurs in the preliminary and varied writings in the field, and these fieldnotes often prefigure the final texts!

In sum, the fluid, open-ended processes of writing fieldnotes resonate with the imagery of all these approaches and, yet, differ from them in important ways. Never a simple matter of inscribing the world, fieldnotes do more than record observations. In a fundamental sense, they constitute a way of life through the very writing choices that the ethnographer makes and the stories that she tells; for through her writing, she conveys her understandings and insights to future readers unacquainted with these lives, people, and events. In writing a fieldnote, then, the ethnographer does not simply put happenings into words. Rather, such writing is an interpretive process: It is the very first act of textualizing. Indeed, this often "invisible" work—*writing ethnographic fieldnotes*—is the primordial textualization that creates a world on the page and, ultimately, shapes the final ethnographic, published text.

2

In the Field: Participating, Observing, and Jotting Notes

Ethnographers ultimately produce a written account of what they have seen, heard, and experienced in the field. But different ethnographers, and the same ethnographer at different times, turn experience and observation into written texts in different ways. Some maximize their immersion in local activities and their experience of others' lives, deliberately suspending concern with the task of producing written records of these events. Here, the field researcher decides where to go, what to look at, what to ask and say so as to experience fully another way of life and its concerns. She attends to events with little or no orientation to "writing it down" or even to "observing" in a detached fashion. Indeed, an ethnographer living in, rather than simply regularly visiting, a field setting, particularly in non-Western cultures where language and daily routines are unfamiliar, may have no choice but to participate fully and to suspend immediate concerns with writing. A female ethnographer studying local women in Africa, for example, may find herself helping to prepare greens and care for children, leaving no time to produce many written notes. Yet in the process of that involvement, she may most clearly learn how women simultaneously work together, socialize, and care for children. Only in subsequent reflection, might she fully notice the subtle changes in herself as she learned to do and see these activities as the women do.

Field researchers using this ethnographic approach want to relate naturally to those encountered in the field; they focus their efforts on figuring out—holistically and intuitively—what these people are up to. Any anticipation of writing fieldnotes is postponed (and in extreme cases, minimized or avoided altogether) as diluting the experiential insights and intuitions that immersion in another social world can provide.[1] Only at some later point does the ethnographer turn to the task of recalling and examining her experiences in order to write them down.

But the ethnographer may also participate in ongoing events in ways that directly and immediately involve inscription. Here, the fieldworker is concerned with "getting into place" to observe interesting, significant events in order to produce a detailed written record of them. As a result, participation in naturally occurring events may come to be explicitly oriented toward writing fieldnotes. At an extreme, the fieldworker may self-consciously look for events that should be written down for research purposes; he may position himself in these unfolding events to be able to observe and write; and he may explicitly orient to events in terms of "what is important to remember so that I can write it down later."

Each mode of field involvement has strengths and drawbacks. The former allows an intense immersion in daily rhythms and ordinary concerns that increases openness to others' ways of life. The latter can produce a more detailed, closer-to-the-moment record of that life. In practice, most field researchers employ both approaches at different times, sometimes participating without thought about writing up what is happening and, at other times, focusing closely on events in order to write about them. Indeed, the fieldworker may experience a shift from one mode to another as events unfold in the field. Caught in some social moment, for example, the field researcher may come to see deep theoretical relevance in a mundane experience or practice. Conversely, a researcher in the midst of observing in a more detached, writing-oriented mode may suddenly be drawn directly into the center of activity.[2]

In both approaches, the ethnographer writes fieldnotes more or less contemporaneously with the experience and observation of events of interest in the spirit of the ethnographer who commented, "Anthropologists are those who write things down at the end of the day" (Jackson 1990b:15). In the experiential style, writing may be put off for hours or even days until the field researcher withdraws from the field and, relying solely on memory, sits down at pad or computer to reconstruct important events.[3] In the participating-to-write approach, writing—or an orientation to writing—begins earlier when the researcher is still in the field, perhaps in the immediate presence of talk and action that will be inscribed. The ethnographer may not only make mental notes or "headnotes"[4] to include certain events in full fieldnotes, but he may also write down, in the form of jottings or scratch notes, abbreviated words and phrases to use later to construct full fieldnotes.

Furthermore, in both styles, field researchers are deeply concerned about the quality of the relationships they develop with the people they seek to know and understand. In valuing more natural, open experience of others' worlds and activities, field researchers seek to keep writing from intruding into and affecting these relationships. They do so not only to avoid distancing themselves from the ongoing experience of another world but also because writing, and research commitments more generally, may engender feelings of betraying those with whom one has lived and shared intimacies. Ethnographers who participate in order to write, in contrast, pursue and proclaim research interests more openly as an element in their relationships with those studied. But these field researchers often become very sensitive to the ways in which the stance and act of writing are very visible to, and can influence the quality of their relationships with, those studied. And they also may experience moments of anguish or uncertainty about whether to include intimate or humiliating incidents in their fieldnotes.

In the remainder of this chapter, we focus on a participating-in-order-to-write fieldwork approach that confronts writing issues directly and immediately in the field. This approach brings to the fore the interconnections between writing, participating, and observing as a means of understanding another way of life; it focuses on learning how to look in order to write, while it also recognizes that looking is itself shaped and constrained by a sense of what and how to write. We will begin by examining the processes of participating in order to write in detail, considering a number of practices that ethnographers have found useful in guiding and orienting observations made under these conditions. We then take up issues of actually writing in the presence of those studied by making jottings about what we see and hear, even as these interactions are occurring. Here, we first present illustrations of actual jottings made in different field settings and discuss a number of considerations that might guide the process of making jottings. We then consider choices confronting field researchers in deciding how, where, and when to make jottings in field settings.

PARTICIPATING IN ORDER TO WRITE

In attending to ongoing scenes, events, and interactions, field researchers take mental note of certain details and impressions. For the most part, these impressions remain "headnotes" until the researcher sits down at some later point to write full fieldnotes about these scenes and events. In the flux of their field settings, beginning students are often hesitant and uncertain about what details and impressions they should pay attention to as potential issues for writing. We have found a number of procedures to be helpful in advising students how initially to look in order to write.

First, ethnographers should take note of their *initial impressions*. These impressions may include those things available to the senses—the tastes, smells, and sounds of the physical environment, and the look and feel of the locale and the people in it. Such impressions may include details about the physical setting, including size, space, noise, colors, equipment, and movement, or about people in the setting, such as their number, gender, race, appearance, dress, movement, comportment, and feeling tone. Writing down these impressions provides a way to get started in a setting that may seem overwhelming. Entering another culture where both language and customs are incomprehensible may present particular challenges in this regard. Still, the ethnographer can begin to assimilate strange sights and sounds by attending to and then writing about them.[5]

Furthermore, this record preserves these initial and often insightful impressions, for observers tend to lose sensitivity for unique qualities of a setting as these become commonplace. Researchers who are familiar with the setting they study, perhaps already having a place in the setting as workers or residents, have lost direct access to their first impressions. However, such fieldworkers can indirectly seek to recall their own first impressions by watching any newcomers to the setting, paying special attention to how they learn, adapt, and react.

Second, field researchers can focus on their personal sense of *what is significant or unexpected* in order to document key events or incidents in a particular social world or setting. Particularly at first, fieldworkers may want to rely on their own experience and intuition to select noteworthy incidents out of the flow of ongoing activity. Here, for example, the fieldworker may look closely at something that surprises or runs counter to her expectations, again paying attention to incidents, feeling tones, impressions, and interactions, both verbal and nonverbal.

Similarly, field researchers may use their own personal experience of events that please, shock, or even anger them to identify matters worth writing about. A fieldworker's strong reaction to a particular event may well signal that others in the setting react similarly. Or a fieldworker may experience deeply contradictory emotions, for example, simultaneously feeling deep sympathy and repulsion for what he observes in the field. These feelings may also reflect contradictory pressures experienced by those in the setting.

To use personal reactions effectively, however, requires care and reflection. One must first pay close attention to how others in the setting are reacting to these events; it is important to become aware of when and how one's own reactions and sensitivities differ from those of some or most members. But in addition, in taking note of others' experiences, many beginning ethnographers tend to judge the actions of people in the setting, for better or worse, by their own, rather than the others', standards and values. Prejudging incidents in outsiders' terms makes it difficult to cultivate empathetic understanding and to discover what import local people give to them (see chapter 5). The field researcher should be alive to the possibility that local people, especially those with very different cultures, may respond to events in sharply contrasting ways. For example, an ethnographer in a Chokwe village may react with alarm to an unconscious man drugged by an herbal drink in a trial-for-sorcery court, only to realize that others are laughing at the spectacle because they know he will soon regain consciousness.

Yet, fieldworkers should not go to the other extreme and attempt to manage strong personal reactions by denial or simply by omitting them from fieldnotes. Rather, we recommend that the ethnographer first register her feelings, then step back and use this experience to ask how others in the setting see and experience these matters. Are they similarly surprised, shocked, pleased, or angered by an event? If so, under what conditions do these reactions occur, and how did those affected cope with the incidents and persons involved? Whether an ethnographer is working in a foreign or in a familiar culture, she needs to avoid assuming that others respond as she does.

Third, in order to document key events and incidents, field researchers should move beyond their personal reactions to attend explicitly to *what those in the setting experience and react to as "significant" or "important."* The field researcher watches for the sorts of things that are meaningful to those studied. The actions, interactions, and events that catch the attention of people habitually in the setting may provide clues to these concerns. Specifically: What do they stop and watch? What do they talk and gossip about? What produces strong emotional responses for them? "Troubles" or "problems" often generate deep concern and feelings. What kinds occur in the setting? How do people in the setting understand, interpret, and deal with these troubles or problems? Such "incidents" and "troubles" should move the field researcher to jot down "who did what" and "how others reacted."

Often, however, a researcher who is unfamiliar with a setting may not initially be able to understand or even to identify local meanings and their significance. Hence, the researcher may have to write down what members say and do without fully understanding their implications and import. Consider, for example, the following fieldnote written by a student ethnographer making her first visit to a small residential program for ex-prostitutes:

> We walk inside and down the hallway, stopping in front of the kitchen. One of the girls is in there, and Ellen [the program director] stops to introduce me. She says, Catherine this is our new volunteer. She says, "Oh, nice to meet you," and thanks me for volunteering. We shake hands, and I tell her it's nice to meet her as well. Ellen adds, "Well most people call her Cathy, but I like the way Catherine sounds so that's what I call her." Catherine is wearing baggy, navy blue athletic shorts and a loose black tank top. Her thick, curly hair is pulled into a bun resting on the side of her head. She is barefoot. She turns to Ellen, and the smile leaves her face as she says, "Julie cut her hair." Ellen responds that Julie's hair is already short, and asks, "Is it buzzed?" Catherine responds no, that it's cut in a "page boy style and looks really cute." Ellen's eyebrows scrunch together, and she asks, well, is she happy with it? Catherine smiles and says, "Yeah, she loves it." To which Ellen responds, "Well, if she's happy, I'm happy," and that she's going to finish taking me around the house. I tell Catherine, "See you later."

Here, the program director's response to Catherine's report treats Julie's haircut as simply a decision about personal style and appearance—"is she happy with it?" On its face, it does not seem to be an important or significant statement and could easily have been left out in the write-up of this encounter.[6]

But events immediately following this encounter made it clear that Julie's haircut had important implications for the institution and its program. Leaving Catherine, the program director continued to show the ethnographer around the home:

> [In an upstairs bedroom] Ellen tells me to take a seat while she "makes a quick phone call." She begins the conversation, "Hey, so I just got home, and Catherine told me that Julie cut her hair." She listens for awhile, and her voice becomes more serious as she says, "Yeah, I know. I'm just thinking she's headed toward the same bullshit as last time." [Later in her office] Ellen explains to me

that Julie used to be a resident of the house but left and went back into prostitution. When Julie wanted to come back "we took her back on one condition, that she doesn't focus on her physical appearances but works on what's inside instead." That is why she was so concerned about the haircut: "It seems like she's going back to the same things as before," because this is how it starts.

The program director's phone call, immediately reporting Julie's haircut to someone else connected with the program, displays the local importance of this event. Later, the program director explains to the observer that, given Julie's history in the program, her haircut is a likely indicator of a troubled psychological state and weakening commitment to the program.

As this incident illustrates, the field researcher discerns local meanings, not so much by directly asking actors about what matters to them, but more indirectly and inferentially by looking for the perspectives and concerns embedded and expressed in naturally occurring interaction. And in gleaning indigenous meanings implicit in interaction, the ethnographer is well placed to apprehend these meanings, not simply as static categories, but, rather, as matters involving action and process. This requires not just that the ethnographer describes interactions but that she consistently attends to "when, where, and according to whom" in shaping all fieldnote descriptions. Those in different institutional positions (e.g., staff and clients) may evaluate different clients as doing well or poorly in "working the program" and may do so by invoking different evaluative criteria. Indigenous meanings, then, rarely hold across the board but, rather, reflect particular positions and practical concerns that need to be captured in fieldnote descriptions.

Fourth, ethnographers can begin to capture new settings by focusing and writing notes as systematically as possible, focusing on *how routine actions in the setting are organized and take place*. Attending closely to "how" something occurs encourages and produces *"luminous descriptions"* (Katz 2001c) that specify the actual, lived conditions and contingencies of social life. Consistent with our interactionist perspective, asking *how* also focuses the ethnographer's attention on the social and interactional processes through which members construct, maintain, and alter their social worlds. This means that field researchers should resist the temptation to focus descriptions on *why* events or actions occur; initially focusing on "why" stymies and prematurely deflects full description of specific impressions, events, and interactions because determining "why" is a complex and uncertain process requiring explanation and, hence, comparison with other

instances or cases. Consider the difference in understanding that Katz develops between asking *why* one decides to get gas for one's car and *how* one
does so:

> I can describe how I did that on a given occasion, but why I did it is never really
> as simple as top-of-the-head explanations suggest, for example, "because I
> was low on gas" or "because I needed gas." I needed gas before I entered the
> station; I did not rush to the station the first moment I noticed the gas gauge
> registering low; and usually I get there without having to push the car in be-
> cause it ran completely dry. In any case, my "need" for gas would not explain
> the extent to which I fill the tank, nor why I pay with a credit card instead of
> cash, nor which of the pumps I choose, nor whether I accept the automatic
> cut-off as ending the operation or top up with a final squeeze. As the descrip-
> tion of how the act is conducted improves, the less convincing becomes the
> initially obvious answer to "why?" (Katz 2001c:446)

Finally, ethnographers' orientations to writable events change with time
in the field. When first venturing into a setting, field researchers should
"cast their nets" broadly; they should observe with an eye to writing about
a range of incidents and interactions. Yet, forays into a setting must not be
viewed as discrete, isolated occasions that have little or no bearing on what
will be noted the next time. Rather, observing and writing about certain
kinds of events foreshadow what will be noticed and described next. Identifying one incident as noteworthy should lead to considering what other
incidents are similar and, hence, worth noting. As fieldwork progresses and
becomes more focused on a set of issues, fieldworkers often self-consciously
document a series of incidents and interactions of the "same type" and look
for regularities or patterns within them.

Even when looking for additional examples of a similar event, the field researcher is open to and, indeed, searches for, *different forms* of that event, and
for *variations from, or exceptions to, an emerging pattern*. Beginning field researchers are often discouraged by such discoveries, fearing that exceptions to a pattern they have noted will cast doubt upon their understanding
of the setting. This need not be the case, although noting differences and
variations should prod the field researcher to change, elaborate, or deepen
her earlier understanding of the setting. The field researcher, for example,
might want to consider and explore possible factors or circumstances that
would account for differences or variations: Are the different actions the
result of the preferences and temperaments of those involved or of their dif-

ferent understandings of the situation because they have different positions in the local context? Or the ethnographer may begin to question how she decided similarity and difference in the first place, perhaps coming to see how an event that initially appeared to be different is actually similar on a deeper level. In these ways, exploring what at least initially seem to be differences and variations will lead to richer, more textured descriptions and encourage more subtle, grounded analyses in a final ethnography (see chapter 7).

In summary, ethnographic attention involves balancing two different orientations. Especially on first entering the field, the researcher identifies significant characteristics gleaned from her first impressions and personal reactions. With greater participation in that local social world, however, the ethnographer becomes more sensitive to the concerns and perspectives of those in the setting. She increasingly appreciates how people have already predescribed their world in their own terms for their own purposes and projects. A sensitive ethnographer draws upon her own reactions to identify issues of possible importance to people in the setting but privileges their "insider" descriptions and categories over her own "outsider" views.

WHAT ARE JOTTINGS?

While participating in the field and attending to ongoing scenes, events, and interactions, field researchers may, at moments, decide that certain events and impressions should be written down as they are occurring in order to preserve accuracy and detail. In these circumstances, the field researcher moves beyond mere "headnotes" to record jottings—a brief written record of events and impressions captured in key words and phrases. Jottings translate to-be-remembered observations into writing on paper as quickly rendered scribbles about actions and dialogue. A word or two written at the moment or soon afterward will jog the memory later in the day when she attempts to recall the details of significant actions and to construct evocative descriptions of the scene. Or, more extensive jottings may record an ongoing dialogue or a set of responses to questions.

In order to convey how field researchers actually write and use jottings, we provide two illustrations. Each identifies specific scenes, observed actions, and dialogue rather than making evaluations or psychological interpretations. But each researcher approaches interaction in their settings in different ways, noting different sensory and interpretive details. (We will consider the full fieldnotes written from both these sets of jottings in chapter 3.)

"Too Many Sexual References"

A student ethnographer jotted the following notes while sitting in on an after-school staff meeting attended by a continuation school principal, four teachers, and the school counselor:

> Sexual Harassment
> Andy—too many sexual references
>   PE frisbee game "This team has too many sausages"
> Reynaldo—*(Carlos—in jail for stealing bicycle, 18 yrs old) [circled]*
> Laura → Wants to propose sexual harassment forms
>   Thinking about detention for these students but already too much work
>   for keeping track of tardies/truancies/tendencies

Here, the observer begins by marking off one of the topics that came up during this meeting—"sexual harassment." His jottings then identify a student—Andy—who has been accused of making "too many sexual references." The next line records a specific incident: When placed on a team composed mostly of boys during an Ultimate Frisbee game on the physical education field, Andy had commented that "this team has too many sausages." There follows the name of another student—Reynaldo—but no indication of what he said or did. Adjacent to this name was a circled phrase, including another name "Carlos" and a comment "in jail for stealing bicycle, 18 yrs old." The rest of the jotting names a teacher—Laura—and sketches her proposal to create "sexual harassment forms" to be filled out in response to such "inappropriate" sexual talk by students. Detention is mentioned as one possible punishment for such offenders, but this idea is countered by the observation that staff already has too much paperwork in dealing with students in detention.

"You Can Call His Doctor"

In contrast to the focus on named individuals and a variety of events linked to them, the following jottings focus strictly on dialogue, recording bits of talk in a formal court proceeding. The case involved a woman seeking a temporary restraining order against her two landlords, one of whom is not present in the courtroom. The landlord who is present disputes the woman's testimony that the missing landlord is "well enough to walk" and, hence, could have come to court:

you can call his doctor at UCLA and
he can verify all this
I just don't call people on the
telephone—courts don't operate that way—
it has to be on paper or
(in person)[7]

Here, only spoken words are recorded; specific speakers are not indicated but can be identified by content—the landlord defendant in the first two lines and the judge in the last four lines. The words represent direct quotes, written down as accurately as possible when spoken; an exception occurs in the last line where the observer missed the judge's exact words ending this sentence (because of jotting down the preceding dialogue) and inserted a paraphrase "in person" (indicated by parentheses). As in the prior illustration, there is no indication of what the ethnographer had in mind in noting these pieces of the flow of social life; they "speak for themselves," making no reference as to why they were recorded or about their possible implications.

Each of the jottings in these illustrations is "a mnemonic word or phrase [written] to fix an observation or to recall what someone has just said" (Clifford 1990:51). As preludes to full written notes, jottings capture bits of talk and action from which the fieldworker can begin to sketch social scenes, recurring incidents, local expressions and terms, members' distinctions and accounts, dialogue among those present, and his own conversations.

Making jottings, however, is not only a writing activity; it is also a mindset. Learning to jot down details that remain sharp and that easily transform into vivid descriptions on the page results, in part, from envisioning scenes as written. Writing jottings that evoke memories requires learning what can be written about and how. We have found the following recommendations helpful for making jottings useful for producing vivid, evocatively descriptive fieldnotes.[8]

First, jot down details of what you sense are key components of observed scenes, events, or interactions. Field researchers record immediate fragments of action and talk to serve as focal points for later writing accounts of these events in as much detail as can be remembered. The field researcher studying the continuation school staff meeting, for example, relied on the jotted names of two youth, supplemented by one direct quote, to recall two accounts provided by the complaining teacher about students' "inappropriate" sexual comments. In this way, jottings serve to remind the ethnographer of what was happening at a particular time, providing a marker around which to collect other remembered incidents. But the fieldworker does not have to have a specific reason or insight in mind to make a jotting about what she has seen and heard. For example, one field researcher teaching in a Headstart Program described a series of incidents that occurred while supervising children playing in a sandbox. Included in her jottings, but not in her full fieldnotes, was the phrase, "Three new bags of sand were delivered to the sandbox." In discussing this scratch note later, she commented: "I don't think it is so important as I would want to include it in my notes because I think it is just—I wrote it down to remind me more what the day was like, what was happening."[9]

Second, jot down concrete sensory details about observed scenes and interactions. Sensory details will later help to reconstruct the feel of what happened. Pay particular attention to details you could easily forget. Since jottings must later jog the memory, each field researcher must learn which kinds of details that they best remember and make jottings about those features and qualities that they might easily forget. Thus, fieldworkers come to develop their own jotting styles reflecting their distinctive recall propensities, whether visual, kinetic, or auditory. Some focus on trying to capture evocative pieces of broader scenes, while some jot down almost exclusively dialogue; others record nonverbal expression of voice, gesture, and movement; still others note visual details of color and shape. Through trial and error, field researchers learn what most helps them to recall field experiences once they sit down to write up full notes.

Third, avoid characterizing scenes or what people do through generalizations or summaries. Many novice field researchers initially tend to jot down impressionistic, opinionated words that lend themselves better to writing evaluative summaries than to composing detailed, textured descriptions. For example, it is problematic for a field researcher to characterize the way someone works as "inefficient." Such cryptic, evaluative jottings are likely to evoke only a vague memory when the fieldworker later on attempts to write a full description of the social scene. Such jottings also convey nothing of how people in the setting experience and evaluate worker performance. Similarly, jottings that a probation officer "lectures about school" and that a youth is "very compliant—always agrees" during a probation interview are overly general; such summary statements are not helpful for writing close descriptions of how the probation officer and the youth actually talked and acted during a particular encounter.

Fourth, fieldworkers use jottings to capture detailed aspects of scenes, talk, and interaction; short or more extended direct quotes are particularly useful for capturing such detail, as reflected in the previous two illustrations of jottings. In general, field researchers note concrete details of everyday life that *show*, rather than tell, about people's behavior (see chapter 3). By incorporating such details, jottings may provide records of actual words, phrases, or dialogue that the field researcher wants to preserve in as accurate a form as possible. It is not enough, for example, to characterize an emotional outburst simply as "angry words." Rather, the ethnographer should jot the actually spoken words, along with sensual details such as gestures and facial expressions, suggesting that the speaker's emotional experience involved "anger." Jotting these words should evoke recall, not only of the details about what happened, but also of the specific circumstances or context involved: who was present, what they said or did, what occurred immediately before and after, and so on. In this way, jottings may be used to reconstruct the actual order or sequence of talk, topics, or actions on some particular occasion.

Fifth, use jottings to record the details of emotional expressions and experiences; note feelings such as anger, sadness, joy, pleasure, disgust, or loneliness as expressed and attended to by those in the setting. Beginning ethnographers sometimes attempt to identify motives or internal states when recording observed actions. Having witnessed an angry exchange, for example, one is often tempted to focus on the source or "reason" for this emotional outburst, typically by imputing motive (e.g., some underlying feeling such as "insecurity") to one or both of the parties involved. But such psychologized explanations highlight only one of a number of possible internal states that may accompany or contribute to the observed actions. Anger could, for example, result from frustration, fatigue, the playing out of some local power struggle, or other hidden factors; the ethnographer who simply witnesses a scene has no way of knowing which factors are involved.[10] When witnessing social scenes, then, the ethnographer's task is to use his own sensibilities and reactions to learn how others understand and evaluate what happened, how they assess internal states, and how they determine psychological motivation. Useful jottings should correspondingly reflect and further this process of writing textured, detailed descriptions of interactions rather than attributing individual motivation.

Sixth, use jottings to signal your general impressions and feelings, even if you are unsure of their significance at the moment. In some cases, the ethnographer may have only a vague, intuitive sense about how or why something may be important. Such feelings might signal a key element that in the future could enable the field researcher to see how incidents "fit together" in meaningful patterns. For example, at another point the ethnographer in the Headstart Program made a jotting about a student, "Nicole showing trust in me," which she decided not to write up in her full notes: "It was just an overall feeling I had throughout the day; . . . at that point when I wrote the jottings I couldn't remember an exact incident." But this jotting served as a mental note, subsequently stimulating her to appreciate (and record) the following incident as a revealing example of "children trusting teachers":

> At one point, Nicole got on the swings without her shoes on and asked me for a push. I told her that I would push her after she went and put her shoes on. Nicole paused and looked at me. I repeated my statement, telling her that I would save her swing for her while she was gone. Nicole then got off of the swing and put her shoes on. When she came back to the swing, I praised her listening skills and gave her a hug. I then gave her a push. I found this incident to be a significant accomplishment for Nicole, as usually she doesn't listen to the teachers.[11]

Through thinking about whether or not to write this jotting up as full notes, this student developed sensitivity to the issue of "trust." The jotting later acted as a stimulus to observe and write up a "concrete event" involving such "trust."

In summary, by participating in a setting with an eye to making jottings, an ethnographer experiences events as potential subjects for writing. Like any other writer, an ethnographer learns to recognize potential writing material and to see and hear it in terms of written descriptions. Learning to observe in order to make jottings thus is keyed to both the scene and to the page. Ethnographers learn to experience through the senses in anticipation of writing: to recall observed scenes and interactions like a reporter; to remember dialogue and movement like an actor; to see colors, shapes, textures, and spatial relations as a painter or photographer; and to sense moods, rhythms, and tone of voice like a poet. Details experienced through the senses turn into jottings with active rather than passive verbs, sensory rather than evaluative adjectives, and verbatim rather than summarized dialogue.

MAKING JOTTINGS: HOW, WHERE, AND WHEN

Making jottings is not simply a matter of writing words on a notepad or laptop. Since jottings are often written close to or even in the immediate pres-

ence of those whose words and deeds are at issue, producing jottings is a
social and interactional process. Specifically, how and when an ethnographer makes jottings may have important implications for how others see
and understand who she is and what she is about. There are no hard and fast
rules about whether to make jottings and, if so, when and how to do so. But
with time spent in a setting and by benefitting from trial and error, a field
researcher may evolve a distinctive set of practices to fit writing jottings to
the contours and constraints of that setting.

One initial choice involves the selection of writing materials. Traditionally, fieldworkers have relied on pen and paper. Many have used small note-
pads that fit easily into pocket or purse. Others prefer even less obtrusive
materials, using folded sheets of paper to record jottings about different
topics on specific sides. Writers also frequently develop idiosyncratic preferences for particular types of pens or pencils. But with the spread and common use of electronic and computer technologies in many contemporary
settings, many field researchers now avoid pen and paper entirely and make
jottings directly onto laptop computers, netbooks, smartphones, or audio
recorders.

Field researchers actually write jottings in different ways. It is time-
consuming and cumbersome to write out every word fully. Many fieldworkers use standard systems of abbreviations and symbols (for pen-and-paper
ethnographers, a formal transcribing system such as shorthand or speed
writing; for those using electronic devices, the evolving codes of texting).
Others develop their own private systems for capturing words in shortened
form in ways appropriate to their particular setting; in studying highly technical judicial mediation sessions, for example, Burns (2000:22) "developed a
system of shorthand notation and abbreviations for commonly used terms"
that allowed her to produce minutely detailed accounts of these events. Abbreviations and symbols not only facilitate getting words on a page more
quickly; they also make jotted notes incomprehensible to those onlookers
who ask to see them and, hence, provide a means for protecting the confi-
dentiality of these writings.

Field researchers must also decide when, where, and how to write jottings. Clearly, looking down to pad or keyboard to write jottings distracts
the field researcher (even if only momentarily), making close and continuous observation of what may be complex, rapid, and subtle actions by others
very difficult. But beyond limited attention, jotting decisions can have tre-
mendous import for relations with those in the field. The researcher works
hard to establish close ties with participants so that she may be included in

activities that are central to their lives. In the midst of such activities, however, she may experience deep ambivalence: On the one hand, she may wish
to preserve the immediacy of the moment by jotting down words as they are
spoken and details of scenes as they are enacted, while, on the other hand,
she may feel that taking out a notepad or smartphone will ruin the moment
and plant seeds of distrust. Participants may now see her as someone whose
primary interest lies in discovering their secrets and turning their most intimate and cherished experiences into objects of scientific inquiry.[12]

Nearly all ethnographers feel torn at times between their research commitments and their desire to engage authentically those people whose
worlds they have entered. Attempting to resolve these thorny relational and
moral issues, many researchers hold that conducting any aspect of the research without the full and explicit knowledge and consent of those studied
violates ethical standards. In this view, those in the setting must be understood as collaborators who actively work with the researcher to tell the outside world about their lives and culture. Such mutual collaboration requires
that the researcher ask permission to write about events and also respect
people's desire not to reveal aspects of their lives.

Other field researchers feel less strictly bound to seek permission to conduct research or to tell participants about their intention to record events
and experiences. Some justify this stance by insisting that the field researcher has no special obligations to disclose his intentions since all social
life involves elements of dissembling with no one ever fully revealing all of
their deeper purposes and private activities. Other researchers point out
that jottings and fieldnotes written for oneself as one's own record will do no
direct harm to others. This approach, of course, puts off grappling with the
tough moral and personal issues until facing subsequent decisions about
whether to publish or otherwise make these writings available to others.
Finally, some advocate withholding knowledge of their research purposes
from local people on the grounds that the information gained will serve the
greater good. For example, if researchers want to describe and publicize the
conditions under which undocumented factory workers or the elderly in
nursing homes live, they must withhold their intentions from the powerful
who control access to such settings.

Many beginning researchers, wanting to avoid open violations of trust
and possibly awkward or tense encounters, are tempted to use covert procedures and to try to conceal the fact that they are conducting research; this
practice often requires waiting until one leaves the field to jot notes. While
these decisions involve both the researcher's conscience and pragmatic

considerations, we recommend, as a general policy, that the fieldworker in-form people in the setting of the research, especially those with whom he has established some form of personal relationship. In addition to making these relations more direct and honest, openness avoids the risks and likely sense of betrayal that might follow from discovery of what the researcher has actually been up to. Concerns about the consequences—both discov-ery and ongoing inauthenticity—of even this small secret about research plans might mount and plague the fieldworker as time goes on and rela-tions deepen.

Of course, strained relations and ethical dilemmas are not completely avoided by informing others of one's research purposes. While participants might have consented to the research, they might not know exactly what the research involves or what the researcher will do to carry it out.[13] They might realize that the fieldworker is writing fieldnotes at the end of the day, but they become used to his presence and "forget" that this writing is going on. Furthermore, marginal and transient members of the setting may not be aware of his research identity and purposes despite conscientious efforts to inform them.

By carrying out fieldwork in an overt manner, the researcher gains flexi-bility in when, where, and how to write jottings. In many field situations, it may be feasible to jot notes openly. In so doing, the fieldworker should act with sensitivity, trying to avoid detracting from or interfering with the ordinary relations and goings-on in the field. If possible, the fieldworker should start open jottings early on in contacts with those studied. If one es-tablishes a "note-taker" role, jotting notes comes to be part of what people expect from the fieldworker. Here, it helps to offer initial explanations of the need to take notes; an ethnographer can stress the importance of accu-racy, of getting down exactly what was said. People often understand that such activities are required of students and, therefore, tolerate and accom-modate the needs of researchers who, they believe, want to faithfully repre-sent what goes on. When learning a new language in another culture, the field researcher can explain that she is writing down local terms in order to remember them. By saying the word as she writes, people might offer new terms and become further interested in teaching her.

Although taking down jottings may at first seem odd or awkward, after a time, it often becomes a normal and expected part of what the fieldworker does. In the following excerpt from a Housing and Urban Development (HUD) office, the office manager and a worker jokingly enlist the fieldworker as audience for a self-parody of wanting to "help" clients:

> Later I'm in Jean's office and Ramon comes up and waxes melodramatic. Take this down, he says. Jean motions for me to write, so I pull out my notepad. "I only regret that I have but eight hours to devote to saving" . . . He begins to sing "Impossible Dream," in his thick, goofy Brooklyn accent. . . . "Feel free to join in," he says. . . .

Here, the ethnographer and his note-taking provide resources for a spontaneous humorous performance.[14]

Yet even when some people become familiar with open writing in their presence, others may become upset when the researcher turns to a notepad or laptop and begins to write down their words and actions. Ethnographers may try to avoid the likely challenges and facilitate open, extensive note-taking by positioning themselves on the margins of interaction. Even then, they may still encounter questions, as reflected in the following comment by a field researcher observing divorce mediation sessions:

> I tried to take notes that were as complete as possible during the session. My sitting behind the client had probably more to do with wanting to get a lot of written notes as unobtrusively as possible as with any more worthy methodological reason. While taking copious amounts of notes (approximately 50 pages per session) did not seem to bother the clients, a few mediators became quite defensive about it. One mediator wanted to know how I "decided what to write down and what not to write down." At staff meetings, this same mediator would sit next to me and try to glance over to see what I had written in my notebook.

Given the delicacy of this and similar situations, fieldworkers must constantly rely upon interactional skills and tact to judge whether or not taking jottings in the moment is appropriate.[15]

Furthermore, in becoming accustomed to open jotting, people may develop definite expectations about what events and topics should be recorded. People may question why the fieldworker is or is not taking note of particular events: On the one hand, they may feel slighted if she fails to make jottings on what they are doing or see as important; on the other hand, they may react with surprise or indignation when she makes jottings about apparently personal situations. Consider the following exchange, again described by the field researcher studying divorce mediation, which occurred as she openly took notes while interviewing a mediator about a session just completed:

> On one occasion when finishing up a debriefing, . . . [the mediator] began to apply some eye makeup while I was finishing writing down some observations. She flashed me a mock disgusted look and said, "Are you writing *this* down too!" indicating the activity with her eye pencil.

Open jotting, then, has to be carefully calibrated to the unfolding context of the ongoing interaction.[16] Open jottings not only may strain relations with those who notice the writing, but, as noted previously, jottings can also distract the ethnographer from paying close attention to talk and activities occurring in the setting. A field researcher will inevitably miss fleeting expressions, subtle movements, and even key content in interactions if his nose is in his notepad.

Taking open jottings is not always advisable for other reasons as well. In some settings, the fieldworker's participation in ongoing interaction might be so involving as to preclude taking breaks to write down jottings; in such instances, he may have to rely more upon memory, focusing on incidents and key phrases that will later trigger a fuller recollection of the event or scene. For example, in a setting where only a few people write and do so only on rare occasions, an ethnographer who writes instead of participating in an all-night village dance might be perceived as failing to maintain social relationships—a serious offense in a close-knit village.

As a result of these problems, even ethnographers who usually write open jottings may, at other times, make jottings privately and out of sight of those studied. Waiting until just after a scene, incident, or conversation has occurred, the ethnographer can then go to a private place to jot down a memorable phrase. Here, it is often useful for the fieldworker to adopt the ways members of the setting themselves use to carve out a moment of privacy or to "get away." Fieldworkers have reported retreating to private places such as a bathroom (Cahill 1985), deserted lunchroom, stairwell, or supply closet to record such covert jottings. Depending upon circumstances, the fieldworker can visit such places periodically, as often as every half hour or so, or immediately after a particularly important incident. Another option is to identify the natural "time-out" spaces that members of the setting also rely on and use as places to relax and unwind, to be by oneself, and so on. Thus, fieldworkers can often go to the institutional cafeteria or coffee shop, to outside sitting areas, or even to waiting rooms or hallways to make quick jottings about events that have just occurred. Other researchers avoid all overt writing in the field setting but immediately upon leaving the field, pull out a notepad or laptop to jot down reminders of the key incidents, words, or reactions they wish to include in full fieldnotes. A similar procedure is to record jottings or even fuller notes on some kind of recording device while driving home from a distant field site. These procedures allow the fieldworker to signal items that she does not want to forget without being seen as intrusive.

Finally, an ethnographer may write jottings in ways intermediate between open and hidden styles, especially when note-taking becomes a part of her task or role. In settings where writing—whether pen on paper or on a computer or laptop—is a required or accepted activity, fieldworkers can take jottings without attracting special notice. Thus, classrooms, meetings where note-taking is expected, organizational encounters where forms must be filled out (as in domestic violence legal aid clinics), or in public settings such as coffee shops and cafeterias where laptops are common, jottings may be more or less openly written. Those in the field may or may not know explicitly that the fieldworker is writing jottings for research purposes. Though many activities do not so easily lend themselves to writing jottings, fieldworkers can find other naturally occurring means to incorporate jottings. For example, fieldworkers often learn about settings by becoming members. For the fieldworker who assumes the role of a novice, the notes that as a beginner he is permitted or even expected to write may become the jottings for his first fieldnotes.

Strategies for how, where, and when to jot notes change with time spent in the field and with the different relationships formed between fieldworker and people in the setting. Even after the ethnographer has established strong personal ties, situations might arise in fieldwork when visibly recording anything will be taken as inappropriate or out of place; in these situations, taking out a notepad or laptop would generate deep discomfort to both fieldworker and other people in the setting.[17] One student ethnographer studying a campus bookstore who had grown quite friendly with bookstore workers—with whom she had spoken openly about her study—nonetheless reported the following incident:

> One of the younger cashiers came up to me after having seen me during two of my last observation sessions. She approached me tentatively with a question about me being a "spy" from the other campus bookstore or possibly from the administration. Trying to ease the situation with a joke, I told her I was only being a spy for sociology's sake. But she didn't understand the joke, and it only made the situation worse.

Sometimes people may be uncomfortable with a jotting researcher because they have had little experience with writing as a part of everyday life. Especially in oral cultures, watching and writing about people may seem like a strange activity indeed. In other instances, people have unpleasant associations with writing and find jottings intrusive and potentially dangerous. On one occasion, an elder in a Zambian village became very hesitant to continue speaking after the ethnographer jotted down his name on a scrap of paper simply to remember it. She later learned that government officials in colonial times used to come by and record names for tax purposes and to enlist people into government work projects.

Finally, even with permission to write openly, the tactful fieldworker will want to remain sensitive to and avoid jotting down matters that participants regard as secret, embarrassing, too revealing, or that put them in any danger. In other instances, the people themselves might not object and, in fact, urge the researcher to take notes about sensitive matters. Even though she thinks they may be embarrassing or bring them harm if they were to be made public, the researcher might take jottings but then later decide not to use them in any final writing.

All in all, it is a defining moment in field relations when an ethnographer begins to write down what people are saying and doing in the presence of those very people. Therefore, fieldworkers take very different approaches to jottings, their strategies both shaping and being shaped by their setting and by their relationships. Hence, decisions about when and how to take jottings must be considered in the context of the broader set of relations with those in the setting. In some situations and relations, taking open jottings is clearly not advisable. In others, fieldworkers decide to take jottings but must devise their own unique means to avoid or minimize awkward interactions that may arise as a result. When deciding when and where to jot, it is rarely helpful or possible to specify in advance one "best way." Here, as in other aspects of fieldwork, a good rule of thumb is to remain open, flexible, and ready to alter an approach if it adversely affects the people under study.

REFLECTIONS: WRITING AND ETHNOGRAPHIC MARGINALITY

Starting as outsiders to a field setting, many fieldworkers find themselves pulled toward involvement as insiders in ways that make maintaining a research stance difficult. The student-ethnographer working in a bookstore, for example, noted this tension:

> There were times when I wanted to be free to listen to other individuals talk or to watch their activities, but friends and acquaintances were so "distracting" coming up and wanting to talk that I wasn't able to. Also, there was this concern on my part that, as I got to know some of the staff people better, their qualities as human beings would become so endearing that I was afraid that I would lose my sociological perspective—I didn't want to feel like in studying them, I was exploiting them.

Many field researchers similarly find themselves unable to consistently sustain a watching, distancing stance toward people they are drawn to and toward events that compellingly involve them.[18] Indeed, some may eventually decide to completely abandon their commitment to research (a possibility that has long given anxiety to anthropologists concerned about the dangers of "going native"). Others may abandon their research commitment in a more limited, situational fashion, determining not to write fieldnotes about specific incidents or persons on the grounds that such writing would involve betrayals or revelations that the researcher finds personally and/or ethically intolerable (see Warren 2000:189–90).

But more commonly, ethnographers try to maintain a somewhat detached, observational attitude, even toward people whom they like and respect, balancing and combining research commitments with personal attachments in a variety of ways.[19] One way to do so is to take occasional time-outs from research, not observing and/or writing fieldnotes about selected portions of one's field experience while continuing to do so about other portions. When living in a village on a long-term basis, for example, an ethnographer may feel drawn into daily, intimate relations as a neighbor or perhaps even as a part of a family. On these occasions, she may participate "naturally"—without a writing orientation or analytic reflection—in ongoing social life. But on other occasions, she participates in local scenes in ways that are directed toward making observations and collecting data. Here, her actions incorporate an underlying commitment to write down and ultimately transform into "data" the stuff and nuances of that life.

Several practical writing conflicts arise from these opposing pressures toward involvement and distance. The inclination to experience daily events either as a "natural" participant or as a researcher shows up in writing as shifts in point of view as well as in varying kinds of details considered significant for inscription. Even where and when to jot notes depends on the person's involvement, at a particular moment, as a participant or as an observer. Whether a researcher-as-neighbor in the village or as a researcher-as-intern on a job, ethnographers experience tension between the present-oriented, day-to-day role and the future-oriented identity as writer; this tension will shape the practical choices they make in writing both jottings and more complete notes.

While a primary goal of ethnography is immersion in the life-worlds and everyday experiences of others, the ethnographer inevitably remains in significant ways an outsider to these worlds. Immersion is not merging; the ethnographer who seeks to "get close to" others usually does not become one of these others. As long as, and to the extent that, he retains commitment to the exogenous project of studying or understanding the lives of others, as opposed to the indigenous project of simply living a life in one way or another, he stays at least a partial stranger to their worlds, despite sharing many of the ordinary exigencies of life that these others experience and react to (see Bittner 1988; Emerson 1987).

Writing fieldnotes creates and underlies this socially close, but experientially separate, stance. The ethnographer's fieldnote writing practices—writing jottings on what others are doing in their presence, observing in order to write, writing extended fieldnotes outside the immediacy of the field setting—specifically create and sustain separation, marginality, and distance in the midst of personal and social proximity. Overtly writing jottings interactionally reminds others (and the ethnographer herself) that she has priorities and commitments that differ from their own. Observing in order to write generates moments when the fieldworker is visibly and self-consciously an outsider pursuing tasks and purposes that differ from those of members.[20] And going to tent, home, or office to write fieldnotes regularly reminds the ethnographer that she is not simply doing what members are doing but that she has additional and other commitments.

In sum, in most social settings, writing down what is taking place as it occurs is a strange, marginalizing activity that marks the writer as an observer rather than a full, ordinary participant. But independently of the reactions of others, participating in order to write leads one to assume the mind-set of an observer, a mind-set in which one constantly steps outside of scenes and events to assess their "write-able" qualities. It may be for this reason that some ethnographers try to put writing out of mind entirely by opting for the more fully experiential style of fieldwork. But this strategy simply puts off, rather than avoids, the marginalizing consequences of writing, for lived experience must eventually be turned into observations and represented in textual form.

3

Writing Fieldnotes I:
At the Desk, Creating Scenes
on a Page

After hours participating in, observing, and perhaps jotting notes about ongoing events in a social setting, most fieldworkers return to their desks and their computers to begin to write up their observations into full field-notes. At this point, writing becomes the explicit focus and primary activity of ethnography: Momentarily out of the field, the ethnographer settles at her desk, or other preferred spot, to write up a detailed entry of her day's experiences and observations that will preserve as much as possible what she noticed and now feels is significant. At first glance, such writing up might appear to be a straightforward process to the fieldworker. It might seem that with sufficient time and energy, she can simply record her observations with little attention to her writing process. While having enough time and energy to get her memories on the page is a dominant concern, we suggest that the fieldworker can benefit by considering several kinds of basic writing choices.

To view writing fieldnotes simply as a matter of putting on paper what field researchers have heard and seen suggests that it is a transparent process. In this view, ethnographers "mirror" observed reality in their notes; they aim to write without elaborate rhetoric, intricate metaphors, or complex, suspenseful narration. Writing a detailed entry, this view suggests, requires only a sharp memory and conscientious effort.

A contrasting view insists that all writing, even seemingly straightforward, descriptive writing, is a construction. Through his choice of words, sentence style, and methods of organization, a writer presents a version of the world. As a selective and creative activity, writing always functions more as a filter than a mirror reflecting the "reality" of events. Ethnographers, however, only gradually have deepened their awareness and appreciation of this view; they see how even "realist" ethnographies are constructions that rely upon a variety of stylistic conventions. Van Maanen (1988:47) draws ethnographers' attention to a shift from "studied neutrality" in writing to a construction through narrating conventions. He identified studied neutrality as a core convention in realist ethnography; through this convention, the narrator "poses as an impersonal conduit, who unlike missionaries, administrators, journalists, or unabashed members of the culture themselves, passes on more-or-less objective data in a measured intellectual style that is uncontaminated by personal bias, political goals, or moral judgment" (1988:47). The increasing awareness of writing as a construction, whether in realist or other styles, has led to closer examination of how ethnographers write.

While these analyses of ethnographic writing focus primarily on completed ethnographic texts, fieldnotes also draw on a variety of writing conventions. Ethnographers construct their fieldnote entries from selectively recalled and accented moments. Whether it be an incident, event, routine, interaction, or visual image, ethnographers recreate each moment from selected details and sequences that they remember or have jotted down: words, gestures, body movements, sounds, background setting, and so on. While writing, they further highlight certain actions and statements more than others in order to portray their sense of an experience. In other words, ethnographers create scenes on a page through highly selective and partial recountings of observed and re-evoked details. These scenes—that is, moments re-created on a page—represent ethnographers' perceptions and memories of slices of life, enhanced or blurred by their narrating and descriptive skills in writing. An ethnographer's style of writing (whether describing, recounting/narrating, or analyzing) inevitably draws on conventions in order to express and communicate intelligibly to readers, whether they be simply the ethnographer herself or others.

This chapter explores the relations between an ethnographer's attention to people's sayings and doings, processes for recalling these moments, and writing options for presenting and analyzing them. Of course, no writing techniques enable an ethnographer to write up life exactly as it happened or even precisely as she remembers it. At best, the ethnographer "re-creates" her memories as written scenes that authentically depict people's lives through selected, integrated details. But in mastering certain descriptive and narrating techniques, she can write up her notes more easily in that first dash of getting everything down; and she can depict more effectively those scenes that she intuitively selects as especially significant. Whether she writes up key scenes first or goes back to them to fill in details, more explicit awareness and exploration of writing strategies enables her to more vividly and fully create those scenes on the page.

In this chapter, we focus on how ethnographers go about the complex tasks of remembering, elaborating, filling in, and commenting upon field-notes in order to produce a full written account of witnessed scenes and events. We begin by discussing the process of writing up full fieldnotes as ethnographers move from the field to desk and turn their jottings into detailed entries. Next, we explain various writing strategies that ethnographers often draw on as they depict remembered slices of life in fieldnotes and organize them in sequences using conventions of narrating and describing. Although we discuss depicting and organizing strategies separately, in actual fieldnote writing, one does both at the same time. Finally, we discuss several analytic options for reflecting on fieldnotes through writing *asides* and/or more extended *commentaries* in the midst of or at the end of an entry. Whereas strategies for "getting the scene on the page" create a sense of immediacy that allows readers—whether self or others—to envision a social world, analytic strategies explore the ethnographer's understandings about that world but do not portray it. Thus, these strategies complement each other, assisting the ethnographer both to recall events and also to reflect on them.

Throughout the chapter, we make suggestions and offer examples in order to increase fieldworkers' awareness of their options for writing. For example, first-time fieldworkers typically have little difficulty in writing snippets about brief interactions; however, they are often uncertain about how to write about more complex, key scenes by sequencing interactions, creating characters, reporting dialogue, and contextualizing an action or incident with vivid, sensory details. Though we offer many concrete suggestions and examples, we do not attempt to prescribe a "correct" style or to cover all the writing options an ethnographer might use. Yet, we do suggest that one's writing style influences how one perceives what can be written. Learning to envision scenes as detailed writing on a page is as much a commitment to a lively style of writing as it is to an intellectual honesty in recording events fully and accurately.

MOVING FROM FIELD TO DESK

In this section, we discuss several practical issues that surround the shift of context from the field to desk (or other preferred writing spot). Here we answer some of the novice ethnographer's most basic questions: How much time should one allow for writing fieldnotes? How long should one stay in the field before writing fieldnotes? What is the most effective timing for writing fieldnotes after returning from the field? What writing tools and equipment does one need? How does the goal of "getting it down on the page," quickly before forgetting, shape one's writing style?

Writing requires a block of concentrated time. Sometimes, incidents that span a few minutes can take the ethnographer several hours to write up; he tries to recall just who did and said what, in what order, and to put all that into words and coherent paragraphs. Indeed, an ethnographic maxim holds that every hour spent observing requires an additional hour to write up.

Over time, fieldworkers evolve a rhythm that balances time spent in the field and time writing notes. In some situations, the field researcher can put a cap on time devoted to observing in order to allow a substantial write-up period on leaving the field. Limiting time in the field in this way lessens the likelihood that the fieldworker will forget what happened or become overwhelmed by the prospect of hours of composing fieldnotes. We recommend that beginning ethnographers, when possible, leave the field after three to four hours in order to begin writing fieldnotes.

In other situations, the fieldworker might find it more difficult to withdraw for writing. Anthropologists working in other cultures generally spend whole days observing and devote evenings to writing. Field researchers who fill roles as regular workers must put in a full workday before leaving to write notes. In both cases, longer stretches of observation require larger blocks of write-up time and perhaps different strategies for making note writing more manageable. For example, once having described basic routines and daily rhythms in the first sets of notes, the ethnographer who spends hours in the field might focus subsequent notes on significant incidents that occurred throughout the day. At this stage, longer periods spent in the field might in fact prove advantageous, allowing greater opportunities for observing incidents of interest.

Alternatively, the field researcher with regular workday responsibilities might find it useful to designate certain hours for observing and taking jottings, giving priority to these observations in writing up full fieldnotes. Varying these designated observation periods allows exploration of different patterns of activity throughout the day. Of course, while using this strategy, the fieldworker should still write notes on important incidents that occur at other times.

More crucial than how long the ethnographer spends in the field is the timing of writing up fieldnotes. Over time, people forget and simplify experience; notes composed several days after observation tend to be summarized and stripped of rich, nuanced detail. Hence, we strongly encourage researchers to sit down and write full fieldnotes as soon as possible after the day's (or night's) research is done. Writing fieldnotes *immediately* after leaving the setting produces fresher, more detailed recollections that harness the ethnographer's involvement with and excitement about the day's events. Indeed, writing notes immediately on leaving the field offers a way of releasing the weight of what the researcher has just experienced. It is easier to focus one's thoughts and energies on the taxing work of reviewing, remembering, and writing. In contrast, those who put off writing fieldnotes report that with the passage of time, the immediacy of lived experience fades, and writing fieldnotes becomes a burdensome, even dreaded, experience.

Often, however, it is impossible for an ethnographer to find time to write up notes immediately upon leaving the field. Long or late hours, for example, often leave him too tired to write notes. Under these circumstances, it is best to get a good night's sleep and turn to writing up first thing in the morning. Sometimes, even this rest is impossible: A village event might last through several days and nights, confronting the anthropological researcher with a choice between sleeping outside with the villagers or taking time out periodically to sleep and write notes.

When a researcher has been in the field for a long period and has limited time immediately afterward for writing full fieldnotes, she has several alternatives. First, she could make extensive, handwritten jottings about the day's events, relying on the details of these notes to postpone writing full fieldnotes, often for some time.[1] Second, she could dictate fieldnotes into a tape recorder. One can "talk fieldnotes" relatively quickly and can dictate while driving home from a field setting. But while dictation preserves vivid impressions and observations immediately on leaving the field, dictated notes eventually have to be transcribed, a time-consuming, expensive project. And in the meantime, the field researcher does not have ready access to these dictated notes for review or for planning her next steps in the field.

When writing immediately or soon after returning from the site, the fieldworker should go directly to computer or notebook, not talking with intimates about what happened until full fieldnotes are completed. Such "what happened today" talk can rob note writing of its psychological immediacy and emotional release; writing the day's events becomes a stale recounting rather than a cathartic outpouring.[2]

Ethnographers use a variety of different means to write up full notes. While the typewriter provided the standard tool for many classic ethnographers, some handwrote their full notes on pads or in notebooks. Contemporary ethnographers strongly prefer a computer with a standard word-processing program. Typing notes with a word-processing program not only has the advantage of greater speed (slow typists will soon notice substantial gains in speed and accuracy) but also allows for the modification of words, phrases, and sentences in the midst of writing without producing messy, hard-to-read pages. Fieldnotes written on the computer are also easily reordered; it is possible, for example, to insert incidents or dialogue subsequently recalled at the appropriate place. Finally, composing with a word-processing program facilitates coding and sorting fieldnotes as one later turns to writing finished ethnographic accounts.

In sitting down at a desk or computer, the ethnographer's most urgent task or writing purpose is to record experiences while they are still fresh. Thus, ethnographers write hurriedly, dashing words "down on the page." Their notes read like an outpouring, not like polished, publishable excerpts. Knowing that a memorable event fades and gets confused with following ones as time passes, a fieldworker writes using whatever phrasing and organization seems most accessible, convenient, and doable at the time. He need not worry about being consistent, and he can shift from one style, one topic, or one thought to another as quickly as the fingers can type. In that initial writing, the field researcher concentrates on a remembered scene more than on words and sentences. If the ethnographer focuses too soon on wording, she will produce an "internal editor," distracting her attention from the evoked scene and stopping her outpouring of memory. The goal is to get as much down on paper in as much detail and as quickly as possible, holding off any evaluation and editing until later. But in this process, the ethnographer tries to strike a balance between describing fully and getting down the essentials of what happened. One student explains her struggle to describe an incident:

> Here I'm going to stop and go back later because I know what I'm trying to say, but it isn't coming out. . . . So there's a little more to it than that, but I have to think about how to say it, so I'm just going to leave it. When I write my fieldnotes, I just try to get it all down, and I go back through and edit, take time

away from it and then come back and see if that's really what I meant to say or
if I could say that in a better way, a clearer way.

Fieldworkers may write down all the words that come to mind and later
choose a more evocative and appropriate phrasing. Many writers produce
a first round quickly, knowing that they will make additions, polish wording, or reorganize paragraphs at some other time. Thus, in that first rush of
writing, finding the absolutely best word or phrase to persuade a future audience should not be of such concern that it slows down the flow of getting
words to paper.

Beginning ethnographers should not be surprised to experience ambivalence in writing fieldnotes. On the one hand, the outpouring of thoughts
and impressions as the writer reviews and reexperiences the excitement and
freshness of the day's events might bring expressive release and reflective insight. Having seen and heard intriguing, surprising things all day long, the
fieldworker is finally able to sit down, think about, and relive events while
transforming them into a permanent record. On the other hand, after a long,
exciting, or draining stint in the field, a busy schedule might inhibit finding
enough time to write up notes, turning the writing-up process into an intrusive, humdrum burden. This experience is more likely to occur after the ethnographer has spent weeks or months in the field; writing notes more selectively and/or focusing on new and unexpected developments not described
in previous writings can provide some relief to these feelings.

RECALLING IN ORDER TO WRITE

In sitting down to compose fieldnotes in a fluid, "get it down quickly" fashion, the fieldworker seeks to recall in as much detail as possible what he observed and experienced earlier that day. This process of recalling in order to
write involves reimagining and replaying in one's mind scenes and events
that marked the day, actively repicturing and reconstructing these witnessed
events in order to get them down on a page. Sometimes replaying and reconstructing are keyed to jottings or lists of topics written earlier; at others, the
ethnographer works only with "headnotes" and other memories to reconstruct detailed accounts of the day's events. In both cases, the descriptions
that result must make sense as a logical, sensible series of incidents and experiences, even if only to an audience made up of the fieldworker himself.

Ethnographers often use a mix of standard practices for recalling the day's events in order to organize and compose detailed, comprehensive fieldnotes. One strategy is to trace one's own activities and observations in chronological order, recalling noteworthy events in the sequence in which one observed and experienced them. Another strategy is to begin with some "high point" or an incident or event that stands out as particularly vivid or important, to detail that event as thoroughly as possible, and then to consider in some topical fashion other significant events, incidents, or exchanges. Or, the ethnographer can focus more systematically on incidents related to specific topics of interest in order to recall significant events. Often ethnographers combine or alternate between strategies, proceeding back and forth over time in stream-of-consciousness fashion.

As noted, ethnographers often compose full fieldnotes without any prior writings, working strictly from memory and the recollection of what was seen and heard in the field. In other cases, they can work from jottings made in the field or soon after. Some ethnographers also find it useful, on moving to the desk in preparation for writing, to write up a list of topics—brief references to key events that unfolded that day or to the sequence of action that marked a key incident—using the list to get started on and to organize notes on these events. In these later instances, the fieldworker fills in, extends, and integrates these abbreviated bits and pieces of information by visualizing and replaying the events, incidents, and experiences they refer to. Jottings and lists of topics, then, can anchor the writing process, providing links back to the field; the fieldworker simply turns to the start of that day's jottings or topics and moves through in the order recorded, filling in and making connections between segments on the basis of memory.

To explore the process of using memory and abbreviated writings to construct full fieldnotes, we consider how fieldworkers turn brief jottings into extended texts. Looking at the movement back and forth between jottings and the fuller, richer recollection of events in the final fieldnotes provides a grounded way of examining the generic processes of recalling in order to write. Here, we return to the two illustrations of jottings provided in chapter 2, examining how each was used to produce sets of full fieldnotes.

1. *"Too Many Sexual References"*

A. Jottings
Sexual Harassment
Andy—too many sexual references
        PE frisbee game "This team has too many sausages"

Reynaldo—(*Carlos—in jail for stealing bicycle, 18 yrs old*) [*circled*]
Laura—Wants to propose sexual harassment forms
      Thinking about detention for these students but already too much work
      for keeping track of tardies/truancies/tendencies

B. Full Fieldnotes

Next Laura goes off topic and mentions that some of the students keep making sexual comments that are "inappropriate." She says that Andy is particularly bad and recounts an instance where the class was out on the PE field and she split the class into teams for Ultimate Frisbee. I split the boys and girls evenly but you know how the girls tend to just switch teams so they can be together. Most of the boys ended up on one team, and the other team, the team with Andy, had a lot of boys. Andy says, "Jezz, this team has too many cocks!" right in front of me! Then Laura focuses on Reynaldo. Someone used lotion at my desk and it squirted out onto the table in front of my desk. Reynaldo comes in and says, Wow, somebody had an accident over here! Don't worry, Laura, I'll clean it up for you. And he did, he took some Kleenex and cleaned it up, but still, do you really think that it's appropriate to mention to me, someone in her 50s, that someone excreted ejaculatory fluid on my desk?! I mean, I'm in my 50s, I have three sons, and I have a Master's degree!

The other teachers nod their heads and agree this is wrong. Marie says, I feel exactly the same way. She wanted to say something else but Ms. Diaz interrupts her: The other day I was trying to teach Jerry something and he yelled at me, "Get off my nuts!" Can you believe that? The principal mentions, Oh yeah, I remember you came down to tell me about that. Laura then says, We need a system to control this. I think that we should type out a statement that shows exactly what they said and have the student who said it sign and date it. If they have three of those, we punish them somehow. The teachers debate the merits of this system and ask what kinds of punishment they could realistically enforce. Laura says they could give students detention. Rose says, Yeah, but look at how much paperwork we already have to do for the students who are already in detention, so you want to make more work in general for all of us? No, we can't give the students detention, it'd have to be something else. In the end, there is a consensus that this system is good but has kinks to work out. (The punishment of the students is contingent on the workload of the staff.)

Note the contrasts in content, texture, and comprehensibility between the initial jottings and the full fieldnotes. The fieldworker uses the references to Andy and Reynaldo to recollect and reconstruct the teacher's accounts of inappropriate "sexual references" recently made by each boy. Nothing is written here from the jotting about Carlos being in jail for stealing a bicycle; presumably one of the staff mentioned this as a side issue in the midst of this talk. That these words were circled suggests that they have been included elsewhere in the notes, perhaps to document staff plans to dismiss students who were eighteen or older whom the school was not legally mandated to retain. The second paragraph fills in the discussion generated by Laura's proposal to create "sexual harassment forms" and to punish students who accumulate three such forms. Note that it is only here that the school staff use the term "sexual harassment," although the ethnographer has used this heading to mark and recall these exchanges in his jottings.

Furthermore, a discrepancy between the jottings and the full notes is evident: in the former, Andy is reported to have referred to "too many sausages," while in the full notes Laura quotes Andy as having said "too many cocks." The student ethnographer explained what happened here (personal communication): "Reynaldo told me Andy used the words 'too many cocks.' I got mixed up when creating the fieldnotes. It should have been Laura 'too many sausages' and Reynaldo 'too many cocks.'"[3]

2. *"You Can Call His Doctor at UCLA"*

A. Jottings
[case number]
Snow, Marcia
Thomas

> atty—AIDS Mike
> Murphy
> legal guardian

---

are you prepared to proceed against
the one individual—(both)
massive doses of chemother(apy)
I don't think he's ever going to come in
> here
I know he's well enough to walk–
came in (returned heater)—when?
you can call his doctor at UCLA and
he can verify all this
I just don't call people on the
telephone—courts don't operate that way—it has to be on paper or (in person)

———

Mr. M returned my heaters–

was walking

———

Let me be clear
You don't want to proceed against
only one of these individuals?
I want to proceed against (no, but)
—if he is his guardian both—but

———

unravel it
Dept 10—J(udge) Berkoff
Ms. S, hold on just a

B. Full Fieldnotes

Marcia Snow has longish, curly, dark brown hair, in her 20s, dressed informally in blue blouse and pants. No wedding ring, but with a youngish looking guy with glasses. Robert Thomas is in his 40s, light brown hair, shaggy mustache, jacket with red-black checked lining.

Judge begins by asking RT if he has an atty; he does, but he is not here. He explains that his business partner, Mike Murphy, who is also named in the TRO, is not here today; he has AIDS and is very ill. "I'm his legal guardian," so I can represent his concerns. J asks MS: "Are you prepared to proceed against this one individual?" MS answers that she wants the order against both of them. RT then explains that MM has had AIDS for three years, has had "massive doses of chemotherapy," and adds: "I don't think he's ever going to come in here." J asks MS if from what she knows that MM is this sick. MS hesitates, then says: "I know he's well enough to walk." I saw him walking when he returned the heaters that they stole. J: When was this? (I can't hear her answer.) RT: He's had his AIDS for three years. He's very sick. "You can call his doctor at UCLA, and he can verify this." J: "I just don't call people on the telephone. Courts don't operate that way. It has to be on paper" or testified in person. RT repeats that MM is very ill, that he has to take care of him, and he is not getting better. But MS again counters this, saying again: "Mr. Murphy returned my heaters—he was walking then . . ."

J then looks to MS, asking: "Let me be clear—you don't want to proceed against only one of these individuals?" MS: "No, I want to proceed against both. But if he is his guardian," then I can go ahead today with it. J agrees to this, saying he will let another judge "unravel it," and assigns the case to Dept. 10, Judge Berkoff. MS and RT turn to leave, but J says: "Ms. Snow, hold on just a minute until the clerk has your file." MS waits briefly, then gets file and goes out with the guy with her.

Compared to the highly selected, partial, and abbreviated jottings, the full fieldnotes tell a coherent, step-by-step story of what was observed in the courtroom. Most of this story consists of details that have been filled in from memory. The brief "background" of the case provided by the jottings, for example, has been fleshed out into relatively full descriptions of the two litigants (but not of the judge or other regular courtroom personnel). In addition, the notes tell a story about one specific topic—the problems arising from the absence of a codefendant, the questions the judge raises about this absence, and a sequence of responses to this problem by the petitioner and defendant. The story, however, is missing key elements (for example, the fact that this case involves a tenant-landlord dispute) and contains elements of unknown meaning (for example, Marcia's comment about how the absent defendant "returned the heaters that they stole").

Also consider the handling of direct quotations in moving from jottings to fieldnotes. Only those words actually taken down at the time are placed in quotes; a portion of the direct speech missed at the time is paraphrased outside the direct quotes. Thus, the jotted record of the judge's remark, "it has to be on paper or (in person)," is written in fieldnote form as "'It has to be on paper' or testified in person." As a general practice, speech not written down word for word at the time should either be presented as indirect quotation or paraphrased (see discussion of "dialogue" below).

Ethnographers rely upon key words and phrases from their jottings to jog their memories. But writing fieldnotes from jottings is not a straightforward remembering and filling in; rather, it is a much more active process of constructing relatively coherent sequences of action and evocations of scene and character (see below). In turning jottings and headnotes into full notes, the fieldworker is already engaged in a sort of preliminary analysis whereby she orders experience, both creating and discovering patterns of interaction. This process involves deciding not simply *what to include* but also *what to leave out*, both from remembered headnotes and from items included in jottings. Thus, in writing full fieldnotes, the ethnographer might clearly remember or have jottings about particular incidents or impressions but decide, for a variety of reasons, not to incorporate them into the notes. The material might seem to involve matters that are peripheral to major activities in the setting, activities that members appear to find insignificant, or that the ethnographer has no interest in.

However, in continuing to write up the day's fieldnotes or at some later point in the fieldwork, the ethnographer might see significance in jottings or headnotes that initially seemed too unimportant or uninteresting to include in full fieldnotes. The student ethnographer who, in writing full notes, had initially passed over a jotting about the "delivery of three new

bags of sand" to the sandbox at a Headstart Program (chapter 2) saw relevance and meaning in this incident as she continued to write up and reflect
on the day's observations:

> Now that I'm thinking back, when we got the sand, it was a really hot day so
> that actually that jotting did help me remember because it was so warm out
> that Karen, the teacher, said that the children could take their shoes off in the
> sandbox. This became a really tough rule to enforce because the children aren't
> allowed to have shoes off anywhere else. They would just run out of the sand-
> box and go into the parking lot, and so it was a really tough rule to enforce.
> And I have an incident about that.

In the comments made here, the student comes to appreciate (and construct) a linkage between the three new bags of sand included in her jottings
and what she sees as significant issues of rule enforcement and control in
the setting; with this appreciation, she decides to incorporate the delivery
of the sand as an incident in her notes. Moreover, this focus on enforcement
and control leads her to review her memory for "relevant" events or "incidents"; here she recollects "an incident about that," signaling her intent to
write up this incident in her notes.

In light of the ways "significance" shifts and emerges in the course of
writing notes and thinking about their import, we encourage students to
write about as many of these "minor" events as possible, even if they seem
insubstantial or only vaguely relevant at the moment. They might signal important processes relevant to other incidents or to emerging analytic themes
in ways the ethnographer can only appreciate at some later point. Even when
writing the story of one rather cohesive event, writers should include apparently tangential activities and comments, for they might turn out to provide
key insights into the main action.

WRITING DETAILED NOTES: DEPICTION OF SCENES

The ethnographer's central purpose is to portray a social world and its
people. But often beginning researchers produce fieldnotes lacking sufficient and lively detail. Through inadvertent summarizing and evaluative
wording, a fieldworker fails to adequately describe what she has observed
and experienced. The following strategies—description, dialogue, and
characterization—enable a writer to coherently depict an observed moment
through striking details. As is evident in several of the included excerpts,

ethnographers often merge several strategies. In this section, we explain and provide examples of these writing strategies; in the next section, we discuss various options for organizing a day's entry.

Description

"Description" is a term used in more than one way. Thus far, we have referred to writing fieldnotes as descriptive writing in contrast to analytic argumentation.[4] Here, we refer more specifically to description as a means of picturing through concrete sensory details the basic scenes, settings, objects, people, and actions the fieldworker observed. In this sense, writing descriptive images is just one part of the ethnographer's storytelling about the day's events.

As a writing strategy, description calls for concrete details rather than abstract generalizations, for sensory imagery rather than evaluative labels, and for immediacy through details presented at close range. Goffman (1989:131) advises the fieldworker to write "lushly," making frequent use of adjectives and adverbs to convey details. For example, details present color, shape, and size to create visual images; other details of sound, timbre, loudness, and volume evoke auditory images; those details describing smell or fragrance recreate olfactory images; and details portraying gestures, movements, posture, and facial expression convey kinetic images. While visual images tend to predominate in many descriptions, ethnographers find that they often combine these various kinds of images in a complete description.

When describing a scene, the writer selects those details that most clearly and vividly create an image on the page; consequently, he succeeds best in describing when he selects details according to some purpose and from a definite point of view. For example, the writer acquires a clearer sense of what details to accent if he takes as his project describing, not the office setting in a general sense, but, rather, the office environment as a cluttered place to work, perhaps as seen from the perspective of a secretary who struggles with her boss's disorder every day. However, frequently the fieldworker sits down to write about a setting he does not yet understand. In fact, the beginning ethnographer often faces the dilemma of not knowing what counts as most important; under these circumstances, his purpose is simply to document the impression he has at that time. Wanting to recall the physical characteristics and the sensory impressions of his experience, a fieldworker often describes the setting and social situations, characters' appearances, and even some daily routines.

Ethnographers often select details to describe the ambience of a setting or environment that is important for understanding subsequent action. For example, during initial fieldwork in a village in southeastern Congo (formerly Zaire), an ethnographer might reflect on the spatial arrangement and social relations as she has observed them thus far. In her fieldnotes, she might describe how the houses all face toward an open, cleared area; that the village pavilion where men visit is situated in the center; that the women cook by wood fires in front of their houses, often carrying babies on their backs as they work and are assisted by younger girls; and that some men and boys sit under a tree in the yard near two other men weaving baskets. How she perceives these details and the way she frames them as contextualizing social interactions determines, in part, the details she selects to create this visual image of a small village in the late afternoon.

An ethnographer should also depict the appearance of characters who are part of described scenes in order to contextualize actions and talk. For example, in looking at how residents adapted to conditions in a psychiatric board-and-care home, Linda Shaw described someone who others living in the home thought was especially "crazy":

Robert and I were sitting by the commissary talking this afternoon when a new resident named Bruce passed by several times. He was a tall, extremely thin man with straggly, shoulder-length, graying hair and a long bushy beard. I had heard that he was only in his thirties, even though he looked prematurely aged in a way that reminded me of the sort of toll that harsh conditions exact from many street people. He wore a long, dirty, gray-brown overcoat with a rainbow sewn to the back near the shoulder over a pair of torn blue jeans and a white tee shirt with what looked like coffee stains down the front. Besides his disheveled appearance, Bruce seemed extremely agitated and restless as he paced from one end of the facility to the other. He walked with a loping gait, taking very long strides, head held bent to his chest and his face expressionless, as his arms swung limply through the air, making a wide arc, as though made of rubber. As Bruce passed by on one of these rounds, Robert remarked, "That guy's really crazy. Don't tell me he's going to be recycled into society."

Here the ethnographer provides a detailed description of a newcomer to the home, providing the context necessary to understand a resident's comment that this person was too crazy to ever live outside of the home. In fact, the final comment, "Don't tell me he's going to be recycled into society," serves as a punch line dramatically linking the observer's detailed description of the new resident with the perceptions and concerns of an established resident.

While describing appearance might initially seem easy, in fact, many observers have difficulty doing so in lively, engaging ways. Part of the problem derives from the fact that when we observe people whom we do not know personally, we initially see them in very stereotyped ways; we normally notice and describe strangers in terms of gender, age, or race, along with other qualities in their physical appearances.[5] Thus, beginning fieldworkers invariably identify characters by gender. They frequently add one or two visible features: "a young woman," "a young guy in a floral shirt," "two Latina women with a small child," "a woman in her forties," "a white male with brown/blond medium length hair." Indeed, many fieldnotes present characters as *visual clichés*, relying on worn-out, frequently used details to describe others, often in ways that invoke common stereotypes: a middle-aged librarian is simplistically described as "a bald man wearing thick glasses," a youth in a juvenile hall as having "slicked back hair," a lawyer as "wearing a pin-striped suit" and "carrying a briefcase." Such clichés not only make for boring writing but also, more dangerously, blind the writer to specific attributes of the person in front of him.

The description of a character's appearance is frequently "categoric" and stereotyped for another reason as well: Fieldworkers rely upon these clichés not so much to convey another's appearance to envisioned readers but to label (and thus provide clarity about) who is doing what within the fieldnote account. For example, a fieldworker used the phrase "the floral shirt guy" a number of times to specify which character he was talking about when he described the complicated comings and goings occurring in a Latino street scene. Thus, the initial description does not provide many details about this character's appearance but merely tags him so that we can identify and follow him in the subsequent account.

However, the ethnographer must train herself both to notice more than these common indicators of general social categories and to capture distinctive qualities that will enable future readers (whether herself in rereading the notes or others who read excerpts) to envision more of what she saw and experienced. A *vivid image* based on actual observation depicts specific details about people and settings so that the image can be clearly visualized. For example, one fieldworker described a man in a skid row mission as "a man in the back who didn't have any front teeth and so spoke with a lisp." Another described a boy in a third-grade classroom as "wiggling his butt and distorting his face for attention" on entering the classroom late. Such images use details to paint more specific, lively portraits and avoid as much as possible vague, stereotypic features.

Ethnographers can also write more vivid descriptions by describing how characters dress. The following excerpt depicts a woman's clothes through concrete and sensory imagery:

> Today Molly, a white female, wore her African motif jacket. It had little squares on the front which contained red, yellow, green, and black colored prints of the African continent. Imposed on top was a gold lion of Judah (symbol of Ethiopian Royal Family). The sleeves were bright—red, yellow, and green striped. The jacket back had a picture of Bob Marley singing into a microphone. He is a black male with long black dreadlocks and a little beard. Written in red at the top was: "Rastafari."

This description advances the ethnographer's concern with ethnic identity and affiliation. The initial sentence, "Today Molly, a white female, wore her African motif jacket," sets up an unexpected contrast: Molly is white, yet she wears an item of clothing that the researcher associates with African American culture. "African motif" directs attention to particular attributes of the jacket (colors, insignia, and symbols) and ignores other observable qualities of the jacket, for example, its material, texture, style, cleanliness, or origins. Consequently, this description frames the jacket as an object publicly announcing its wearer's affiliation with African Americans.[6]

Furthermore, rather than simply *telling* the reader what the ethnographer infers, this passage *shows* affiliation with African Americans in immediate detail through actions and imagery. Contrast this descriptive strategy with the following (hypothetical) abstract and evaluative depiction that generalizes, rather than specifies, details: "Today, Molly, a white girl, *assertively* wore her *bright African* jacket. She always *shows off* in these clothes and *struts* around pretending to act *like a black*." Not only does this summary rely on a vague adjective ("bright"), but it also obscures the actions with evaluative adverbs and verbs ("assertively," "struts," and "shows off") and categorizing labels ("like a black").

Because an ethnographer wishes to depict a scene for a reader, he does not condense details, avoids evaluative adjectives and verbs, and never permits a label to stand for description. While all writing entails grouping and identifying details, the ethnographer resists the impulse to unself-consciously label others according to received categories from his own background. Nonetheless, it is not enough to avoid evaluative wording. In descriptions, the writer's tone of voice unavoidably reflects his personal attitude toward the people described. A better-than-thou attitude or objectifying the other (as odd, a foreigner, from a lower class, from a less civilized culture, from another ethnic group) always "shows" in subtle ways: Tone, like a slip of the tongue, appears in word choice, implicit comparisons, and even in rhythms as in the staccato of a curt dismissal. A self-reflective ethnographer should make his judgments explicit in written asides. But, the best antidote to these evaluative impulses is to keep in mind that the ethnographer's task is to write descriptions that lead to empathetic understanding of the social worlds of others.

In addition to describing people, places, and things, an ethnographer might also depict a scene by including action. For example, she might portray a character's talk, gesture, posture, and movement. In contrast to describing a person's appearance, action sequences highlight a character's agency to affect her world; a character acts within a situation in routine ways or in response to set conditions. The following fieldnote excerpt of a grocery stocker working in a nearly empty store reveals how sensory details about action can create a vivid description of a scene:

> As I conclude my first "lap" [around the store] and begin my second, I find myself slowly making my way through the frozen food aisle when I come across a female "stocker." She seems to be pretty young (college age) and is thin with dark, heavily lined eyes. Although her eyes are dark, the makeup is not to the point where she looks gothic. Her brown hair is pulled back in a loose bun, and she is in the process of restocking TV dinners into the freezer. She is like a robot: she seems to be in her own space as she opens the freezer door and props open the door using her body. She then grabs a few TV dinners from their original boxed container and sorts and loads them into the new and appropriate location within the freezer. As she turns around to reload, she fails to prop open the freezer door with something other than her body. This causes the door to involuntarily close when she shifts her body in order to grab more boxes. This action causes the freezer door to slam shut with a loud "snap" sound. As strange as it may seem, the sound that the door makes is almost as if the freezer is mocking the female stocker. But this does not seem to distress her as she turns around and repeats the whole process, again and again.

Here, the ethnographer sets the scene, using an evocative image (eyes are dark, but the makeup is not gothic-looking) to enable the reader to visualize the stocker's appearance. Notice how she uses a familiar metaphor, for example "robot," as a starting point to call up a visual image, but she avoids creating a stereotyped character by providing the details of actions to create a fuller, in-depth picture of what the stocker is doing. She employs visual images of the stocker's physical movement (using her body to keep the freezer door open), as well as auditory images (the freezer door slams shut with a loud "snap" sound), to give the door a human-like character (the ability to mock the stocker). Thus, she effectively portrays both the physical and emotional effort required to place the TV dinners in the freezer. When ethnographers occasionally use figurative language, such as this robot metaphor, they always should supplement the image with descriptive detail as this ethnographer does. Otherwise, later on when reading her fieldnotes, she might not remember why she chose this metaphor or what actions it represented.

Dialogue

Ethnographers also reproduce dialogue—conversations that occur in their presence or that members report having had with others—as accurately as possible. They reproduce dialogue through direct and indirect quotation, through reported speech, and by paraphrasing. We hold that only those phrases actually quoted verbatim should be placed between quotation marks; all others should be recorded as indirect quotations or paraphrases.

The following example illustrates how direct quotation, indirect quotation, and reported speech work together to convey back-and-forth conversation:

> For a minute or so before I left, I talked with Polly, the black woman who guards the front school entrance. As we were talking, a black girl, wearing dark blue sweats, walked by. Polly pointed to her. "Did you see that girl?" she asked me. I told her I had, and Polly confided that the girl had hassled her. Polly said the girl tried to leave school without permission and had started arguing. She said the principal had been walking by and he had tried to deal with the disturbance. And the girl had answered, "This is my school. You can't control me!" and then she had called the principal a "white MF." Polly told me, "It's usually a black MF, but she changed it." She said that girl had a "bad attitude" and shook her head.

Writing up this conversation as predominately indirect quotation preserves the back-and-forth flow of the spoken interaction. Interspersing quoted fragments livens up the dialogue and lends a sense of immediacy. By clearly marking the direct quotation, indirect quotation, and reported speech, we can see how they work together.

Direct: "Did you see that girl?"
Indirect: I told her I had . . .
Indirect: . . . and Polly confided that the girl had hassled her. Polly said that the girl
            tried to leave school without permission and had started arguing. She said
            the principal had been walking by and he had tried to deal with the distur-
            bance.
Reported speech, direct: And the girl had answered, "This is my school. You can't con-
            trol me!" and then she called the principal a "white MF."
Direct: "It's usually a black MF, but she changed it."
Indirect: She said that the girl has a
Direct: "bad attitude" . . .

Indirect quotation more closely approximates dialogue than paraphrasing does. Paraphrasing this conversation with Polly might have preserved
the basic content. But in paraphrasing, a writer translates speech into her
own words and too readily starts to summarize. For example, a paraphrase
of the last portion of this excerpt might read: "The girl talked back to the
principal and called him names. . . . She has some attitude problems." This
paraphrasing obscures the flavor of chatting and offering confidences, and
it fails to voice the student's remarks to the principal, which thus would
have been unheard.

Clearly, this ethnographer has a lively style that moves easily because the
fieldnote varies the phrasing and only uses "she said" as needed. In writing
direct or indirect quotations, ethnographers do not need to repeat "she said
that . . ." each time they introduce dialogue. Instead, one can keep the pace
of the dialogue moving by immediately stating the verbatim-recalled wording or the approximately recalled phrase. For example, "Polly said that the
girl had hassled her," could also be written as, "Polly replied, the girl hassled
me," or, sometimes when it is clear who is speaking, simply as "the girl hassled me." Too many repetitions of "she said" or "he said" begin to echo and,
thus, detract from the flow of the dialogue.

Members' own descriptions and "stories" of their experiences are invaluable indexes to their views and perceptions of the world (see chapter 5) and
should be documented verbatim when possible. Writing this exchange as
a "story" told verbatim to the fieldworker preserves two different kinds of
information. First, it shows that "something happened" between a student,
a guard, and the principal. Second, the account provides the guard's experience of that something. As the guard's story, this fieldnote conveys more
about the teller and her concerns than it does about the girl and her trouble.

Writing up dialogue is more complicated than simply remembering talk or replaying every word. People talk in spurts and fragments. They accentuate or even complete a phrase with a gesture, facial expression, or posture. They send complex messages through incongruent, seemingly contradictory and ironic verbal and nonverbal expression as in sarcasm or polite putdowns. Thus, ethnographers must record the meanings they infer from the bodily expression accompanying words—gesture, movement, facial expression, tone of voice. Furthermore, people do not take turns smoothly in conversations: They interrupt each other, overlap words, talk simultaneously, and respond with ongoing comments and murmurs. Such turn taking can be placed on a linear page by bracketing and overlapping speech.

Although accurately capturing dialogue in jottings and full fieldnotes requires considerable effort, ethnographers have a number of reasons for peppering their notes with verbatim quoted talk. Such dialogue conveys character traits, advances action, and provides clues to the speaker's social status, identity, personal style, and interests. Dialogue allows the field researcher to capture members' terms and expressions as they are actually used in specific situations. In addition, dialogue can point to key features of a cultural worldview. The following excerpt comes from a discussion in an African American history course:

> Deston, a black male with Jheri curls, asked Ms. Dubois, "What's a sellout? I hear that if you talk to a white person—you sell out. If you go out with a white girl—you sell out." She replied that some people "take it to the extreme." She said that a sellout could even be a teacher or someone who works at McDonalds. Then she defined a sellout as "someone who is more concerned about making it . . . who has no racial loyalty, no allegiance to people."

The writer uses direct quotation to capture an ongoing exchange about racial identity and to retain a key member's term.

The use of indirect, along with direct, quotation also allows an ethnographer to represent the back-and-forth character of everyday interaction in accurate and effective ways. In the following excerpt from a swap meet, for example, directly quoting the actual negotiations over price highlights and focuses the reader's attention on this aspect of the interaction.

> She (swap meet vendor) had many different items including a Sparkletts water dispenser, some big outdoor Christmas lighted decorations, a blanket, wooden shoes from China, salt and pepper shakers, a vacuum cleaner, mini wooden mantels, clothes, small pieces of furniture, and shoes. I see a beaded curtain jumbled up on the tarp and walk toward it. I point to it and ask the vendor how

much she wants for it. She takes a moment to think and then says, "Ummm, five dollars." She stands up slowly and walks over to it. She picks it up off the ground. She shows us that it is in good condition by holding it up high and letting all the bead strands hang down. "Will you take three?" I ask as I look it over. It has a fancy top that the beads hang off of. It is all one color—ivory or light brown. "How about four?" she says. "Alright, I'll take it," I say. She tells me that she will bag it up for me, and she turns around to get a plastic bag from the inside of the van. I rummage through my pockets looking for the one dollar bills. All I have left are three ones and a five. I hand her the five and she gives me the bag. She puts the five dollar bill into her fanny pack and withdraws a one dollar bill. She hands it to me and says thank you. I say thank you back and turn to leave.

In addition to contributing to a lively description of a scene at the swap meet, the presentation of dialogue furthers sensitivity to the interactional processes through which members construct meanings and local social worlds in such routine exchanges.

These issues and choices in writing dialogue become even more complex when the local language differs from the researcher's. How well the researcher knows the language certainly determines the extent of verbatim quoting. When the ethnographer hears slang, nonstandard English, or grammatically incorrect phrasing, she should resist correcting this wording but, instead, put such expressions in quotation marks. In addition, when a fieldworker does research in a second language, not only will she frequently miss what someone said because she did not understand a particular word, but she also will have difficulty capturing the verbatim flow of a dialogue even when she does understand. By working with a local assistant and checking to make sure she understands correctly what people are saying, she can compensate for some of her difficulty. Similar problems arise when working in English in a setting with much technical lingo or other in-group expressions such as slang. Unable to follow all the talk, the researcher paraphrases as much as she can and occasionally includes the snippets of verbatim talk she heard and remembered clearly.

In response to these language difficulties, many ethnographers supplement their fieldnotes by tape recordings. They might also make recordings in order to preserve as detailed a record of naturally occurring talk as possible so that they can pursue particular theoretical issues. For example, field researchers interested in recurrent patterns of interaction in institutional settings might make special efforts to tape-record at least some such encounters.[7] Still, most ethnographers do not regard recordings as their primary or exclusive form of data; rather, they use them as one way among others for closely examining the meaning events and experiences have for those studied.

By way of illustration, consider how Rachel Fretz worked with recordings of storytelling performances among the Chokwe people in Bandundu, Congo (formerly Zaire). She recorded and carefully transcribed all verbal expressions of both narrators and audience, since listeners actively participate in the storytelling session. The following is an excerpt from the beginning of one such performance; the narrator (N), a young man, performs to an audience (A) of women, men, and children one evening around the fire (Fretz 1995a).

N: Once upon a time, there were some young boys, myself and Fernando and Funga and Shamuna.

A: Is it a story with a good song?

N: They were four persons. They said, "Ah. Let's go hunting."
    Pia they went everywhere. *Pia* they went everywhere.

A: Good.

N: They went this way and that way, this way and that way. No game. "Let's return.
    Let's go." They saw a large hut.
    Inside there was a container with honey in it.
    "My friends, this honey, *mba*, who put it here?"
    He said, "Who?"
    Another said, "Who?"
    [Another said,] "Let's go. We can't eat this."
    Then, *fwapu*, Funga came forward and said, "Ah! You're just troubled. Even
        though you're so hungry, you won't eat this honey?"
    "Child. The man who put the honey here is not present. You see that this house
        was built with human ribs, and you decide to eat this honey."
    He [Funga] said, "Get out of here. I'll eat it. Go on ahead. Go now." He took some
        honey; he ate it.
    "Shall we wait for him? We'll wait for him."
    He came soon. "Let's go."
    Liata, liata, liata, they walked along. "We're going a long way. We came from
        a great distance." They arrived and found, ah! *Kayanda* [my goodness], a
        large river.
    "My friends, what is this?"
    "My friends, such a large river. Where did it come from?"
    He said, "Ah! Who can explain it?"
    "We can't see its source or where it's going."
    "Let's cross the river. I'll go first.

First Singing

N: Oh Papa. Eee, Papa, it's I who ate the honey.
A: This large river God created, I must cross it.
N: Papa! Eee, Papa, I'm going into the water.
A: This large river God created, I must cross it.
N: Papa! Eee, Papa, I didn't it.
A: This large river God created, I must cross it.
N: Papa! Eee, Papa, I'm crossing to the other side.
A: This large river God created, I must cross it.

Transcribing a performance involves catching all the teller's words and audience responses (often requiring the help of a native speaker) despite such
interfering sounds as a dog barking and children crying. Accurate transcription also requires close attention to the rhythm and pauses in speaking so
that the punctuation and line breaks reflect the storytelling style (cf. Hymes
1991; Tedlock 1983).

But transcribing and translating the tape is only one part of the ethnographer's efforts to learn about and understand storytelling performances. She
also wrote extensive fieldnotes describing the situation and participants.[8]
For example, she noted that the storytelling session took place by the fire
in the chief's pavilion at an informal family gathering including the chief,
his seven wives, and their children and grandchildren. She observed that the
women participated primarily by singing the story-songs and by answering
with exclamations and remarks. The ethnographer also recorded her conversations with these participants and the general comments Chokwe people
offered about telling such stories, called *yishima*. She found out that in this
performance, listeners know that the house-made-of-human-ribs probably
belongs to a sorcerer, that eating his honey is dangerous because it will cast a
spell over them, that the river that appeared from nowhere across their path
had been created by the sorcerer, and that Funga who ate the honey most
likely will drown as a consequence of not listening to his older brother. She
learned that the recurring song, sung four times during the performance,
created a tension between hope and panic about the consequences of eating
the honey and between trusting that it was a natural river created by God
("This large river God created") and fearing that it was a sorcerer's invention
("Eee, Papa, it's I who ate the honey").

Thus, a transcription of recorded speech is not a straightforward and
simple means of documenting an event. The ethnographer needs to observe
and listen to more than the words; she needs to ask many follow-up ques-

tions and write down what she learns. As a result, much field research uses a variety of recording and encoding processes, combining fieldnotes with audio and video recording.[9]

Characterization

Ethnographers describe the persons they encounter through a strategy known as *characterization*. While a simple description of a person's dress and movements conveys some minimal sense of that individual, the writer more fully characterizes a human being through also showing how that person talks, acts, and relates to others. An ethnographer most effectively characterizes individuals in context as they go about their daily activities rather than by simply listing their characteristics. Telling about a person's traits never is as effective as *showing* how they act and live. This entails presenting characters as fully social beings through descriptions of dress, speech, gestures, and facial expressions, which allow the reader to infer traits. Traits and characteristics thus appear in and through interaction with others rather than by being presented as isolated qualities of individuals. Thus, characterization draws on a writer's skills in describing, reporting action, and presenting dialogue.

In the following set of fieldnotes, Linda Shaw describes an encounter with a couple living in the kitchen area of an apartment in a psychiatric board-and-care facility. The woman, in particular, emphasizes the efforts they have made to create a "normal" living environment and the futility they feel in doing so:[10]

I went with Terri and Jay today as they offered to show me the "apartment" they had created out of the small converted kitchen area that was their room. Terri escorted me from one space to another, taking great pride in showing me how they had made a bedroom area at one end, a living room next to it, and a kitchen area next to that. They had approximated an entire apartment in this tiny space, and she showed me features of each "room" in detail. The bed, they said, had a real mattress, not like the foam pads on all the other beds. There was a rug on the living room floor and a TV at the foot of the bed. Then Terri opened the cupboards. She pointed out the spice rack and counted each glass out loud. She took particular pride in the coffeepot she uses to fix Jay's morning coffee and a warmer oven where they sometimes heat take-out pizza.

Terri tried very hard to demonstrate all they had done to make their apartment like one that any married couple might have; yet, the harder she tried, the more apparent it became how different their lives really were. Terri spoke of the futility she felt in spite of all these efforts: "All the noise, the screaming, the tension really bothers me. I'm married, and I can't even be a normal wife here. I want to get up in the morning, fix my husband breakfast—a cup of coffee, eggs, bacon, orange juice—before he goes to work, clean the house, take care of the kids and then fix him a nice dinner and drink or whatever he wants when he gets home. Here, I get up and can fix him a cup of instant coffee. You know, it's not as good to just pick up the apartment, but then there's nothing else to do."

Terri comes across as a fully human individual whose actions and talk reveal her character. She has done her best to create the normal way of life she wishes for but cannot sustain in this quasi-institutional setting. Through her actions and words, we see her struggle in vain to construct this private space as a refuge against the debilitating forces of institutional life.

Pressed to finish his notes, a writer might be tempted to characterize by using some convenient label ("a retarded person," "a homeless person," a black/white/Asian, etc.) rather than looking closely at that person's actual appearance and behavior. Such quick characterization, however, produces a stock character who, at best, comes across as less than fully human and, at worst, appears as a negative stereotype. For example, one student, in describing people in a shopping mall, characterized an older woman as a "senile bag lady" after noting that she muttered to herself while fumbling absentmindedly in a shabby, oversized purse. Such labeling sketches only a pale type and closes the writer's attention to other relevant details and actions.

While ethnographers try to avoid characterizing people by stock characters, they do include members' remarks and actions that stereotype or mock others. The following excerpt describes a student who mockingly acts out typical gestures and postures of a Latino "cholo" before some classmates:

> As the white male and his friend walked away, he said "chale homes" [eh! homies] in a mock Spanish accent. Then he exaggerated his walking style: he stuck his shoes out diagonally, placed his arms at a curved popeye angle, and leaned back. . . . Someone watching said, "Look at you fools."

In this group of bantering young men, the white teenage male enacts a ludicrous caricature of a Latino "cholo." Ethnographers take care to distinguish members' characterizations from their own by providing details that clearly contextualize the talk and behavior as delivered from a member's point of view.

An ethnographer usually characterizes in detail those persons who act centrally in a scene. Although the full picture of any person develops through time in a series of fieldnotes, each description presents lively and significant details that show a primary character as completely as possible through appearance, body posture, gesture, words, and actions. In contrast, a peripheral figure might indeed be referred to simply with as few details as necessary for that person to be seen doing his small part in the scene.

A number of criteria shape the field researcher's decision about who is central and who is peripheral. First, the researcher's theoretical interests will focus his attention toward particular people. For example, the central characters in a study of teamwork among "support staff" in a courtroom were courtroom clerks and bailiffs rather than attorneys, witnesses, or the judge. Second, methodological strategies also focus the ethnographer's attention. For example, a strategy for depicting a social world by describing distinctive interactional patterns might shape his decision to focus on someone who presents a particularly vivid illustration of such a pattern. Finally, if members in a scene orient to a particular person, then a description that makes that person central to the scene is called for. Conversely, even those who are central figures in a setting might get slight attention from the field researcher if they are so treated by those in the scene. For example, in a scene focusing on students talking in the quad at lunchtime, the "principal walking across the courtyard and looking from side to side" might not be described in much more detail if no one seems to notice him.

As a practical matter, an individual already well known through previous entries does not need to have a full introduction each time he enters a scene. Even for a main character, one describes only those actions and traits relevant to the current interaction or those that were previously unnoted. But continuing contacts with people greatly expand the field researcher's resources for writing fuller, richer characterizations; greater familiarity enables the researcher to note and to write about qualities that are harder to detect. Yet many ethnographers tend to describe even main characters only upon first encountering them, leaving that first characterization unchanged despite coming to know more about that person. Hence, we suggest taking time as research progresses to periodically reflect on and try to capture on paper the appearance and feel of major characters, now known as persons with unique features and special qualities. Each entry is only a partial record, and as notes accumulate, fieldworkers notice that they have assembled enough observations to present some persons as full-fledged individuals ("rounded" characters), leaving others as less well-known figures ("flat" characters), and a few individuals as types such as a bus driver or a policeman ("stock" characters).

Fieldnotes should also include the ethnographer as a character in the interactions. The presence of the ethnographer who truly stands at the side watching might only be noted to identify the position from which the event is seen. But an ethnographer who directly participates in the action becomes a relevant character in the fieldnote, especially when a member clearly interacts with him. Indeed, a researcher might act as a central character in the incident in unanticipated ways. He might shift from his stance as an outside observer and become fully engaged in the interactions. In the following excerpt, students in a deaf-and-hard-of-hearing class encourage each other to speak while playing an educational game. The fieldworker, having had a stuttering problem all of his life, clearly empathizes with the students. Though essentially an outsider in the class, he becomes a pivotal figure at one juncture:

> Lynn keeps on telling Caesar to say what the answers are by speaking (rather than through sign language). The teacher says, "Very good Lynn. . . . That's right, Caesar, you should try to speak what the answers are as well so that we can all understand you." Caesar looks over at me a little red in the face and looks down at his desk with a half smile. The teacher asks him (while pointing at me), "Are you afraid of speaking because he is here?" Lynn and Jackie and Caesar all seem to answer at once in sign that he is afraid of having me hear him speak. I tell Caesar, "You don't have to be afraid of what I think. I have a hard time speaking too."
>
> Caesar seems interested by my statements and points a finger at me questioningly. The teacher says, "Yes, it's okay, you speak fine. You don't have to be afraid of what anybody thinks about you. Just say one sentence, and he'll tell you if he can understand you."
>
> Caesar reluctantly says something and then looks at me, his head still slightly down and his face still red. A faint smile lines his lips as he waits for my answer. I had not understood a single word and was feeling desperate. What if they asked me to repeat what he had said? I reply, "Yes, that was fine. I understood you." The teacher quickly turns to Caesar and gives him the appropriate signs for my answer and goes directly into saying that he shouldn't be so intimidated by what other people think. Caesar looks at me and smiles. The game continues, and Caesar starts answering in both sign and speech. And I began to understand some of the things they were saying.

Clearly, this ethnographer's past experiences and presence played a central role in this scene, and his empathetic responses color the description in essential ways. Had he tried to write up these notes without including himself—his own interactions and feelings—the scene would have been deeply distorted.

When describing their own participation in scenes, field researchers generally write in the first person (see chapter 4). If this observer had described the scene in the third person, referring to himself by name, much of the impact would have been lost:

> Caesar reluctantly says something and looks at Paul, his head still slightly down and his face still red. A faint smile lines his lips as he waits for his answer. . . . He replies, "Yes, that's fine. I understood you." The teacher quickly turns to Caesar and gives him the appropriate signs for Paul's answer and goes directly into saying that he shouldn't be so intimidated by what other people think. Caesar looks at Paul and smiles. The game continues, and Caesar starts answering in both sign and speech.

In the original segment, the writer carefully stuck to Caesar's observable behavior ("looks over at me with a red face" and "looks down at his desk with a half smile") and did not attribute nervousness. But in the third-person account, we miss an essential part of Caesar's struggle to speak. This struggle was conveyed through the ethnographer's empathetic and self-revealing comment, "I had not understood a single word . . . ," and by his closing observation, "And I began to understand some of the things they were saying." Through the writer's careful attention to details of behavior and talk, as well as through his own revealed personal feelings, readers can sense the fear and later the relief in speaking and in being understood.

Finally, along with writing in the first person, we also recommend that ethnographers use active rather than passive verbs. Some researchers use passive verbs because they think that it makes their writing more objective (Booth, Colomb, and Williams 2008). Yet, ethnographers prefer active verbs to show how people act together to construct their social worlds (Becker 2007). Consider, for example, the loss of crucial detail about the unfolding interaction among actors in the classroom scene above had the ethnographer used passive rather than active verbs.

> Something is said by Caesar to Paul, his head still slightly down and his face still red. His lips are lined with a faint smile as he waits for his answer. . . . He replies, "Yes, that's fine. I understood you." Caesar is given the appropriate signs and is told he shouldn't be so intimidated by what other people think. A smile is received by him. The game is continued, and answers are given in both sign and speech.

The use of passive verbs obscures the agency of those in the setting and the clarity of the moment-by-moment sense of who did what with/to whom that the ethnographer portrayed so effectively in the original excerpt. Hence, we recommend the use of active verbs to show more vividly, clearly, and directly who is engaged in an activity, the meanings that others in the setting give to it, and how they use meanings to shape subsequent interactions.

NARRATING A DAY'S ENTRY: ORGANIZATIONAL STRATEGIES

When first returning from the field to her desk, an ethnographer, worried about getting everything down, writes spontaneously, hurriedly, and in fragments. But at the same time, in order to describe scenes and actions effectively, she needs to balance speed and clarity by organizing her writing into *units* that create coherence and mark beginnings and endings. While some ethnographers consider these units as descriptive writing (in contrast to analytic writing), we find it beneficial to discuss these units as narrating or recounting the day's experiences. By drawing on narrating conventions, ethnographers can sustain their memories by grouping and sequencing details and interactions into coherent units. When they remember observed interactions as a series of moments to be narrated, they can more easily sustain that memory as a perceived whole or unit.

Perhaps the most general unit of writing is simply the day's entry—the ethnographer's telling of the day's experiences and observations in the field. Seeking to document fully all remembered interactions with no specific point or theme in mind, the ethnographer relates his experiences in the field, implicitly drawing on narrating conventions. In this sense, the day's entry is an episodic tale with many segments—perhaps telling about an interaction, next transitioning to a different location, now sketching in the scene of the new context, then recounting another episode of action—on and on until finishing by returning from the field as the tale's ending. Within this overall narrative of the day's entry, the ethnographer might also create other tales that stand out as more focused sequences of interconnected actions and episodes (see chapter 4).

The most basic unit within the day's entry is the paragraph, used to coherently depict one brief moment or idea. By convention, a *paragraph* coheres because the writer's attention focuses on one idea or insight.[11] When he perceives some actions as a gestalt and concentrates on them, he writes about them in a paragraph. While continuing to write, he also shifts attention from one recalled moment to another, for example, from one person or activity to another within a classroom. These slight shifts are often indicated by paragraph breaks.

In narrating an entry, ethnographers work with a number of different organizing units that build on the paragraph. Sketches and episodes, which may be several paragraphs, create larger units of detailed scenes and interactions within that day's fieldnotes. In this way, the writer coherently sequences moments—those remembered interactions and specific contexts. Though these units or segments have no explicit connections between them, the ethnographer might write a few transitional sentences, briefly summarizing what happened in the interim or explaining that he shifted his focus to another activity or person to observe.

Sketches

In a sketch, the fieldworker, struck by a vivid sensory impression, *describes* a scene primarily through detailed imagery. Much as in a photograph, sequencing of actions does not dominate. Rather, the writer, as a more distanced observer looking out on a scene, describes what she senses, pausing for a moment in recounting the action to create a descriptive snapshot of a character or a setting. As a result, sketches might be short paragraphs or a few sentences within the overall narrative. Such static snapshots help orient the reader to the relevant details of the contexts in which actions take place.

While the term "sketch" employs a visual metaphor, this form of organizing writing need not rely only on visual details but can also incorporate auditory or kinetic details as well. For example, not appearance but the sense of smell might be the primary criterion for recalling and conveying the merits of a particular food. In describing people, settings, objects, and so forth, the writer must evoke all those senses that recall that moment as she perceived it. Often, the sense of vision dominates, however, simply because the fieldworker observes at a distance or aims to give a brief overview of the setting. It also dominates, in part, because the English language for vision is much more detailed and developed than it is for the other senses.[12] Hence, the ethnographic writer might have to expend special effort to evoke and write about nonvisual sensory images.

A sketch typically is a brief segment, which unifies descriptive details about a setting, an individual, or a single incident. Because it is primarily static, it lacks any sense of consequential action (of plot) and any full characterization of people. Consider the following sketch of a Latino street market that presents a close-up picture of one particular character's momentary behavior at a stall with toys:

> An older Latina woman is bent over looking at the toys on the ground. Behind her she holds two plastic bags of something, which she uses to balance as she leans over. She picks up several toys in succession from the ground, lifting them up several inches to turn them over and around in her hand, and then putting them down. After a minute, she straightens up and walks slowly away.

Organizing details into a sketch in this way permits the writer to give a quick sense of the setting by presenting a close-up picture of one particular character's engagement with it.

Often, sketches contextualize subsequent interactions, placing them into a larger framework of events or incidents and allow the reader to visualize more readily the setting or participants involved. On some occasions, however, these entries might stand as independent units of writing. In the following sketch, for example, an ethnographer describes the scene in a high school during an uneventful, uncrowded lunch hour in a way that documents how students group themselves:

> Even though it was cold and windy, there were still about one hundred black students clustered in the central quad. On the far left, one short black male wearing a black starter jacket was bouncing a ball. Next to him, seven black females and two black males were sitting on a bench. Further to the right stood a concentrated group of about thirty or forty black students. I counted about twenty who were wearing different kinds of starter jackets. Further up the quad stood another group of fifteen blacks, mostly females. At the foot of quad, on the far right, was another group of maybe twenty black students, about equally male and female. Some were standing, while others were sitting on a short concrete wall against the auditorium. To the right of this group, I noticed one male, listening to a yellow walkman, dancing by himself. His arms were flung out, pulling as though he were skiing, while his feet ran in place.

This ethnographer was especially concerned with ethnic relations and wanted to track how, when, and where students socialized and with whom. Even when he could not hear or see exactly what the students were doing, he depicted these groupings in an almost snapshot fashion. Although the paragraph includes visual and kinetic details, it creates the scene as a still life rather than as an event in which actions could be sequenced.

In general, sketches are useful for providing an overall sense of places and people that sometimes stand as a background for other fieldnote descriptions. Descriptive sketches of people standing around or of a person's expression and posture as she looks at someone, for example, can reveal qualities of social relations even when apparently nothing much is happening.

Episodes

Unlike a sketch, which depicts a "still life" in one place, an episode recounts action and moves in time to narrate a slice of life. In an episode, a writer constructs a brief incident as a more or less unified depiction of one continuous action or interaction. Consequently, when recalling an incident that does not extend over a long period of time or involve many characters, ethnographers often write up that memory as a one- or two-paragraph episode.[13]

The following excerpt consists of a one-paragraph episode in which the writer describes an interaction between two students during the beginning of class time:

> A black female came in. She was wearing a white puffy jacket, had glasses and straight feathered black hair. She sat down to my right. Robert and another male (both black) came in and sat down. They were eating Kentucky Fried Chicken which they took out of little red and white boxes. Robert's friend kept swiping at the black female, trying to slap her. She kept telling him in an annoyed voice to leave her alone. After a minute of this exchange, the black teacher said to the guy, "Leave her alone, brother." He answered Ms. Dubois with a grin on his face, "Don't worry. She's my sistah." The girl said "Chhh," looking briefly at him. He had gone back to eating his chicken.

Here, the students' and teacher's actions are presented as a sequence, each seeming to trigger the next; the girl responds to the boy's swiping, and the teacher responds to him, and so on. Thus, these actions are linked and appear as one continuous interaction, producing a unified episode.

Not every episode needs to build to a climax as the one above does. Many fieldnote episodes minutely recount one character's routine, everyday actions. In fact, in many entries, ethnographers find themselves writing primarily about mundane activities. In the following excerpt, for example, the ethnographer recounts how several students in an ESL class worked together to complete a group activity:

> One group consisted of six people: two Korean girls, one Korean boy, two Mexican boys, and one Russian girl. Like all of the other groups, they arranged

their chairs in a small circle for the assigned activity. Ishmael, a Mexican boy, held the question card in his hand and read it to the rest of the group: "List five things that you can do on a date for less than $10.00 in Los Angeles." (His English was heavily marked by his Mexican accent, but they could understand him.) Placing his elbows on the desk and looking directly at the group, he said, "Well?" He watched them for a minute or two; then he suggested that one could go for drinks at Hard Rock Café. The others agreed by nodding their heads. Ishmael again waited for suggestions from the group. The other Mexican boy said "going to the beach" and the Russian girl said "roller skating." The Koreans nodded their heads, but offered no other suggestions. (I think that Ishmael waited for others to respond, even though he seemed to know the answers.)

In describing this classroom scene, the ethnographer filled six pages with a series of such more or less isolated episodes occurring during that hour. Thus, she was able to present the small groups as working simultaneously on various activities. The episodes belong together only because they are situated in the same class during one period. Fieldworkers often write up such concurrent actions, loosely linked by time and place, as a series of discrete episodes.

Since episodes present action as progressing through time, a writer should orient the reader to shifts in time, place, and person as the action unfolds, particularly in longer scenes or those without obviously interconnected actions. Writers sequence actions in an order (e.g., first, second, third) and mark action shifts with transitions (e.g., now, then, next, afterward, the next morning). They also locate action with situational markers (e.g., here, there, beyond, behind). In the following excerpt, a researcher studying an outpatient psychiatric treatment facility connects actions through transitional phrases ("as he continues talking" and transitional words ("then," "as"):

I sat down on the bench in the middle of the hall. And as I sat waiting for something to gain my attention, I heard the director yell out, "Take off your clothes in the shower!" as he shuts the door to the shower room. . . . Remaining outside the door of the shower room, the director speaks with Roberta, one of the staff members assigned to look after the clients. Then Karen approaches them with a small, dirty Smurf that she found outside. "Look at it, how pretty, kiss it," she says talking to the director, but he doesn't pay any attention to her. As he continues talking to Roberta, he glances over and notices that I am observing them. As our eyes lock, he opens up his arm toward Karen and requests a hug. Karen, in her usual bashful way, giggles as she responds to his hug.

In this episode, the writer focuses on movement—sat, shuts, approaches, glances, opens—interspersed with talk: "the director yell(s) out, 'Take off your clothes in the shower!'" In observing and reporting actions, ethnographers interested in social interactions view action and talk as interconnected features of what people "do." They write about "talk" as part of people's actions.

Ethnographers often write episodic rather than more extended entries because they cannot track a sequence of actions and learn all the outcomes within one day. They may write an episode about an interaction simply because it bears upon a topic they are interested in. They often write without knowing whether that fieldnote will later be important in the full analysis. Yet, writing these episodes over time might enable the ethnographer to find patterns of behavior and connections between people's actions through different fieldnotes.

Many fieldnote episodes stand on their own, barely associated with others. Particularly in initial entries organized as narratives of the researcher's activities and observations for the day, writing *transitional summaries* can link different episodes. A transitional summary provides a succinct bridge between detailed episodes, enabling a reader to understand how the ethnographer got from one event or episode to another. How the ethnographer got from the school office to the classroom with a brief personal stop in the bathroom, for example, can simply be noted in this summary fashion if there is a need to show continuity. Of course, if something interesting occurred during this movement—a student stopped her to talk about a school fight—then writing detailed notes is advisable.

IN-PROCESS ANALYTIC WRITING: ASIDES AND COMMENTARIES

As the field researcher participates in the field, she inevitably begins to reflect on and interpret what she has experienced and observed. Writing fieldnotes heightens and focuses these interpretive and analytic processes; writing up the day's observations generates new appreciation and deeper understanding of witnessed scenes and events. In writing, a field researcher assimilates and thereby starts to understand an experience. She makes sense of the moment by intuitively selecting, highlighting, and ordering details and by beginning to appreciate linkages with, or contrasts to, previously observed and written-about experiences. Furthermore, she can begin to reflect on how she has presented and ordered events and actions in her notes, rereading selected episodes and tales with an eye to their structuring effects.

To capture these ruminations, reflections, and insights and to make them available for further thought and analysis, field researchers pursue several kinds of analytical writing that stand in stark contrast to the descriptive writing we have emphasized to this point. As the result of such writings, the researcher can bring a more probing glance to further observations and descriptive writing and consequently become more selective and in depth in his descriptions.

The most immediate forms of analytic writing are asides and commentaries, interpretive writings composed while the ethnographer is actively composing fieldnotes.[14] Asides and commentaries consist of brief questions, ideas, or reactions the researcher writes into the body of the notes as he recalls and puts on paper the details of a specific observation or incident. (We will consider a third, more complex form of initial analytic writing, in-process memos, in chapter 4.) The lines between asides and commentaries (and in-process memos) are often blurred; we offer them as heuristic devices that can sensitize the fieldworker to both momentary and more sustained concentration on analytic writing while actively producing fieldnotes.

Asides are brief, reflective bits of analytic writing that succinctly clarify, explain, interpret, or raise questions about some specific happening or process described in a fieldnote. The ethnographer dashes off asides in the midst of descriptive writing, taking a moment to react personally or theoretically to something she has just recounted on paper and then immediately turns back to the work of description. These remarks may be inserted in the midst of descriptive paragraphs and set off by parentheses. In the following example, the ethnographer uses a personal aside to note his uneasy feeling that someone is watching him:

> I turn around, away from the office, and face the woman with the blondish hair who is still smiling. (I can't shake the feeling that she's gazing at me.) "I'll see you Friday," I say to her as I walk by her and out the front door.

Fieldworkers often write somewhat more elaborate asides, several phrases in length, again triggered by some immediate piece of writing and closely tied to the events or scenes depicted in that writing. In the fieldnote below, the fieldworker describes a moment during her first day at a crisis drop-in center and then reacts to that experience in a more extended aside:

Walking up the stairs to the agency office, I noticed that almost every step creaked or moaned. At the top stands an old pine coat hanger, piled high with coats. Behind it is a bulletin board containing numerous flyers with information about organizations and services of various kinds. (Thinking about the scene as I climbed those stairs, I think that if I were an upset, distraught client, I would most probably find it difficult to find helpful information in that disorganized mass.)

In providing her own "lived sense" of the agency, the student incorporates in her description the meaning of physical space, while allowing for the possibility that others might perceive it differently. Asides may also be used to explain something that would otherwise not be apparent or to offer some sort of personal reflection or interpretive remark on a matter just considered. Ethnographers frequently use asides, for example, to convey their explicit "feel" for or emotional reactions to events; putting these remarks in asides keeps them from intruding into the descriptive account.

The ethnographer may also use brief asides to offer tentative hunches when the meaning of an incident to members is not clear or may only be inferred. In the following excerpt, the ethnographer asks questions about the meaning and import of an incident at a food bank in which a shopper rejects an item given to her as part of a preselected grocery cart full of food.

She had a package of frozen turkey meatballs in her hand and said that she didn't want the package because the contents were expired. The meatballs had apparently expired two days prior to today, and she said that she did not like taking expired food to her house. (Why the emphasis on "my house?" Self-respect? Could it be that if she took the expired meatballs, she was somehow accepting hand-me-downs? Just because she is not paying full price doesn't mean she can't receive up-to-par food?)

Using a question in this brief aside to reflect upon the possible meaning of the incident helps the ethnographer avoid reaching premature or unsupported conclusions. The aside also marks the incident as important, reminding her to look for further examples that will clarify and deepen her understanding of similar or contrasting examples.

A *commentary* is a more elaborate reflection, either on some specific event or issue or on the day's experiences and fieldnotes. Focused commentaries of the first sort are placed just after the fieldnote account of the event or issue in a separate paragraph set off with parentheses. A paragraph-long summary commentary of the second sort should conclude each set of field-notes, reflecting on and raising issues and questions about that day's observations. Both types of commentaries involve a shift of attention from events in the field to outside audiences imagined as having an interest in something the fieldworker has observed and written up. Again, in contrast to descriptive fieldnotes, commentaries might explore problems of access or emotional reactions to events in the field, suggest ongoing probes into likely connections with other events, or offer tentative interpretations. Putting a commentary in a separate paragraph helps avoid writing up details as evidence for preconceived categories or interpretations.

Focused commentaries can raise issues of what terms and events mean to members, make initial connections between some current observation and prior fieldnotes, and suggest points or places for further observation, as in the following excerpt:

> M called over to Richard. He said, "C'm here lil' Homey." Richard came over to sit closer to M. He asked Richard about something Richard said earlier (I couldn't completely hear it) . . . something to do with weight lifting. Richard replied, "Oh, I could talk about it for hours . . ." M asked Richard if there was a place where he could lift weights on campus. Richard said there was a weight room, but only "hoops" could use it today. M then asked Richard what "hoops" was. Richard answered that "hoops" was basketball. (Is the word "homey," possibly derived from homeboy, somebody who is down or cool with another person? It seems to me that M, who apparently didn't know Richard, wanted to talk to him. In order to do that, he tried to let Richard know M thought he was a cool person? "Homey" appears to be applied regardless of ethnicity. . . . Their interaction appeared to be organized around interest in a common activity, weight lifting. Judging by the size of M's muscles, this was something he excelled in.)

This ethnographer has been noticing the ways blacks use the terms "cool" and "down" to refer to inclusion of nonblacks in their otherwise black groupings. In this commentary, he reflects on other terms that also seem to be inclusive.

Focused commentaries can also be used to create a record of the ethnographer's own doings, experiences, and reactions during fieldwork, both in observing-participating and in writing up. A researcher-intern in a social service agency, after describing an incident with staff, wrote the following commentary about this moment as a turning point in her relationship with staff members:

Entering the kitchen, where staff often go to socialize alone, I began to prepare my lunch. Soon, several staff had come in, and they began to talk among one another. I stood around awkwardly, not quite knowing what to do with myself. I exchanged small talk for a while until D, the director, asked in her typically dramatic tone loud enough for everyone to hear: "Guess where A (a staff member who was also present) is going for her birthday?" There was silence in the room. Turning in her direction, I realized that she was speaking to me. "Where?" I asked, somewhat surprised that she was talking to me. "To Hershey Park!" she exclaimed. "No way!" I said, and feeling embarrassed, I started laughing. "Yeah," D exclaimed. "She's gonna dip her whole body in chocolate so R (lover) can eat her!" The room filled up with laughter, and I, too, could not restrain my giggles.

(With that, the group broke up, and as I walked back to my desk, I began to feel that for the first time, I had been an active participant in one of their kitchen get-togethers. This experience made me believe that I was being viewed as more than just an outsider. I have been trying to figure out what it takes to belong here, and one aspect undoubtedly is to partake in an occasional kitchen get-together and not to appear above such practices.)

In this commentary, the researcher not only reports her increased feeling of acceptance in the scene but also reflects on the likely importance of these informal, sometimes ribald "get-togethers" for creating a general sense of belonging in the organization.

In writing a summary commentary, the fieldworker takes a few moments to mentally review the whole day's experiences, selecting an important, memorable, or confusing issue to raise and briefly explore. Here, ethnographers have found it useful to ask themselves questions like the following: What did I learn today? What did I observe that was particularly interesting or significant? What was confusing or uncertain? Did something happen today that was similar to or radically different from things that I have previously observed? In the following excerpt, an ethnographer used commentary at the end of his day in the field to reflect his growing understanding of largely Spanish-speaking day laborers' interactions with employers in their efforts to get work.

English seems to be an important resource to acquire work, but even more interesting is the *illusion of knowing English* because even though Jorge does not speak English, he goes about acting to employers as if he does [know English] to increase his chances for hire. Something that was also intriguing was the employer searching for day laborers with legal documentation. It is interesting because day laborers are stigmatized as all being undocumented but employers seem to know that there are many that are documented . . . Jorge believes that when folks are undocumented, employers threaten them with Immigration. Jorge seems to be at odds with this dynamic because as a person with documentation, he is held responsible [by employers] for information on others who may not be documented. And, due to his documentation, he seems to have a sense of entitlement [to work] due to his legal status.

The ethnographer uses this day's commentary to build on his growing understanding of both the strategic ways that day laborers use their knowledge of characteristics desired by employers to compete among themselves for work and day laborers' sense that legal status bring with it extra entitlement to work.

Summary commentaries are also useful for comparing and contrasting incidents that occurred on the same day or earlier in the field experience. In the following commentary, the ethnographer compares two incidents that occurred during the day's observations to further understand parent-child interactions in a public setting, in this case a grocery store:

Both of these incidents help illustrate how two very different parents choose to deal with their children in a public setting. Both children showed "bratty" behavior in two different ways: the first by illustrating his discontent in being forced to go shopping when he would have preferred staying home and the second by making the need to purchase an item within the store known. In both situations, the moms tried to ignore their children in what seemed to be the hope that their kids would realize that they were in a public setting and consequently stop their behavior. However, this was not the case. I believe that just as the moms knew that they were in a location where outside forces (i.e., limits on the ways that they could exercise control of their kids within a public store setting) influenced their ability to discipline the behavior of their children, the children knew this as well. This is all hypothetical, but the children also seem to know that they could continue to push their moms' buttons because the course of action that their parents could have taken at home would not occur in this public place. The first mom's response of "unbelievable" to her son is an indication that she is fully aware that her motherly duties are limited when considering the environment and the forces within it.

The ethnographer uses commentary to suggest possible patterns of parent-child interactions in public places, taking care to avoid "overinterpreting" and drawing conclusions too quickly based on meanings she attributes to just two examples. The understandings gleaned from these incidents should remain suggestive of avenues for further investigation and ongoing comparison.

Finally, daily summary commentaries might identify an issue that came up in the course of the current set of fieldnotes and suggest practical, methodological steps for exploring that issue in future observations. Indeed, it is often useful simply to ask: What more do I need to know to follow up on a particular issue or event? Asking such questions helped a researcher in a battered women's shelter identify gaps in her understanding of how staff viewed and accomplished their work:

> The goals staff have talked about so far of "conveying unconditional positive regard" for clients and "increasing their self-esteem" seem rather vague. How does the staff know when they have achieved unconditional positive regard? Is it based on their interaction with the client or by their refraining from being judgmental or critical of them during staff meetings? I will attempt to discover how they define and attempt to achieve the goal of "increasing a woman's self-esteem." It has been made clear that this goal is not only seen to be achieved when women leave their abusive relationships. If leaving their abusive partners were the primary indicator of achieving raised self-esteem, the organization would be largely unsuccessful, since most of these women go back to their abusive relationships. Yet, while I have learned what raising self-esteem is not, I have yet to learn what it is.

In this series of comments and questions, the fieldworker identifies two matters that shelter staff members emphasize as goals in their relations with clients: "conveying unconditional positive regard" and increasing client "self-esteem." She then considers ways she might look to understand how these general policies/values are actually implemented and how their success or failure is practically assessed in interactions within the shelter. These questions and tentative answers helped direct the ethnographer's attention, focusing and guiding future observations and analysis.

REFLECTIONS: "WRITING" AND "READING" MODES

To characterize fieldnotes as descriptions initially conveys the prospect of simple, straightforward writing. But once we recognize that description involves more than a one-to-one correspondence between written accounts and what is going on, writing fieldnotes raises complex, perplexing problems. Descriptions are grounded on the observer-writer's participation in the setting, but no two persons participate in and experience a setting in exactly the same way. Moreover, there is always more going on than the ethnographer can notice, and it is impossible to record all that can be noticed. Description inevitably involves different theories, purposes, interests, and points of view. Hence, fieldnotes contain descriptions that are more akin to a series of stories portraying slices of life in vivid detail than to a comprehensive, literal, or objective rendering.[15]

The ethnographer, however, needs to avoid getting drawn into the complexities of fieldnote descriptions while actually writing fieldnotes. She must initially work in a *writing mode,* putting into words and on paper what she has seen and heard as quickly and efficiently as possible. In this text-producing mode, the ethnographer tries to "get it down" as accurately and completely as possible, avoiding too much self-consciousness about the writing process itself. She stays close to the events at issue, rekindling her excitement about these events and inscribing them before memory fades. The writing ethnographer tries to "capture what is out there," or more accurately, to construct detailed accounts of her own observations and experience of what is "out there." At this point, too much reflection distracts or even paralyzes; one tries to write without editing, to produce detailed descriptions without worry about analytic import and connections, and to describe what happened without too much self-conscious reflection.

Only subsequently, once a text has actually been produced, can the ethnographer really step back and begin to consider the complexities that permeate fieldnote descriptions; only with fully detailed fieldnotes can the ethnographer adopt a *reading mode* and begin to reflect on how these accounts are products of his own, often implicit, decisions about how to participate in and describe events. That is, only with full notes in hand does it make sense to view these writings as texts that are truncated, partial, and perspectival products of the ethnographer's own styles of participating, orienting, and writing. It is at this point that the ethnographer can begin to treat fieldnotes as constructions and read them for the ways they *create* rather than simply record reality.

One key difference between initially working in a writing mode and subsequently in a reflective reading mode lies in how the ethnographer orients to issues of "accuracy," to "correspondence" between a written account and what it is an account of. In the moment of writing, the ethnographer must try to create some close correspondence between the written account and his experiences and observations of "what happened." The immediate task in writing fieldnote descriptions is to create a detailed, accurate, and comprehensive account of what has been experienced. But once notes have been written, this correspondence criterion loses salience. This shift occurs because "what happened" has been filtered through the person and writing of the observer as it was written onto the page. The resulting text "fixes" a social reality in place but does so in a way that makes it difficult to determine its relationship with realities outside that text. Readers might attempt to do so by invoking what they know from having "been there" or from experience with a similar reality. But readers are heavily constrained by what is on the page; they usually lack any effective means of gaining access to "what actually happened" independently of the written account. In such a reading mode, then, conscious, critical reflection on how writing choices have helped construct specific texts and textual realities becomes both possible and appropriate.

4

Writing Fieldnotes II: Multiple Purposes and Stylistic Options

Ethnographers have multiple purposes in writing fieldnotes; these goals both shape and reflect their choices about styles of writing. So far, we have focused on one initial purpose: to quickly and immediately "get down on the page" the ethnographer's first-time observations and new experiences. But in "getting it down," field researchers also decide how to represent a particular scene, event, or interaction, decisions that involve choices, often implicit, about writing strategies. They develop a range of writing styles in order to implement a number of more complex purposes: to capture the qualities of people and events through details they had previously not recognized; to represent in written form processes and issues that initially they had not appreciated; to express the taken-for-granted features and constraints of everyday life and interaction; and to create comprehensible accounts of often disorderly or even chaotic social life. As writers, they increasingly learn a greater variety of writing strategies and conventions to facilitate these purposes.

In talking about multiple writing "purposes," and about "choosing" writing styles and strategies, we risk overemphasizing the conscious use of writing practices.[1] Rather, we are concerned with strategies of writing—often referred to as writing or literary "conventions"—and with the different effects that these conventions can produce. Though ethnographers sometimes consciously draw on certain conventions and aim for certain effects in using them, at other times, they employ writing strategies almost unthinkingly, as a matter of reflex and writing habit. In using terms like "choices," "purposes," and "goals," we seek to increase awareness of the different ways that social life can be represented in written texts, to enhance fieldworkers' ability to invoke ways of writing that effectively capture the subtle processes and complex issues they want to document. In brief, we contend that awareness and understanding of writing strategies enable fieldworkers to more easily make writing choices that realize their ethnographic purposes.

In this chapter, we explore writing styles and conventions that facilitate more complex purposes beyond quickly "capturing it on the page." We begin by examining how different stances or orientations toward research and toward anticipated future readers also influence the writing of fieldnotes. We then discuss writers' choices about perspective by examining how "point of view" determines whose view appears more fully represented on the page and how time perspective ("real time" or "end point") shapes what is revealed. Next, we turn to the possibilities and constraints in writing more cohesive narratives, namely, those extended narrative segments that depict an ongoing experience or event. Finally, we close the chapter with a consideration of in-process memos whereby the ethnographer reflects analytically about experiences and observed events.

STANCE AND AUDIENCE IN WRITING FIELDNOTES

Sitting down to write full fieldnotes, ethnographers make decisions: what to write, in what order, and how to express what they have to say. While some of these decisions are relatively straightforward, others are more implicit, arising from the particular *stance* adopted in writing fieldnotes. On a fundamental level, a researcher's stance in fieldwork and note writing originates in her outlook on life. *Prior experience, training, and commitments* influence this stance, predisposing the fieldworker to feel, think, and act toward people in more or less patterned ways. Whether from a particular gender, social, cultural, political, or theoretical position or orientation, the fieldworker not only interacts with and responds to people in the setting from her own orientation but also writes her fieldnotes by seeing and framing events accordingly. The effects of this fundamental stance appear in fieldnote writing in subtle ways. These range from how she identifies with (or distances herself from) those studied and thus writes about them sympathetically (or not), to the kinds of local activities that draw her attention and result in more detailed descriptions, and to the way she prioritizes and frames certain topics and writes more fully about any events she sees as relevant or salient (Wolfinger 2002).

By self-consciously recognizing his fundamental orientation, the fieldworker can write fieldnotes that highlight and foreground issues and insights made available by that orientation. This recognition might also make him more sensitive to the ways his orientation shapes key interactions with others. For example, in writing up fieldnotes about a school for gays and lesbians, one heterosexual male often wrote about the ways students pressed him to reveal his sexual orientation and watched for his responses to their jokes and teasing. But an openly identified gay male researcher in the same field site became sensitive to how students "sexualized" stories about their experiences as they constructed gay identities in everyday talk. Indeed, he then began to ask and write about students' talk about sexual activities, as in the following fieldnote:

> "Wait," I said, interrupting his story. "Where was this?" "Over by Circus Books," Adam said. "And what was he doing?" I asked as I leaned forward smiling slightly. "He was cruising," Adam said. "What's that?" I asked. "It's a meeting place," answered John. "And this is at a bookstore," I said sounding a bit confused. "Yeah," they both said reassuringly.

The more the field researcher acknowledges those factors influencing his fundamental stance toward people in the setting, the more he can examine and use the insights and appreciations opened up by this stance in fieldnote writing. Furthermore, he can better guard against any overriding, unconscious framing of events—for example, by avoiding evaluative wording or by focusing on members' views of events.

As fieldwork progresses, the researcher's stance toward people and issues often changes. As she learns through interactions with individuals in the setting to look at activities, events, and issues in new ways, she might adjust her prior views and reorient herself vis-à-vis others. Having readjusted her stance toward people in the setting, she more frequently can write fieldnotes in ways that not only highlight members' views but that also reveal her ongoing resocialization. Over time, a fieldworker's personal views and theoretical commitments often veer and transform; her stance in writing fieldnotes shifts accordingly, particularly as she more frequently comes to see and respond to events as members do.

Another key component determining the stance expressed in written fieldnotes is *intended or likely audience*. How a field researcher writes about observed events is linked to often unacknowledged assumptions about those for whom he is writing. We first consider anticipated actual readers and then turn to the subtle, but significant, relevance of more diffusely envisioned audiences.

Under most circumstances, a researcher writes fieldnotes immediately for herself as a future reader. This absence of an actual reader allows the researcher to write in relaxed and shifting styles, moving from audience to audience without worrying (at that point) about consistency or coherence. In this sense, fieldnotes should be written "loosely" and flowingly. If and when fieldnotes are shown to another reader—usually in a more comprehensive paper or article—the field researcher at this time can take control of this process; she can select, focus, and edit any notes before making them available to others. As a future reader of her own fieldnotes, the researcher anticipates a detailed reading in order to code and analyze the notes for a paper or article.

In practice, however, the researcher-writer might have in mind actual readers other than herself. Student researchers, in particular, ordinarily submit their fieldnotes to an instructor and write notes for that reader. Similarly, field researchers in team projects (Douglas 1976) write notes to be read by coworkers and colleagues. Here, field researchers might self-consciously write with actual readers in mind, producing accounts explicitly oriented to these others' knowledge and concerns. One common effect of writing with such readers in mind is to include more details of background and context to make fieldnotes more accessible. The ethnographer should, nonetheless, try to maintain a loose, flowing, and shifting approach without trying to write with consistency of voice and style.[2]

The effects of envisioned audiences on writing fieldnotes are more subtle and complex than those of actual readers.[3] The ethnographer's stance in writing fieldnotes involves trying to convey something about the world she has observed to outside audiences made up of those who are unfamiliar with that world. In this sense, fieldnotes are ultimately intended for outsiders of one sort or another. Indeed, it is in this respect that fieldnotes differ from a personal diary. Fieldnotes are not merely the personal reactions of the writer, intended to heighten self-awareness and self-insight; rather, they are more fundamentally accounts framed and organized to be read—eventually—by some other, wider audience.

Many ethnographers envision and write for a professional audience, forming their fieldnotes with eventual publication in mind. These sorts of notes often need some polishing and smoothing, but the writing is intended to be comprehensible to other professionals who are unfamiliar with the people and customs being written about, so there is less need for it to be further adapted for its audience. To the extent that the researcher-writer is self-conscious about writing for an ultimate, broader audience, notes will be richer; they will provide more background, context, and detail.

This is not to say that fieldnotes in "raw" form would be immediately comprehensible to professional or other outside readers. Fieldnotes are an accumulating body of writings, and the sense of later portions often depends upon what has been written earlier. People or events described in earlier notes, for example, need not be described in later ones. And indeed, just who the people are in particular incidents might not be evident to outside readers because of abbreviated names and lack of socially identifying information.[4] Only with filling in and contextualizing would such a fieldnote actually become comprehensible to someone other than the writer. Thus, accumulating fieldnote entries have an open-endedness that allows for new information and insights and an unfinished, in-progress quality that calls for editing later on.

In writing fieldnotes, most ethnographers shift between self and outside readers as envisioned future audiences. When writing in the first person about one's own direct involvement in field events, or when reflecting on one's emotional reactions or intuitions about next steps to take in the field, for example, the ethnographer assumes that these accounts will only be read by, and, hence, only need to be comprehensible to, oneself. In contrast, when writing up an event that was deeply "important" to those in the setting and that is likely to be excerpted for the final ethnography, the writer often strives for completeness and detail.

In sum, stance and envisioned audience significantly prefigure the way a researcher composes fieldnotes, even though both take on heightened salience when the field researcher self-consciously prepares texts for wider audiences. Writing fieldnotes involves a series of intricate, moment-by-moment choices in abstracting and processing experience. These choices involve not only what to look at and perhaps jot down but also *for whom*. Intended and anticipated audiences, as well as the theoretical commitments they reflect, linger as an influential presence over every ethnographer's shoulder.

NARRATING CHOICES ABOUT PERSPECTIVE

In using narrative strategies, an ethnographer not only draws on conventions for sequencing episodes (see chapter 3), but also makes choices about perspective. In our approach to ethnography, we do not ignore the presence of the ethnographer as both the observer of, and often participant in, the interactions occurring in the field site. Nor do we try to obscure the consequential effects of that presence in fieldnotes, acknowledging the ethnographer's presence, both explicitly as a character interacting with people in the field site and implicitly in stylistic choices that reveal, rather than obscure, the writer's perspective. Our approach to ethnography, therefore, shapes the following suggestions that we offer about *different points of view* (as revealing some voices and views more so than others) and about *time perspective* (whether writing in "real time" or from an "end-point" orientation).

Multiple Voices and Points of View

In writing fieldnotes, an ethnographer not only remembers and envisions a scene; he also presents that scene from a selected angle that highlights some of its features more than others. As noted in our discussion of stance above, this angling arises, in part, from theoretical concerns of the researcher's discipline; it also results from the nature of his participation in the field, for example, from his selective positioning and from identifying with certain members' experiences. In writing, the ethnographer thus reconstructs memories, prompted by jottings and headnotes, which privilege certain observational perspectives and certain members' experiences and voices over others.

The selective tendencies of field participation and memory construction are augmented by the fact that ethnographers, like all writers recounting events, must unavoidably tell their story through a particular "point of view." By convention, point of view refers to the writing techniques that express the narrator's (here the ethnographer's) perspective on events, namely, through whose eyes events are seen as well as through whose voices events are described. Point of view, then, is the writing perspective (and techniques) through which a story gets told, through whose view the characters, actions, setting, and events are presented to the reader.[5] Although authors have developed varied and complex ways to tell a story, the most general distinctions are between first-person, third-person, and omniscient points of view (Abrams and Harpham 2009:144–48). Each of these points of view privileges different "voices": First person foregrounds not only the perspective but also the "I" voice of the narrator; third person highlights the perspective and voices of others from the field site.[6]

In the following discussion, we explain and adapt the conventions of point of view to fit the purposes of writing fieldnotes from a participant observer perspective. When writing fieldnotes, an ethnographer *unavoidably* documents events from this perspective and, in that sense, always is writing from a first-person orientation readily expressed through "I" statements. However, since the ethnographer's primary goal is to recount the activities of others in the setting and to reveal their meanings, she also often writes segments using the techniques of the third-person point of view. We suggest that through an awareness of the conventions of perspective (those techniques commonly linked with each point of view), the ethnographer more readily can choose the option that expresses her purpose in any moment of writing. We invite ethnographers to remain flexible and to maximize their choices as they write.

FIRST-PERSON POINT OF VIEW. In fieldnotes, the first-person "I" recounting the day's entry is the ethnographer himself. A first-person mode "limits the matter of the narrative to what the first-person author knows, experiences, or finds out by talking with other characters" (Abrams and Harpham 2009:274). Since this perspective most readily encourages the writer to recount his own experiences, responses, and commentary, as well as the actions and talk of others, we suggest that an ethnographer often write in the first person. However, as noted above, we are not advocating that fieldnotes resemble journals or travelogues with the implicit purposes of personal understanding and expression of one's own views and experiences; instead, first-person fieldnotes focus on the "ethnographer as a tool" for understanding members' worlds.

Writing in the first person is particularly effective when the ethnographer is a member of the group she is studying. Seeing incidents through her eyes allows the reader to see an insider's view of actions as filtered through her concerns as an ethnographer. In addition, the first-person point of view allows the ethnographer to present the natural unfolding of experience as seen from her participant's viewpoint. The following fieldnote, written in the first person, illustrates these qualities. In this excerpt, an observer employed in an upscale eyeglass establishment recounts an upsetting incident of sexual harassment by one of the owners of the store:

> About halfway through the day, I am standing in the front section with Richard, one of the owners, and Al, the manager, who's on door duty. I reach down to get a sunglass to try on and say, "Oooo, these are great," as I pull out the plastic stop-sign shaped frames. Richard mutters something like "No" to tell

me that they won't be good on me. I notice that they are Lunettes, the man-
ufacturer of VVO glasses, and am surprised that I've never seen these and
that Richard is so quick to judge the result. I put them on and ask Richard,
"What do you think?" He looks at me and says, "You've got really great tits,
don't you." I think he has said, "You've got really great taste, don't you," so
I say, "Yeah, these are great," as I look at myself in the mirror. (I also believe
that when I don't have my glasses on, and I can't see, that I also cannot hear.
I have reconstructed Richard's words as he said them, from his next clarifying statement and did not just put in my interpretation.) I look at Richard. He
says, "They're really great tits." I utter a low "Huh?" (I now go back to his first
statement in my mind, and understand that I had misheard his suggestion of
my great taste in eyeglasses. Maybe on some level, I heard him correctly the
first time but recast it as something else; denial restores equilibrium.) He continues, "Really firm and high—really firm," gesturing at this point with his
hands like he's feeling breasts. I am stunned and cross my arms over my chest
(I did this unconsciously, as it wasn't until Richard's next line that I had realized I had done this gesture of protection.) He continues, "You cover yourself
up." He folds his arms: "Never seen you get shy before." He then puffs up his
chest as if to strut (as if to show me what I usually do, or what he expects me to
usually do). "That's not appropriate," I say softly.

By writing in the first person, this ethnographer not only can present what
the offender, Richard, said and what she said and did in response, but
also she can reveal how she felt and thought about her experience: "I am
stunned . . ." In this instance of abusive remarks inserted into an otherwise
innocuous conversation, the ethnographer's expression of her feelings of
withdrawal and self-protection reveal, more fully than any mere record of
his words ever could have, how truly distasteful and offensive his remarks
were to her. If it had been written in the third person, the fieldnote would
have lost her inner thoughts and feelings and how they changed as the incident unfolded. Nor would the fieldnotes have revealed the way the owner's
insistence in repeating the offensive remark transforms her earlier hearing
of the comment and causes her "to cross my arms across my chest" in a "gesture of protection."

In addition, by using the first person, the fieldnote can portray both the
author's experience as a member and her reflections as a writing ethnographer. For example, she reconstructs and presents her experience of sexual
harassment so that we see how she initially experienced it as a salesperson
talking to the store owner, mishearing him to say "You have great taste,"
a remark more appropriate to their work relationship and to presenting
glasses to customers. But we also hear her commentary on her experience,

inserted in an aside, on why she initially misheard his offensive comment: "Maybe on some level, I heard him correctly the first time but recast it as something else; denial restores equilibrium."

THIRD-PERSON POINT OF VIEW. Although such first-person field-notes allow the researcher to express her thoughts and feelings well, the primary aim of ethnography is to describe what others are doing and saying. Writing in the third-person point of view is particularly effective for conveying others' words and actions. When using the third person, the writer narrates as an observer of the scene, focuses fully on others, and refers to all characters as "he," "she," and "they." Sometimes known as an *impersonal narrator*, the third-person writer "reports from the outside what can be seen but makes no effort to get inside the minds of any characters" (Beiderwell and Wheeler 2009:393). The techniques of third person highlight others' activities and their concerns by attending to their interactions but without implying (or commenting on) their motivations and thoughts. We suggest that, in addition to first person, ethnographers also write many segments of their fieldnotes from this perspective to report what they see others doing and saying.

When using any of the third-person variations, the writer-narrator speaks through others in the narration, in effect, obscuring her presence as writer by never using the first-person pronoun "I" or invoking her interpretation. One novice ethnographer who had an internship with a probation officer commented that when writing in the third person, she "was able to focus more on what members were seeing and how they were reacting to certain situations that would arise during the interview with clients. . . . I can see myself take a step back and pay attention to details and words in a different manner [than in first person]. It's almost as if my writing becomes more observant." When this ethnographer writes about a probation officer interviewing a potential probationer and her mother, she uses third person.

Ms. Brown begins the interview and tells them both that she's putting the seventeen-year-old girl in probation. Then she starts asking Taquesha what her crime was. She explains that she went into a store with two friends to pick up some items and take them without paying. When Taquesha walked out of the store, she was detained by store personnel, and when the other two girls saw this, they left their items and walked out of the store without being arrested. At that point, the mother starts telling Ms. Brown that one of the girls is twenty-three years old and turns to look at her daughter, and says, "I don't know what she be doing hanging out with them twenty-three-year-olds." Ms.

Brown asks who this person is, and Taquesha tells her it's her friend's cousin. Then, Ms. Brown tells her, "Oohh, so you're the only one who got arrested?" Taquesha nods and smiles a little. Her mother starts saying she got caught because she is a "child of God," and the Lord has done this in order to set her daughter straight. Ms. Brown asks the girl in a serious tone, "Is this what you want? A life of crime? Stealin?" The girl turns to look at her and says "Nooo." Then Ms. Brown asks what classes she took last quarter, and she says she can't remember. Ms. Brown asks her if she's on drugs or something because that would be the only way she wouldn't remember. The girl laughs."

The ethnographer's careful attention to the interactions of the probation officer, the mother, and the daughter unfold clearly in this third-person account. The writer stays focused on what others are doing and saying, catching nuances of the back-and-forth between the characters. Uninterrupted by the writer's first-person comments, the third-person point of view creates a sense of immediacy and a flow of interactional exchanges.

FOCUSED THIRD-PERSON POINT OF VIEW. Field researchers might self-consciously write in ways that convey the point of view of one person directly involved in the scene or action. They can do so by describing an event from that person's actual physical location, by focusing on what the person saw, did, and said, by selecting details the person seems to notice, and by including the person's own words describing the event. Such accounts are written from a focused third-person point of view. For example, in telling about a fight between parents from the child's point of view, a writer might not only narrate using many of the child's words but also describe only those details a child might notice, such as the loud voices, threatening movements, and the large size of those fighting. Though the researcher might make inferences about thoughts and feelings, he would base them on observable facial expressions, gestures, and talk, and describe these from the child's perspective.[7]

An ethnographer writing about a domestic violence legal aid clinic often chose to write with a focus on the woman being interviewed by the intake officer. In the following excerpt, she effectively uses focused third person to reveal the distress of the woman, Graciela, struggling to tell Meredith, the intake officer, about the most recent incident of abuse.

Graciela pauses for a moment and rubs her earlobes. She looks up at Meredith and begins speaking: "On January 21st, 2010, Robert called me on the phone and told me he wanted to see his son. I told him he could see him on the 21st but not on the weekend . . ." He then called me a "dumb B" and hung up the phone. Meredith pauses, looks at Graciela, and says, "Okay, I need you to be as specific as you can, so that means you're going to have to tell me what he called you, exactly." Graciela smiles, laughs slightly, and says that she wants to avoid using "foul language" in front of her son because he tends to "repeat everything I say." Meredith nods her head and says, "I understand." She takes out a piece of green paper and pen from the desk drawer and places it on top of the desk. "Why don't you write it, that way I can know what he said—exactly," says Meredith. Graciela grabs the pen and writes down, "Dumb Bitch." She points to the paper and says, "That's what he called me," and lets out a sigh while shaking her head. "Okay, go on," says Meredith. Robert called back a second later and "insisted that I change my plans for him" in which he said _____. Graciela picks up the pen and writes: "Fuck that." . . . Robert then arrived at my house that day to see our son and upon leaving said, "I'll see you in court you Dumb B." She once again points to her written words. . . . Graciela hands her son in the stroller a stuffed animal that she pulls out from her diaper bag. She continues by saying that she asked Robert to leave after he used foul language, but he insisted on staying and "kept on calling me a trick." "I decided to call the police because I wanted him to leave my house. He got scared and left," Graciela says, as she blinks several times. She says that when the police came, "they told me to get a restraining order."

This ethnographer uses focused third person to stay centered on Graciela, her words and gestures: her nervous smiles and laughter, her sighs, her hesitancy to actually repeat the foul language directed at her by her partner. These details, underscored by her gesture of pulling out a stuffed animal for her son, depict the woman as a distressed mother. Although Meredith is present in the scene, her questions do not detract from the ethnographer's focus on Graciela's responses during the intake interview. Using the focused third person effectively conveys Graciela as struggling and nervous while making a litigant's claim.

Many ethnographers find that use of the focused third person in writing enables them to more fully sense an individual member's outlook and to pursue questions and issues of interest to that person. For example, while studying traditional healing methods in an African culture, the researcher might track the activities of a healer for a day: going with him to make his medicines, sitting beside him as he treats his patients, and resting with him after his duties (cf. Yoder 1982). By staying closely involved in one member's activities and then describing what that person pays attention to, does, and says, the ethnographer is more likely to get a sense of his perspective. Moreover, by taking up different observational positions and participating empathetically with different people, the field researcher can effectively write from different focused third-person perspectives and document the multiple voices in the setting. In studying traditional healing, for example, the ethnographer can easily shift position and focus, tracking the experiences and talk of particular patients.[8]

OMNISCIENT POINT OF VIEW. In taking an *omniscient point of view*, the writer/narrator "knows everything that needs to be known about the agents, actions, and events, and has privileged access to the characters' thoughts, feelings, and motives; also the narrator is free to move at will in time and place, to shift from character to character, and to report (or conceal) their speech, doings, and states of consciousness" (Abrams and Harpham 2009:272). Writing from this point of view, ethnographers use an "objective" tone and style to report events as "realist tales" (Van Maanen 1988), a style much more prevalent in past ethnographies.

However, writing from an omniscient point of view often introduces serious distortions into writing fieldnotes. For example, had Rachel Fretz, the fieldworker studying *mukanda* rituals in Zambia, taken an omniscient perspective, she would have recounted the intense and frenzied dancing, drumming, and singing of the whole village throughout the prior night. Then she might have described the feelings of the young boys—perhaps fear and excitement—waiting to be rushed at dawn into the camp for circumcision. Certainly, the masked figure dancing to the drumming would also have drawn her attention, and she would have described his raffia costume and the black-and-red decorations on the mask. From her unlimited perspective, she also might have described the circumcision taking place in the boy's camp out in the bush, with the fathers, brothers, and uncles attending (her descriptions of this gender-delineated, all-male place would have had to be based on interviews). Next, she might have turned to the mothers, other women, and children back in the village to report not only the singing and the ritual pouring of water on the mothers' heads but also to describe their thoughts—whether nervousness or joy—as they waited to hear from the camp leader that their sons had been successfully circumcised. Narrating these events from an omniscient perspective, she would have created a *realist tale* with an objective tone but at the cost of obscuring how these activities and meanings unfolded for members and how she came to understand them. Of course, this ethnographer did not actually write her fieldnotes in such an omniscient manner.

In sum, our interactionist and interpretive approach, along with our presence in the fieldnotes, militates against using an omniscient perspective in writing fieldnotes. The omniscient style produces fieldnotes that merge the ethnographer's participatory experience with reports from others; conceal the complex processes of uncovering the varied understandings of what an event is about; reduce and blend multiple perspectives into accounts delivered in a single, all-knowing voice; and ignore the highly contingent interpretations required to reconcile and/or prioritize competing versions of the event. In fact, because this point of view positions the writer as a detached observer above or outside events, it encourages her to depict characters and actions with near-divine insight into prior causes and ultimate outcomes. For these reasons, we recommend against narrating fieldnotes from an omniscient point of view.[9]

SHIFTING POINTS OF VIEW—FIRST- AND THIRD-PERSON VARIATIONS. As emphasized previously, fieldnotes provide less a picture of the daily life and concerns of others than a picture of this life and these concerns as seen, understood, and conveyed by the participant observer ethnographer. As a result, the ethnographer tends to write from a stance that acknowledges self as the lens through which one sees and that, at the same time, stays focused on depicting others. He implements this bifurcated stance in practice by moving back and forth between recounting participant experiences in the first person and observations of others in the third person. But, in shifting between first- and third-person points of view, the ethnographer faces an ongoing challenge in handling the tensions of this bifurcated practice. On the one hand, he attends to and writes about routine events that occur frequently in that setting with an eye toward what events mean to members, often using a focused third-person point of view and frequently quoting members so that their voices can be heard. On the other hand, he cannot neglect his own involvement in observed scenes in making the observations and in writing them up. These recurring shifts of attention from self to others appear as substantive shifts in point of view marked by either a frequent use of "I" or a predominance of "he," "she," and "they" and then back again. While these shifts are based in participant observations, the ethnographer—as writer—also can make choices about point of view that highlight the details and voices they experienced in the field.[10]

This bifurcated approach, however, does not necessarily result in precise divisions between different points of view, namely, in discrete first-person and third-person segments of writing; rather, the ethnographer as writer might shift from first to third person and back again within a single segment or episode. Writing from a predominantly third-person point of view does not demand that the ethnographer entirely avoid first-person pronouns or invariably absent herself from her fieldnotes. Within primarily third-person fieldnotes about others, for example, the writer might include herself as a bystander-participant who frames the scene; or as a witness throughout the scene, she might insert her own responses to the action in first-person asides. If the writer *shifts intentionally* to more fully express views from a different perspective, the writing is revelatory and clear, not a confusing "mish-mash" of first and third person.

For example, one intern doing research in a home for recovering prostitutes commented that writing in third person helped her get "a better sense of the scene and what the dialogue meant" to the young women; however, she could not avoid her presence in the predominately third-person writing, as the house had only six residents, and her interactions were a significant part of the conversations. In the following fieldnote, she begins by mentioning her presence with the resident women, chatting together in the garage, but then switches entirely to focusing on them.

> Silvia, Kelly, Sandra and I sit out in the garage. . . . Silvia is holding a beanie doll and says, Check this out. Silvia is wearing a blue sweater jacket with a red tanktop underneath. . . . Her hair is a new color this week, a shade of purple. The v-neck tank top reveals her tattoo. The name, "Mookie," goes across her chest with a star above it. She is shorter, Latina-looking, with large, pink lips. She looks younger (than the others), in her late twenties. Kelly looks at the doll, laughs, and says, That looks just like you! Silvia says, I know, it's my sister. Kelly asks her, Where'd you get that? Silvia tells her, Julie found it for me in the donation. . . . They smoke their cigarettes, and Sandra asks, How was your day, Silvia? . . . Silvia says, Okay I had to do a bunch of stuff, and I lost ten dollars. Sandra says, Oh, that sucks, I'm sorry. Kelly opens her eyes wide, raises her eyebrows and says, You lost ten?? Silvia nods. She mumbles quietly, I'm losin money like it grows on trees or something. She looks down at the ground and fiddles with the cigarette in her hand.

The fieldnotes continue with the conversation between the women, depicting the women's clothes, gestures, and small talk as they relax in the garage. Only when the conversation turns to include her, does the ethnographer's presence become more obvious in the fieldnotes. For example, when the women leave the garage and join the others back in the house, the case manager asks the ethnographer for help in figuring out the financial complexities facing a resident:

Jennifer, the case manager, walks back in the room and says, Catherine, did you figure out your financial stuff? Catherine says, Yeah, kinda. Jennifer looks at me and says, Can you help us figure out some of it? I tell them, Sorry, I don't have much experience with that kind of stuff. Jennifer nods and heads back into the staff office.

These third-person fieldnotes focus on reporting about others and only bring the ethnographer into the scene as a *framing at the beginning and end*: She sits in the garage and listens to the women talk; she walks back into the house with them and answers the case manager's question. The primary attention remains on the women; her use of the third person centers more fully on others than does the first-person perspective and portrays the activities of members of the community more so than her own experiences.[11]

Sometimes an ethnographer focuses on an account as *a witnessed event*, emphasizing her close-up view and involvement even though she is not an actor in the scene. Thus, the attention stays on others, offering what initially seems to be a predominately third-person report. Yet, because she offers her occasional response in an aside (such as "I was horrified,"), one has the sense of watching the scene with her. This rhetorical strategy draws the reader closer and convinces one that this "really happened as I saw it." The ethnographer might include features and occurrences that are unexpected, that stand in contrast with what she is used to, or that generate strong emotional reactions. In writing such fieldnotes, the ethnographer often interjects first-person asides when she focuses on her reactions to events and people. For example, in observing and participating in the *mukanda* rituals (initiations for boys) in Zambia, Rachel Fretz often wrote fieldnotes that described the activities of others.[12] In the following excerpt, she looks out at what others are doing and occasionally inserts "I" statements in recounting moments of more active involvement and in describing her responses.

That afternoon we heard the women and children hollering as though a *lyishi* had come and we [another researcher and I] ran down [to the center of the village] with our cameras. It was *Kalulu*, the rabbit mask. He is a small, lithe figure dressed in a grass skirt and grass shirt around his neck. On his arms and legs he wears the usual fiber costume, a net-like fitted body "overall," and his mask is a small red and white painted face with two large cloth ears. He calls out a nasalized, "Wha, wha." It sounds like a child's cry. He hopped around the yard and half-ran toward the children. Then the Headman told the women to dance with him; so D, his daughter, called some women and children together and they turned their backs toward the Rabbit, *Kalulu*, and sang and danced . . . Now and then Kalulu rather listlessly chased a woman or child. And then all of a sudden, he used his small switch and ran right up to a girl and switched her. The children ran away shrieking, and the Rabbit ran over to J's house. Shortly it came back.

And then it seems that the Headman called John over and gave him some directions because after that, John went and found Kianze, the eight-year-old girl who lives with N (she's her grandchild) and grabbed her firmly by the arm and held on and dragged her screaming over toward *Kalulu*, the Rabbit, who reached to catch her.

She ran screaming in the other direction and John went after her again and grabbed her and pulled her toward the Rabbit. Kianze, looking over her shoulder, seemed thoroughly terrified and screamed and screamed with tears running down her face. (I felt horrified as I watched.) This time the Rabbit swatted her and she ran still screaming into her house. And the mask ran after her and entered the house. But she managed, I was told later, to hide under a bed.

Then, *Kalulu* ran after Jinga and he caught her and picked her up in his arms. Jinga screamed too, but she did not seem so terrified and did not cry. Someone said later that N [her grandmother] yelled at him to get her back, for the mask had started to carry her down the path toward the *mukanda* camp.

The next day I asked John why he grabbed Kianze and Jinga; he said it was because they were supposed to go to school, but that they just left home but did not actually go into the school every day. After a while, the mask ran off down the *mukanda* path, and I went home, still shocked by the mask's treatment of the two girls.

Although the ethnographer in writing these fieldnotes focuses primarily on others—the masked dancer, the screaming girls, the grandmother—she occasionally includes her responses to the frightened girls as "I" remarks inserted within her description. Had she quoted the outcries of the young girls and of the grandmother calling for someone to rescue her granddaughter, she could have augmented the sense of seeing the chase from a more immediate, close-up position. However, since she was doing research in the Chokwe language in a multilingual area, and these particular people were speaking Lunda and Luvale, she could not provide direct quotes. Her descriptions report their actions, screams, and what others speaking Kichokwe told her. Her own presence and asides in the fieldnotes thus add a sense of immediacy.

By convention, the inclusion of "I" makes this a first-person tale, as told through the narrator's experience of the event. But it is not the first-person use we described above, through which we learned the ethnographer's first-person feelings and insights as an insider participating in the exchange. Rather it is another use of first person as one who speaks as the witness about other central characters and thus portions appear to be third person. The writer-narrator "I" shifts between her own responses and her close attention to others who are the central characters; as a consequence, the narrator-as-witness becomes a persuasive presence in the fieldnotes. The juxtaposition of voices—here the ethnographer-as-witness and the persons-running-from-the-mask—has a rhetorical effect that convinces (cf. Atkinson 1990:82–103).

In closing, we contend that the degree to which the researcher becomes involved in people's doings implicitly shapes the perspective from which he can write about incidents. Choices about perspective go deeper than the use of pronouns; how one writes creates an overall impression of the ethnographer's understanding and appreciation for another world. For instance, involvement can allow the ethnographer to write from a "near" perspective and to present details as seen by a member and, by quoting, to present a member's voice. In contrast, even when writing in the first person, a physically or emotionally "distant" stance often results in more generalized descriptions presented in a reportorial and impersonal tone. Finally, shifts in point of view also mark the nature of fieldnotes as unfolding, in-process writing rather than polished, edited work in which a consistent point of view aims for a certain effect. Thus, even though an ethnographer might write particular segments from a single point of view, the fieldnotes as a whole shift. The fieldworker moves from depicting events observed at one position, point in time, and perspective to fieldnotes constructed from other points of view.

"Real-Time" and "End-Point" Perspectives

In writing descriptive accounts, ethnographers face an additional choice: whether to describe an event "in real time," from a perspective of incomplete or partial knowledge, or to describe it from some end point of more complete knowledge.

In real-time descriptions, the writer seeks to characterize events using only what she knows moment by moment as the event unfolds; thus, the writer tries to avoid using information that will ultimately come out but, as of yet, is not available for describing what happened at those prior moments. By way of illustration, consider the way in which the following description of approaching a skid row mission excludes key meanings until they are actually discovered by the writer:

> The whole area around the Mission, including the alley, was dense with people, more so than the surrounding blocks. Probably eighty percent of these people were black; about ninety percent were male. People lay, sat, or stood all along the aqua colored walls of the Mission. . . . The people on the left-hand side of the door gave the impression of being in line: they all were standing at fairly uniform distances, and the same people were standing in line throughout the several hours I was around the Mission. When I later read the Mission's literature, I realized that these people were likely waiting in line for the privilege of spending the night in the Mission. The literature noted that "sleep tickets" were given out at 12:30 pm and that the line formed early. Interesting, there were many more people in back of the Mission in what I perceived to be the lunch line than were in the sleep line.

This real-time account preserves the writer's experience of seeing an assemblage of people and not quite knowing what they are doing. That they are "in line" and there for a particular purpose, the ethnographer does not initially use to characterize the scene but, rather, presents as an in-process discovery; the writer makes some effort to describe the initial grounds for showing these people as "in line," for example, "uniform distance," continuity over time. The later discovery of the "purpose" of these activities—to get a "sleep ticket" allowing one to spend the night in the Mission—is explicitly described only when the ethnographer discovers it; only then, does he characterize this assemblage as "the sleep line."

In contrast, field researchers might describe events from an "end-point" position by making full use of what they ultimately came to know and understand about them. This procedure incorporates "facts" or understandings established at some later point to describe what was going on at earlier stages of observation and understanding. In describing a formal business meeting in this way, for example, an observer would, from the very start of the notes, describe participants by name and position, even though he had only learned about these matters over the course of the meeting.

In observing new scenes, we often use what we ultimately come to know to describe events and meanings that we had initially not understood or had understood partially or incorrectly. Indeed, observation involves continuous processes of such *retrospective reinterpretation* as the observer shapes into more definitive form what at some earlier point had been hazy, ambiguous, or downright confusing (Garfinkel 1967). A fieldworker observing on a bus, for example, might note that a "crazy woman" boarded and talked to the driver. If this woman's "craziness" only became apparent as she talked to the driver and other passengers, it represents an evaluation inferred later from an ongoing course of interaction: To characterize her as "crazy" from her initial appearance in the scene obscures these processes and strips the written account of any consideration of how her disorientation became visible to the observer or to members of the setting.

But, it might have been that her presenting appearance and initial demeanor made this passenger's "craziness" evident "at a glance" to the fieldworker (and presumably to any culturally competent member of American urban society). In this case, to characterize this person as "crazy" right from the start raises an issue of adequate description rather than of retrospective interpretation; "crazy" is a highly evaluative term that should be accompanied by some description of whatever observable features led to such a judgment in the first place. In general, descriptively effective fieldnotes enable a reader to distinguish initial understandings from retrospective reinterpretations.

In many situations, as a practical matter, retrospective reinterpretations are useful and unavoidable. For many purposes, we are not interested either in the initial interpretations that an observer made of people based on woefully incomplete information or in just how the observer figured out who and what these people were and what they were doing. In many cases, ethnographers decide that it is sufficient to characterize matters in terms of meanings that have ultimately been established as true or accurate; tracking exactly how this occurred is often simply too cumbersome, time-consuming, or of little or no relevance to understanding members' core activities and concerns.

Yet, there are times and occasions when the field researcher wants to preserve initial understandings—even if misguided—and to document the actual process of determining meaning. In practical terms, "reliving" the events of the day and writing about them in real time as they unfolded can assist the ethnographer to recall details and result in more lively and complete descriptions of people and events in the setting. In terms of methodological self-consciousness, real-time descriptions allow ethnographers to identify and explicate their own processes for discovering or attributing meaning. For example, a fieldworker in a business meeting might focus on describing just what information and cues she attends to in actually determining the identities and status of those present, writing notes in a way that preserves the initial lack of definiteness in these matters. These descriptions could serve not only as documentation of her processes of identifying others but also suggest how ordinary participants in the meeting work out these meanings. These descriptive procedures would then allow the reader to share at least part of the observer-writer's and members' actual experience of discovering meaning. It also brings the observer-writer to the center of the process of establishing meaning and, hence, "de-objectivizes" the description; a description of how a "sleep line" outside a skid row mission came to be discovered as such shows the observer-writer to be an active interpreter of the social world.

Similarly, ethnographers can use real-time descriptions to highlight *members'* processes of inquiry and inference for determining "facts" and attributing meaning, helping to identify subtly consequential processes that are glossed or obscured in end-point versions. For example, real-time descriptions provide useful tools for describing situations in which meanings remain ambiguous or indeterminate for members and/or the researcher. Consider this episode written by an ethnographer examining interactions with a stranger on a train:

> I made a motion, like moving my stuff from the seat next to me to allow the man to sit down, but he just looked at me and smiled. Then he said, "How's it going?" I said, "Good, thanks." He was carrying a black plastic grocery bag and asked me, "Would you like a pomegranate?" As he took it out of his bag to hand it to me, he said, "I just picked them from my tree." I said, "Sure, thanks!" I asked, "Are you from here?" He said, "Yes, I am going from here to San Marcos to visit a friend." He started talking about going to see a play at the civic center. I tried as much as I could to follow what he was saying (I was being bombarded by a lot of information. He talked to me like I knew the people he was talking about.) He talked about the two who were in the play. . . . I noticed he had missing teeth and crooked yellow teeth. . . . He was wearing sandals and I could see he had callous feet. He was talking about the two friends that were in the play at the Civic Center. I asked, "How old are they?" He said, "The girl is 18 years old and the boy 16 years old." I asked, "So you are going there to see the play?" He said, "Yeah, I saw it yesterday. I was very impressed with them that I am treating them to pizza today after their Cinema." While he was talking, he mentioned his age in comparison to the kids, "I am 49 years old." He started telling me bus numbers, like "302," "309" . . . , bus routes that he would often take. He kept talking without me asking questions; I often repeated some key words of his conversation to make sure that I was following him.
>
> The train was approaching my station, and as I got up to move toward the open doors of the train, the man moved to the lower level. He got off at the Civic Center like he said, but he just sat down on the bench and put his hands on his temples, communicating anguish and distress. (It made me think, I wonder if he was just making that story up about going to see his friends. Later, I looked up the San Marcos Civic Center calendar of events to see if they were having a play that weekend, but no play was playing. Sometimes, we don't know how

much we can trust in a conversation. We don't know the strangers we interact with until we talk to them and ask questions, but even then, it is hard to know and judge or interpret their meaning. Who knows—this man could have had a mental disorder that created these scenarios for himself. I just don't know.)

As this encounter with the man on the train unfolds, the ethnographer reveals aspects of his appearance and talk that alternately make his story seem credible but then cast a slight doubt on what he says about the purpose of his journey. By writing in real time and showing her own attempts to put the sometimes discrepant bits and pieces of the man's story together in a way that makes sense, she recreates, from her own experience, the feeling of uncertainty for the reader (This seems plausible, but should I believe him? How do I know?). When the man gets off of the train at the appropriate stop, yet sits down holding his head in anguish, the ethnographer remains open to varied interpretations, continuing to recognize that the meaning of what happened remains unclear. Rather than concluding that the man is mentally ill based on the accumulating discrepancies and inconsistencies in his story, she takes the opportunity in asides to raise further questions that, as her observations accumulate, could provide deepened understanding about interactions among strangers. In general, we recommend that ethnographers avoid the temptation to prematurely decide "what happened" for the sake of bringing closure. Thus, real-time descriptions can be equally important for revealing how members, as well as ethnographers, sometimes struggle to make sense or give meaning—does a situation or a person mean this or mean that?—to the ambiguity and uncertainties that are often important features of social interaction.

In summary, compact and definite, end-point descriptions are effective ways to recount what goes on in the field much of the time. However, they tend to ignore or gloss crucial interactional processes, thus obscuring what might be consequential ways for working through initially contradictory, confusing, incomplete, or uncertain meanings or assumptions. Real-time descriptions, in contrast, document the processes through which members arrive at what they regard as definitive understandings of meanings, facts, or sequences of events. In so doing, these descriptions preserve the qualities of uncertainty and indeterminacy that characterize much of social life.

FIELDNOTE TALES: WRITING EXTENDED NARRATIVE SEGMENTS

When an ethnographer organizes her early fieldnotes into a day's entry of loosely interconnected episodes, the narration coheres primarily through the writer's perspective—as something that she saw or heard (see chapter 3). But right from the start in doing field research, the ethnographer also perceives some activities as intrinsically cohesive, not only due to her interested attention but, more so, because these interactions cohere for members. In writing fieldnotes about such activities—many of which, like court cases or ritual performances, extend through a session or even several days—the ethnographer still writes vivid sketches and episodes but does so as part of a more focused, unified representation of the flow of social life. She writes such a segment as a cohesive sequence, creating a sustained narrative that documents "what happened" from the beginning to the end of the activity or event. Such extended narrative segments, sometimes called "fieldnote tales" (Van Maanen 1988), recount sequences of interconnected episodes and rely more explicitly on the conventions of narration.

Writing a fieldnote tale allows the ethnographer to present an event or activity as unfolding over time and emerging through members' interactions. Often, ethnographers begin their day's entry by first writing such a narrative segment, eagerly relating an incident or event that appeared fascinating or central to members. As only a part of the day's fieldnotes, these narrations easily become the most extended units of writing embedded within an entry. Occasionally, such a fieldnote tale expands into an entire entry; rarely, a tale might spread through several days' entries.

In composing these fieldnote tales, the ethnographer finds (and creates) connections, not so much by using his own experiences to shape his narrative, but, rather, by constructing a narrative focused on moments that mark the activities in the lives of others. Of course, narratives do not tell themselves; inevitably, the ethnographer-as-narrator constructs these tales and their coherence, even when they depict events in the lives of others. Ethnographers can identify and create such narrative coherence in two different, though related, ways. First, they can build extended narratives directly around sequences of interaction as members in the field site orient to the actions. For example, in many legal and social service settings, "the case" stands as one such "natural" unit; interactions in court hearings, intake interviews, and probation supervising are all organized around the processing of targeted individuals. Similarly, in school settings, "the class period" stands as a unit oriented to by teachers and students and demarcates other nonclassroom units, such as "nutrition" breaks, lunch, all-school meetings, and so on. Second, ethnographers can construct coherent sequences by selectively focusing on a series of events involving the same characters or similar activities over time without directly invoking how members organize or refer to these matters. For instance, ethnographers might organize narratives around the "more interesting" portions of "the workday," showing how members' actions progress, develop over time, and sometimes seem to lead to "something happening." But the ethnographer does not abandon all concern for the "natural units" of members. Though he selects and interconnects the activities he chooses to narrate, he does so with an awareness of the broader scope of member-recognized categories. For instance, he might recount certain students' actions as leading to some conflict; or he might tell about the workers' recurring breaks during a day.

In a basic sense, coherent narratives demarcate explicit "beginnings" and "endings": a "case" begins when the court clerk calls the case and the relevant players take their respective positions in the courtroom, and it ends when they leave those positions; a class period begins and ends with the sounding of a bell or buzzer. These beginnings and endings are relatively clear-cut if the narrative segment directly represents a member-used unit, such as the "case" or "period." Beginnings and endings tend to be more variable when the ethnographer selectively tracks a thematic thread and more actively creates narrative coherence, as in choosing when to begin her account of the member's work or workday. But even in delineating member units, narrative "beginnings" and "endings" are never absolute. From the perspective of the defendant, for example, the "beginning" of his case might be the informal consultation with his public defender in the hallway minutes before his hearing; the "ending" might be a debriefing with his attorney, setting up a probation appointment, or paying a fine after the court's decision. Thus, the beginnings and endings that mark extended narratives are heuristic devices, allowing the ethnographer to organize and unify sequences of interactions within her now book-ended tale. Indeed, through exploring what occurs before this beginning and after the chosen ending, the ethnographer can find useful strategies for expanding and deepening her fieldnote tales.

As a result of these two narrative strategies—using a delineated member-unit or following a thematic thread to create the narrative—fieldnote tales range from more cohesively to loosely integrated narrative segments within a day's entry. Inevitably, most fieldnote tales are loosely structured; the writer reports only what he saw and as much as he remembers. For instance, having selectively tracked certain features of the workday, the ethnographer might narrate a series of episodes that highlight several characters or that concentrate on similar activities. He constructs them as an episodic tale because he infers the actions to be loosely interconnected. He writes one episode after another, including all actions he observed and remembers, even though he might not see how they fit in while writing about them. He makes what connections he can at the moment, guided by an intuitive sense for what belongs in this tale, for "what goes with what." Often, the import of an "extraneous" detail or episode becomes clear only later when rereading the tale.

At other times, ethnographers tend to write fieldnote tales as more tightly structured narratives—for very good ethnographic reasons. Committed to members' perceptions of events, the ethnographer writes about the links and sequences of events that members enact or present as a unified series of actions: for example, as activities that have more or less clearcut beginnings, or progressions in which one action causes the next and leads to consequential endings. As noted, many criminal court hearings in American society are structured in these ways, allowing a researcher to write cohesive tales about them. Similarly, the researcher might hear people telling accounts to each other about their day's experiences, talking about past incidents in response to the researcher's queries, or recounting myths and legends learned from their elders.

In writing up such cohesive narratives, the ethnographer appropriately writes fieldnotes with a unified narrative structure in which one action leads to the next and builds to an outcome. Clearly, writing these fieldnote tales or extended narrative segments differs from composing a dramatic narrative through which the narrator intends to make a point. Well-crafted stories not only narrate actions so that a reader can follow them, but they also build suspense into the unfolding action.[13] Such plot-driven narratives make "something happen." Characters act in ways that have consequences and that lead to an instructive, often dramatic outcome, which invites readers to infer a thematic idea. But most everyday incidents and events do not happen like dramatic narratives in which one action neatly causes the next and results in clear-cut consequences; instead, much of life unfolds rather aimlessly. Making all experiences fit the formal demands of a plotted tale falsifies them. Therefore, the cautious ethnographer—wary of imposing a suspenseful narrative structure on all events—avoids overdetermining the connections between actions and their movement toward an outcome.

Depicting life in a cohesive narrative form is highly interpretive writing. Yet, when telling about experiences and observations, narrating conventions offer very effective ways—perhaps the best—of showing interactions as they unfold and as they become the context for the next interactions, thus allowing one to track how members' meanings emerge through inter-actions. We suggest that ethnographers narrate when they track events and incidents unfolding through member interactions and arching over a period of time. But recognizing that narrating is highly interpretive (like other forms of coherent writing), we offer these suggestions: Ethnogra-phers should avoid superimposing their own sense of narrative structure and movement on others' words and actions; when writing up stories that a community member tells about local events, the ethnographer should stick closely to the teller's sequencing and report carefully the connections the teller makes between actions. In addition, ethnographers should resist crafting events into complex, dramatic sequences or into better-sounding, more convincing tales: They should not revise or rearrange actions to make them lead (inevitably) to a particular ending or a climactic outcome; and they should not build suspense into everyday events that lack this quality. Instead, ethnographers should recount interactions as they unfolded, tell-ing the event as they saw it happen. When narrating, they should mute any "great-storyteller" impulse to create dramatic, suspenseful, highly crafted stories. As a consequence, fieldnote tales tend to be episodic, a string of action chunks put down on the page one after another, a sequence of often loosely interconnected episodes *that reveal interactions unfolding and whose meanings might emerge through the telling.*

In the following pages, we present two fieldnote tales as extended narra-tive segments. Both tales present a series of episodes as the researchers saw and remembered them. Though both tales present activities as they un-folded, they exemplify the two different tendencies in narrating we have discussed in this section: tracking the activities of the same characters and tracking a member incident. In telling the first tale, the ethnographer re-counts the activities of a policeman and policewoman over a period of time, only loosely interconnecting their actions. This episodic tale coheres only because the writer has an interest in the activities of the two officers; that is, the episodes hang together by a thematic thread. In contrast, in telling the second tale, the ethnographer tracks an incident driven by one charac-ter's concern, namely, a school dean seeking to locate and discipline a stu-dent. The incident unfolds as a member case about how the dean handles the student who broke school rules. Thus, this tale achieves a tighter narra-tive structure by linking the series of episodes about the dean and student in which one action leads to another and, ultimately, to some sort of resolution.

Fieldnote Tale One: Activities of Police Officers on a Night Patrol

In this first tale, a student ethnographer writes about events he observed while riding one night on patrol with two police officers, Sam and Alisha. He recounts a series of consecutive, but otherwise fairly discrete, episodes. Although these episodes all involve police activities, they are only loosely related to one another and contain several possible "somethings that happened." To discuss these episodes, we label them *a* through *e*.

(*a*) As we were driving, Alisha was telling Sam about women officers in another department. "I can't believe what some of the women and the women trainees have done, and I hate it cause it's always the women that do the stupidest things. And that's what gives a bad name to the women officers. So—"

"You know what the problem is, don't ya?" Sam says. "Women think on the wrong side of the brain."

"What?"

"They think out of the wrong side of their brain."

"Or is it because we don't have a penis to think from?" Alisha burst out laughing.

"NOOO!"

"Is that what you think, Sam?"

"No. I'll probably tell my wife that. She'll get a kick out of it." We pulled down an alley and passed a Hispanic guy about twenty. "That guy was stealing those tires that were down here."

"The kid's bike ones?"

"Yeah."

"Maybe."

"Um, sure. They were back there and they're not there no more."

"I don't know."

"They were there last night, pieces to a bicycle."

"Oh. Should we go get 'em?"

"No, they've been there forever."

(*b*) We pulled out of the alley and were waiting to make a right-hand turn. "I'm gonna stop that." I looked up and there was a white jeep without its lights on. We zoomed ahead and got behind the car. The car got in the turning lane as did we. After the light changed, and we were proceeding through the intersection, Sam flipped on the lights. The jeep pulled into a gas station. . . . Sam walked up to the car and Alisha walked up and flashed her flashlight in the windows. She walked back and stood next to me. The people in the gas station all watched us. The girl (Caucasian) got out of her car, walked to the back and looked at her taillights. Sam spoke to her and then walked back to the car. We got in and Sam said that her headlights were on but not her taillights. He let her off with a warning.

(c) We decided to go to 7-11 to get coffee. We walked in and the lady clerk knew Sam and Alisha. She gave them these big cups and Sam went and filled them with coffee. I walked over and didn't see any of the cups like they had so I just grabbed the largest coffee cup they had and filled mine up. Alisha was looking down the aisle with all the medicines. I told her she should get Tums for her stomach. Sam came over and made some comment. Alisha replied that she had a tough stomach, and she didn't need anything. Sam got a Mounds candy bar. We each paid and then went back to the car and started driving around again. As we were driving, Sam rolled down his window and pretended to throw his candy wrapper out the window. "You didn't?" Alisha asked. With a big smile on his face, Sam said, "no," and showed her the wrapper. Alisha went on to explain that she had a real thing for not littering, especially when they were working. "I think we need to be examples. What does it look like if somebody sees a candy wrapper fly out the window of a cop car?"

(d) As we were driving through a residential area we heard, "Crack! Crack!" I immediately thought, fireworks? In retrospect that seems like such a dumb thought, but having never heard gunshots except at a range, I guess I'm not used to assuming something is gunshots. Sam said something about a car I hadn't seen and it having only one taillight. He floored the car, the engine raced and we flew down the street. Alisha threw her coffee out the window and both she and Sam pulled their guns out. "Get ready to duck if I tell you" she told me. She then called in that we would be out in the area on possible gunshots. "That fucker split." We flew down the street. At one point, we came up on a car coming toward us, and we met the car as it was driving through a narrow spot with cars parked on each side of the road. Sam locked up the brakes, the tires squealed and somehow we made it through. Sam floored it once again and, once again, we were flying down the street. We hit a bump and I flew out of my seat. I heard the things in the trunk bang on the top of the trunk. "I want to find that car Alisha!"

"Did you see the people in it?"

"No. They were just hauling ass and it's got a fuckin' taillight that's out and I don't even know what kind of car it is." We drove around for a while and then gave up the search. "Damn. I want a felony tonight. We have to find a felony tonight, Alisha. I want to point my gun at someone. Where are all the felons? That was a pretty close call there."

"Yeah. But I trust your driving Sam. I had to throw my coffee out though. Maybe we should go see if it's still there." [Sam teases Alisha for having to throw her coffee out the window.]

"How was I supposed to get my gun out and hold my coffee?"

"I did it and I was driving."

"That's because Sam, you're such a stud."

"I kept mine." I said jokingly and they laughed.

"So you're talking to me about not littering and you go and throw your coffee cup out the window."

"Correct me if I'm wrong, I did realize my mistake afterward, and I requested that you go back so I could retrieve my coffee."

"No you said, 'Go back and get my COFFEE!' is what you said." We all laugh.

"But the coffee had to be in a cup in order for me to get it."

"Would you do some police work and run this plate?" (It was a little surprising how fast the atmosphere had transformed from total intensity to carefree joking in minutes.)

(e) Sam began to follow an old beat up American car. He sped up and told Alisha to call it in for wants and warrants. As he pulled in closer, I saw that the registration said 1991 [it's now January 1993]. "Come on. Come back Code 36 Charles." Sam said, hoping the plate would come back with felony wants on it. The plate came back all clear, expired reg. The car made a left off of the main street, and as we turned to follow, Sam flipped on the lights. The driver was a black male. Alisha shined her flashlight in the back seat and Sam walked up to the driver's window. The driver handed Sam his license and registration. Sam spoke with the man for a minute and then walked back to the car. As he got in he said, "That's a responsible father. I'm not going to write up a responsible father. He had his kids' immunization records in his glove box. That's not our crack dealer."

"Just cause someone's a father doesn't mean he doesn't deal."

"That's not what I meant. Fathers can be drug dealers, but responsible fathers aren't drug dealers."

In this fieldnote tale, two patrol officers drive around and react to events observed outside the car and to topics raised in talk within the car. The episodes reveal their now-teasing, now-supportive work relationship. The tale also conveys the tenor of routine police patrol work—ongoing ordinary talk, endless driving, occasional breaks—punctuated by moments of excitement during a chase that, in turn, dissipates as the officers slip back into normal work activities. Clearly, the quick shifts interest the writer who comments in an aside how suddenly the officers turn from tense excitement to informal joking.

These actions clearly provide the material for a narrative or perhaps more accurately several possible narratives. One tale might be of a night's work for two patrol officers; another might be about the ethnographer riding along with two officers, his efforts to figure out what they do and why, and his hopes to gain some acceptance from them. But it is not at all clear that these were narratives the ethnographer intended to tell at the moment of writing. Rather, his concerns were to write up "what happened" as he remembered it. He does so by constructing a series of episodes.

Not all of these episodes are closely connected. Obviously the writer links some actions in one episode to actions in subsequent episodes: For example, the coffees purchased at the 7-11 store (in episode c) play a key role in the subsequent chase episode (d). But no explicit connections are apparent between other episodes. Even though the police stop two cars, there are no indications that the second car-stop was in any way connected to the first, although a reader might well be able to suggest connections (for instance, that the black father in the second stop had to be let off with a warning, since the white woman in the first stop also had been simply warned).

In writing this tale, the ethnographer advances the narrative through time by grouping actions into discrete episodes; in fact he has no need to use an explicit transition term ("then," "immediately," "next") to mark the shift into a new episode. He also avoids using causal transitions such as "because" or "consequently" or "despite" to forward the action and more clearly establish links building to an outcome. Such interpretive transitions overly determine the reasons for actions; this fieldworker, for example, did not know why each person acted the way he or she did. To avoid such interpretation, he simply juxtaposed related actions to show how the interaction developed. In general, transitions should only orient a reader in time, place, and sequence, rather than imply causal connections between actions leading irrevocably to an outcome, especially when writing a loosely structured, episodic fieldnote tale.

Fieldnote Tale Two: A High School Dean Finding and Disciplining a Student

Ethnographers also write tighter, more cohesive narratives. In such fieldnote tales, episodes are clearly connected, and the account builds to an ending or outcome. Consider the following tale in which the fieldworker tracks a single incident handled by the high school dean, Mr. Jones. The ethnographer composed this fieldnote as a sequence of episodes, which for purposes of discussion, we label as *a* through *i*:

(a) Back in his office, Mr. Jones starts going through some of the paperwork on his desk. One whole pile is set aside for those students caught smoking. According to Mr. Jones, smoking is a major violation at the school. "The first time you're caught, you get written up, and you get a record. The second time—it's state policy now—you get suspended." I expressed my astonishment. Mr. Jones also noted with a sigh that "all the kids caught smoking are absent today."

(b) As Mr. Jones went through his files, he talked about "tagging" as another indicator of delinquency. I was unfamiliar with the term so I asked him what it means. He explained that "tagging" is doing graffiti. . . . "Most of the time if we catch you, you go to jail. That's if it's on the scale that we can charge you for it, of course. For the second time, they either get transferred to another school or they have to do fifteen hours service for the school. Usually, what we have them do is scrape down all the walls" [that they painted with graffiti]. I asked if many students get transferred to other schools. He replied that they do and that "We can send them anywhere in the district. The only limit is transportation. We send a lot of the kids out for gang involvement. Most of them go over to Southside. But, then again, we receive a lot of the same type of students from uptown, too." I asked him, "So a lot of the problems are just being shifted back and forth between schools?" He replied, "Well, the idea is that once a student is in a new environment, he might be more inclined to change. So if we can't seem to do anything for him here, we ship him off somewhere else where he might be away from some of his bad influences."

(c) But, flipping through his files, he finds one that he was looking for and stops. "Here's one right here. Yep, second time caught smoking. That means suspended." He turns to me and says with a confidential air, "You know, it can really ruin a student's future to get suspended, because it can lead to not being admitted elsewhere. We try to let them know it's serious." The student's name is Sokoloff (or something very similar and distinctly Russian-sounding). He looks at the schedules to see where Sokoloff is during second period, and we head up there.

(d) Walking into the room where Sokoloff was supposed to be, I see all the kids looking around at each other seriously. Mr. Jones asks the teacher, a middle-aged white man, if he knows if Sokoloff is here. The teacher had to ask the class if there was anyone there by that name. Many of the students look over to a short, white male with long hair and a heavy metal T-shirt. He stood up and acknowledged his name. Mr. Jones looks at him sternly and says, "Get your bags, you'll be needing 'em." We walk out of the room. (I was actually only in the doorway, trying to remain as inconspicuous as possible.)

(e) The kid has a Russian accent. He seems panicked once we are in the hallway. He is walking side by side with Mr. Jones and looking up at him. In a pleading voice, he asks him, "What did I do?" Mr. Jones responds, "You got caught smoking for the second time. That means we have to suspend you." The kid lets out an exasperated sigh of disbelief and whines, "But that was last semester. I don't even smoke [now]. Please do me a favor." Mr. Jones goes into explaining the state policy and tells him there's nothing he can do but suspend him. The kid starts talking about a Ms. Loges who ". . . told me it [the rule] was going to change this semester. You can ask Julio [a classmate]." Mr. Jones seems to be getting frustrated and says, "I have enough trouble. Look! I'm activating school policy." With this, we walked into the attendance office.

(f) (A little uncertain about how I should position myself to be unobtrusive, I sit down at the desk opposite Mr. Jones's and start acting like I'm looking at some of the papers on his desk. The kid is starting to take notice of me now and keeps looking at my notebook.) He keeps on pleading with Mr. Jones to do him a favor. Mr. Jones inquires, "Don't you read what smoking does to you?" He gets on the phone and tells him, "I'm calling your mother. Does she speak English?" The kid replies affirmatively. As he talks to a receptionist where the mother works, he retains his authoritarian tone in introducing himself: "This is Mr. Jones, Dean of Discipline at the High School. Is Mrs. S. there?" The mother is not at work yet.

(g) The kid pleads a little more calmly, "Do me a favor." Mr. Jones replies authoritatively, but with less vigor, "I'm not going to do you a favor. Not since I don't know what Ms. Loges said." The kid continues to plead, while Mr. Jones stays silent for awhile. The kid tells him, "My friend, Igor, got suspended on the third time." Finally, Mr. Jones says, "Well, it is a new policy this year, so I suppose Ms. Loges could have gotten some of her facts turned around."

(h) As he says this, a short, middle-aged Asian woman walks into the room and seems amused by what is going on. (She sees me sitting at the desk and immediately I get the impression that it is hers. I stand up quickly, looking back down at it and then back up at her.) She seems to know exactly what is going on with the student. She turns to him and starts saying, "You've been smoking, hah? Well, don't you know how bad that is for you?" She asks him, "Do your parents smoke?" He says, "Yes, and my cousins. My whole family." (He seems noticeably relieved and more than willing to talk about the acknowledged evils of smoking.) He says, "I have been trying to stop, and I have been doing pretty good. But it's hard, you know?" The Asian woman says, "Ah, you just have to put your mind to it. I used to smoke." Mr. Jones adds, "Me too. I used to smoke." He nods his head knowingly. In a softer voice, he says to her, "I told him I wouldn't suspend him this time because he got some wrong information. But next time, that's it."

(i) Then, the Dean dismisses him with a slight wave of his hand. The kid leaves the office.

In writing this tale, the ethnographer interconnected the separate episodes—the talk and doings—to show actions as unfolding and developing in a chronological order. The tale moves from an opening that initiates the action (dean examines pile of smoking infractions), through a middle that advances actions as they develop (finding a delinquent student, threatening him with punishment) and climaxes in a turning point involving a change in action (offering student another chance), to an end that indicates an outcome or brings the actions to a resting point (student leaving).

But even though this tale, unlike the previous one, moves to a specific ending, the writer does not foreshadow this outcome by building it into his writing. In the last episodes (h and i), we learn only that the male dean and the female administrator work together and that she discusses the smoking habit in greater detail with the student. She might have influenced the dean to change his mind simply through her presence since he changes after she enters. But, we never get a clear sense of why the dean relents or appears to relent: He might, after all, have been intending all along to simply scare the youth rather than to actually suspend him. The ending merely writes a closing to the fieldnote tale and is almost anticlimactic: The student simply exits the scene. But a more definitive ending that makes a point (about discipline or the dean's and student's actions) would have distorted the incident, attributing import that those involved did not or hypothesizing consequences that might or might not occur. Remaining true to his observations, the writer squelched any inclination to craft a more emphatic ending.

Fieldnote Tales as Temporary and Conditional Narrations

Composing these tales often highlights a fundamental tension felt by many ethnographers as they write fieldnotes. The researcher wants to write the actions as she perceived them in the moment of observation and to include as many details as possible. However, writing is a way of seeing, of increasing understanding, and, ultimately, of *creating scenes*. Indeed, writing on a page is a process of ordering; the writer, perforce, selects this and not that, puts details in this order and not that one, and creates a pattern out of otherwise fragmented or haphazard details.

Narrating is a particularly structured way of seeing and ordering life and, consequently, can heighten the strain between trying to write "everything" and creating an intelligible slice of life on the page. The more unified and climactic the narrative he envisions writing, the more compelled the ethnographer feels to interconnect actions and to exclude any details that the building story line renders peripheral or irrelevant. For example, in the story about the dean disciplining the student, only episode *b* about graffiti does not bear directly on the story line about the smoking infraction. Had the ethnographer written down other details more extraneous to this story line, the tale would have been more episodic and less driven by an internal consistency. The tale might have included, for example, extraneous dialogue with a secretary who remarked after she got off the phone, "Your wife called to say you forgot your lunch," or incidental actions such as a student waiting at the office door holding a balloon in her hand. However, he did not include such irrelevant details; his tale has few gaps.

In telling a fieldnote tale, the ethnographer must juggle these contradictory impulses: to include even peripheral actions and to create an ordered progression telling the "something that happened." If she truly writes "everything," she likely will create mumbo jumbo on the page; but if she overdetermines the connections in her story, she might close her mind to other possible interpretations. Faced with this dilemma, we suggest that the ethnographer aim to write a more loosely structured fieldnote tale. Such a tale tends to be episodic: it describes seemingly extraneous actions that happen during the incident recounted; it might have gaps between episodes with no apparent connections leading from one set of actions to the next; or it often begins in the midst of action and closes without necessarily arriving at any consequences or resolution.

Such a fieldnote tale reflects the ethnographer's perceived experience at the moment of writing. It tells the story as he understands it that day. But every fieldnote tale is embedded not only within the day's entry but also within the context of ongoing fieldwork and note-taking. The researcher returns to the field the next day to further explore his hunches about the previous day's events. He sees a character in various situations over time and deepens his understanding of that person's relationships and patterns of action. Thus, as writing continues and fieldnotes accumulate, the ethnographer might begin to see earlier tales differently than when he wrote them. He might reexamine the implicit connections, the gaps he did not understand, and the endings he inferred, and, consequently, he asks himself questions that stimulate a closer look when he returns to the field.

The cohesion of fieldnote tales, then, is temporary and conditional: Ethnographers' understandings of recounted events often change as fieldwork continues. In the light of further observation of related activities and reappearing characters, the ethnographer might reassess connections and disjunctions between episodes in a fieldnote tale. After observing the dean many times, for example, the writer of this tale might come to see the dean's talk about graffiti as an essential unit in what, after all, seems to be a rather cohesive story: the dean talks about graffiti as a serious infraction in order to highlight the minor nature of smoking violations. He would then understand the tale as following this common pattern: an authority threatens punishment for infraction; the student exhibits properly deferential behavior, offers an excuse, and promises to do better; the authority relents and lets the student off with a warning. In this version of the story, the student will not be suspended as long as he is cooperative.

In reviewing his tale, the ethnographer not only should reflect on the implicit connections he made but also reconsider the gaps between (and within) episodes. The apparent gap in the dean's story—between the suspension threat and the remission—might have various interpretations. The ethnographer, for example, could infer any one of the following: (a) that the dean lets all smoking students off the hook if they are deferential; (b) that the dean generally defers to the opinions of the female, Asian administrator; or (c) that the Asian administrator intervenes often for foreign students. To locate grounds for choosing between these possibilities, the ethnographer would further observe the dean as he disciplined students.

Finally, continuing fieldwork and note writing might lead to revised understandings about the ending of a tale, for there is an element of arbitrariness in both the beginnings and endings of stories. The writer begins the tale at the point she began observing an event, key characters, or an interesting situation. She ends her story either when that incident concludes (the dean dismisses the student) or when she shifts her attention to other characters, activities, or situations. Initially, the writer's experience and attention creates the parameters of the fieldnote tale. But as she rereads a tale and thinks about it, she might realize that this tale is inextricably linked to others involving the same characters. The specific endings are mere resting points. For example, although this one police patrol tale ends, Sam and Alisha continued their patrolling for several more hours that evening and during other subsequent observations; and, the story continues through many more pages.[14] In this respect, fieldnote tales have temporary endings because the story about people's lives continues the next day and throughout the fieldnotes.

In sum, ethnographers write fieldnote tales that reflect daily experience, rather than crafted, artful, suspense-driven narratives. They draw on narrating conventions that order actions so that a reader can visualize them and that, nevertheless, remain true to their immediate sense of the incident. But the understanding that a researcher has of any one event often fluctuates and develops as he continues to write and reread his notes. By considering alternate interpretations of a tale in the light of his ongoing research, the ethnographer opens up the tale to more incisive questions. Therefore, ethnographers commit themselves only tentatively to the version they write today, since the "something that happened" might well change. Thus, each narrative links to, and comments on, other episodes and tales within a set of fieldnotes. In that sense, each tale—as one version among many—remains open-ended.

ANALYTIC WRITING: IN-PROCESS MEMOS

As noted in chapter 3, while writing detailed, descriptive fieldnotes, ethnographers simultaneously begin to pen brief, analytically focused writings—asides and commentaries—to identify and explore initial theoretical directions and possibilities. But in addition to creating these analytic comments and leads in the midst of composing a set of fieldnotes, fieldworkers should also devote time and effort to more systematically develop analytic themes from their data. Ethnographic fieldworkers characteristically seek to collect and analyze data simultaneously, allowing analytic concerns generated by initial observation and interviews to guide and focus the collection of new data (Charmaz 2001).[15] Developing potential analyses requires writing: The ethnographer turns from mentally noting theoretical insights and connections to putting these ideas into written form. When insights are simply thought or communicated orally, rather than being put on paper, they remain loose and fluid. As Becker insists, "First one thing, then another, comes into your head. By the time you have thought the fourth thing, the first one is gone" (2007:55). In contrast, "a thought written down . . . is stubborn, doesn't change its shape, can be compared with other thoughts that come after it" (2007:56). Thus written-down analyses acquire structure, depth, and nuance.

Writing *in-process memos* allows the fieldworker to develop these analytic leads and insights early on in the fieldwork process. In comparison with asides and commentaries, in-process memos require a more extended time-out from actively composing fieldnotes in order to do more sustained analytic writing; briefly stepping back from observed events and field routines, the fieldworker shifts her attention to outside audiences, beginning to clearly envision such future audiences in identifying, formulating, and elaborating the theoretical import or implications of such events and routines.

In-process memos are not intended to produce a final, systematic analysis but, rather, to provide insight, direction, and guidance for the ongoing fieldwork.[16] Careful thought and preliminary, tentative analyses can suggest finer-grained aspects of interactions to focus on, new scenes and topics to be investigated, additional questions to be asked and followed up, and interesting comparisons to notice. Writing such memos becomes fruitful when the researcher entertains such questions as the following: What was the sequence of moves and changes in meaning that punctuated a typical or particularly significant event? Is there a relatively consistent pattern across a range of events or interactions? Are there differences, however minute and subtle, between incidents or cases that, at first glance, appeared the same? Are there similarities between events that initially appear unrelated or different?

Although later memos are built on systematic coding of fieldnotes (see chapter 6), many in-process memos are touched off by a particular event, incident, or comment that resonates with something the fieldworker has previously observed. This resonance leads the researcher to think about the connections and/or to make comparisons between current and other similar (or different) matters. Indeed, at times it is helpful to take a specific, "rich" fieldnote and explore its theoretical implications. An ethnographer studying family members caring for persons with Alzheimer's disease, for example, composed the following memo as a series of "observations" on a single, brief, but "suggestive," fieldnote excerpt:

> *Fieldnote:* During the support group Fumiko comments on her husband's behavior: "Once in a while he is a pussycat" (laughter), "but he was a raging bull when the VNA came to give him a bath." She adds that recently he has fought her shaving him, but "this morning he let me do it."
>
> *Memo:* Note how this description suggests that caregivers recognize that *cooperation* can vary independently of ability or condition for the person with Alzheimer's. Thus, it is one issue whether or not the person with Alzheimer's can feed or bathe him/herself, shave himself, etc.; the stance the person with Alzheimer's takes toward these helping/caring for activities is another matter.
>
> Note also how *unpredictable* these matters may be for the caregiver; bathing and shaving go smoothly on some occasions but produce major hassles on others. And the caregiver does not seem able to find a reason or explanation for when and why one outcome rather than another occurs.
>
> Furthermore, it may well be uncooperativeness or *resistance* in caregiving matters, rather than the amount or kind of help per se, that generates critical problems and burdens for caregivers. In this respect, the core of a caregiving management regime may rest on those devices and practices that inhibit, overcome, or sidestep resistance. With someone with Alzheimer's who is cooperative (or nonresistant)—in most matters—the caregiver can say: "I can still guide him." Similarly, a person with Alzheimer's who is cooperative is one who can be "talked to," i.e., convinced to make changes in his/her daily life, more or less "voluntarily."

In this memo, the fieldworker identifies two initial, somewhat unrelated issues in the fieldnote: Some caregivers report that patient cooperation can vary independently of physical condition and that cooperation can wax or wane unpredictably. In the final paragraph, she speculates on the possible relevance of one of these issues—cooperation (and its counterpart, resistance)—in shaping the broader pattern and course of family caregiving for persons with Alzheimer's disease.

In-process memos are also useful for exploring connections between different events and processes or for developing new interpretations of previous observations and understandings. In the following fieldnote, a student clarifies just when staff came to classify late calls to a shelter crisis line as "nuisance calls":

> Several weeks ago, I wrote about a client whom staff found to be quite aggravating and "annoying" because she had been continually calling the crisis line at all hours of the morning. At the time I had been under the impression that staff perceived such calls as unnecessary unless they pertained to immediate threats of physical injury. Through a conversation that took place today (included in earlier notes), I realize that this was an accurate but oversimplified notion. Although the staff finds late night crisis calls quite aggravating, they also acknowledge the necessity of maintaining such an option to deal primarily with violence of an immediate and physical nature. But even if the caller's situation does not fit into that category, she wouldn't necessarily be identified as a "nuisance" unless she had called repeatedly and had enough familiarity with the organization to know better. Each caller seems to be viewed as an individual case and is treated accordingly. It is only when their issues become too time-consuming or chronic that they are identified as nuisance callers.

Here, the student developed a more complex analysis by correcting and extending an earlier analytic claim. Writing this memo helped her clarify her ideas and draw out subtle differences as she reflected on the relevance of new information for her previous understanding.

Despite their value, writing analytic, in-process memos can easily displace time and effort needed for writing core descriptive fieldnotes. The field researcher might experience uncertainty and strain in deciding when to concentrate on writing fieldnotes and when to turn attention to developing and recording analytic insights. There is no easy solution: New ideas, like the descriptive details that make vivid fieldnotes, are fleeting; if not written down immediately, they tend to "get lost" or remain underdeveloped. So, the field researcher constantly must balance the impulse to write down ideas and insights when they occur against the compulsion to "get it all down" as quickly and completely as possible without interruption.

In sum, ongoing reflection and analysis, even as the fieldworker continues to observe in the field and to actively write fieldnotes, is crucial in ethnographic research. Writing in-process memos helps the field researcher carry forward analysis contemporaneously with the collection of field data. Such reflective writing often incites the researcher to pay closer attention to what she sees and, thus, to write more detailed and vivid descriptions. In-process analytic writing, in turn, increases the possibility of making the kinds of observations needed to develop and support a specific analysis. The sooner and more explicitly analytic themes are identified, the better able the field-worker is to "check out" different alternatives, making and recording observations that can confirm, modify, or reject different interpretations. In these ways, the fieldworker lays the groundwork for developing analyses that are both complex and grounded in the data.

REFLECTIONS: FIELDNOTES AS PRODUCTS OF WRITING CHOICES

In writing fieldnotes, ethnographers have as their primary goal description rather than analysis. A researcher writes notes with a specific purpose in mind: to record a slice of life on a page. But these contrasting terms—description and analysis—refer more to recognized kinds of writing than to separate cognitive activities. In that sense, writing fieldnotes is a process of "analysis-in-description." Indeed, all descriptions are selective, purposed, angled, and voiced because they are authored. To "write up life" in this way, an ethnographer uses language conventions to create an envisioned scene. Accounts written from a particular point of view and as real-time or end-point descriptions, constructed and sequenced in extended narrative tales, paint detailed portraits of settings, people, and actions rather than offering causal explanations or building explicit arguments.

All writing, by definition, is an abstracting and ordering process: Clear writing always has internal coherence, the product of the writer's attention to the subject as well as to the potential reader. Ethnographers construct their fieldnotes in a process more accurately captured by the expression, "writing up" than "writing down" or "getting down" people's doings and sayings. Writers do more than inscribe the world. Just as the ethnographer-as-observer participates with members in constructing a social reality, so, too, the ethnographer-as-writer creates the world through language.

In this chapter, we have seen that even though restricted to actual observed details and members' talk, an ethnographer always "creates" the described action or narrated event. Writing fieldnotes *processes* experience, not only through a researcher's attention in the field, but also through a writer's memory and compositional choices at the desk. An ethnographer perceives interactions and selects significant details; in writing she groups these details into coherent wholes according to conventional writing strategies.[17]

Awareness of writing conventions, however, is not meant to lead a writer to be more craftily inventive through the use of persuasive rhetorical skills. Rather, it invites the ethnographer to make more conscious choices when creating fieldnote records that portray social worlds as experienced and perceived by others. Consider the effects of writing: Not only does a writer's theoretical stance influence compositional choices, but the reverse also happens. Even by inadvertently imitating an "objective" social science style, for example, with its measured wording, omniscient viewpoint, and use of the passive voice, descriptions reflect an affinity—though ever so subtle— for that orientation. Certainly, a writing style tends to shape any writer's vision. How researchers see in the field, in part, results from what they find noteworthy and "writable" as a fieldnote. Consequently, students concerned about research integrity must develop a conscientious respect for how their writing choices influence both fieldwork and note-taking.

Whether carefully or haphazardly written, every fieldnote mirrors an author's choices: to include these details rather than those in depicting scenes and characters, to group selected events and actions into sketches and episodes, to represent talk in direct or more indirect and paraphrased forms, to sequence actions in this way or that way. These authorial choices, if only subliminal, result in on-the-page descriptions with certain kinds of detail, *organized and sequenced in particular ways,* displaying and interweaving different voices. These day-to-day renderings of scenes pile up, and writing choices assume a cumulative effect: The notes portray that world through this particular writer's lens. In making writing choices, therefore, *how* ethnographers write fieldnotes becomes as consequential for readers and those depicted as what they write. Whether as privately filed resources or as public excerpts in final documents, fieldnotes persuade.

5

Pursuing Members' Meanings

At first glance, it might seem that the pursuit of members' meanings is fundamentally a matter not of writing but of what one does in the field—of asking questions and of positioning oneself to hear and observe others' concerns. Members' meanings, however, are not pristine objects that are simply "out there" waiting to be "discovered." Rather, these meanings are interpretive constructions assembled and conveyed by the ethnographer. This process certainly begins with looking, asking questions, and paying attention to what is relevant to people in some indigenous group. But the key to the process lies in sensitively representing in written texts what local people consider meaningful and important. Fieldnotes, then, are a major vehicle for beginning to capture local knowledge and indigenous understandings.

Given the complexities of pursuing members' meanings, it is not surprising that field researchers' efforts to do so have been partial or inconsistent in two distinctive ways. First, some field researchers blunt appreciation of members' meanings by importing outside categories to describe local scenes and actions. This sort of imposition obscures indigenous meanings. Second, some researchers present static taxonomies of native terms. The ethnographer's task, however, is more complex: She must not only apprehend and convey members' categories, but she must also explain how members use terms in specific interactional situations and how involved parties differentially evoke, understand, and act upon them.

In this chapter, we discuss how to write fieldnotes that effectively represent member-recognized meanings. We see producing fieldnotes that identify and present members' meanings as a primary ethnographic commitment. How ethnographers should incorporate such meanings into their final analyses is another issue, one about which ethnographers differ. Many maintain that analytic categories are fundamentally incompatible with members' meanings, that ethnographic analysis must transcend indigenous categories (Burawoy 1991; Wacquant 2002). Others, while acknowledging the temptation to transform local meanings into recognized analytic concepts, remain committed to trying to incorporate such meanings into both working memos and polished ethnographic texts (Charmaz 2001; Tavory and Timmermans 2009). In keeping with our commitment to understanding the social processes through which members construct and act upon meanings to shape future interactions, we maintain that ethnographers should initially write fieldnotes that depict and are sensitive to local meanings. Of course, we recognize that what the ethnographer writes is not a "pure" or literal presentation of the meanings of events and interactions the way that members experience them. Rather, ethnographic writings are inevitably filtered through the perceptions, experiences, and commitments of the ethnographer. And, ultimately, the ethnographer writes about members' meanings and the social processes she observed in the field for particular outside audiences whose substantive and theoretical interests differ from those of members in the setting. But, in writing for such outside audiences, ethnographers seek to begin with and build upon members' meanings and theories rather than their own, developing, in Geertz's (1983:57–58) terms, theories that are "experience-near" (rather than "experience-distant") to the concerns and categories of those studied.

In this chapter, we illustrate these processes using both students' original fieldnotes as well as working memos and final ethnographic papers. We begin the chapter by considering how ethnographic accounts often obscure or suppress members' meanings by imposing outside understandings of events. We then suggest ways of writing about what is significant to members and explore the problems involved in conveying local meanings. Finally, we discuss strategies that allow ethnographers to focus on race/ethnicity, gender, and class while remaining sensitive and giving priority to members' meanings.

IMPOSING EXOGENOUS MEANINGS

All too frequently, ethnographic fieldnotes fail to attend consistently to members' meanings, instead importing outside or exogenous categories and meanings. Imposition of outside categories produces fieldnote descriptions that fail to *appreciate* local meanings and concerns (Matza 1969:15–40) and that tend to frame events as what they are *not* (that is, by reference to categories or standards that differ from those recognized and used by members). In general, field researchers concerned with members' meanings are leery of any classifications that do not refer to the categories that the people recognize and actually use among themselves.

Failures to appreciate members' classifications arise from a number of sources. First, lapsing into classic ethnocentrism, researchers may take a category, standard, or meaning from one culture or locale and use it to describe events in another context. For example, based on their own expectations, Westerners in an African or Indian cinema or theater might describe as "disruptive" loud audience remarks to characters and thus fail to appreciate such participation as a locally appropriate way of expressing an evaluation of the performance (Srinivas 2010). Or an observer may employ exogenous criteria to evaluate school classrooms as "noisy" or "chaotic," thereby ignoring teachers' and students' actual understandings of how classroom activities should be conducted. Both procedures caricature, rather than describe, behavior in its own terms.

Second, ethnographers may use a term, category, or evaluation that is recognized, used, and honored by *one group* in a particular social world to describe features or behaviors of another group in that world. For example, psychiatric staff might interpret certain patients' behaviors as "acting out" or "denial," even though the patients understand the actions as common, everyday behavior or even as resistance to institutional control. Often, a field researcher who comes across different local understandings of the same event has a tendency to accept one view as "true," thereby marginalizing competing versions. In one situation in Zambia, for example, a diviner-healer determined that an older man who suddenly could not walk had been bewitched and, after treating him for a year with medicines and massage, cured him. However, the medical doctor at the local hospital, on hearing the account and later meeting the man, concluded that he had had a stroke resulting in paralysis. In writing fieldnotes, a Western ethnographer might be tempted to privilege, though ever so subtly, the medical doctor's "scientific" account and then to describe the diviner's interpretation as "belief," thereby prioritizing one practitioner's explanations as more "accurate" and implicitly more efficacious.

Third, field researchers may adopt a dismissive stance toward members' meanings, treating such meanings as flawed, hypocritical, contradictory, fallacious, or commonsensical. Such stances are particularly tempting when they involve beliefs and practices that seem strange in contemporary American society. For example, a student ethnographer working in Los Angeles observed weekly meetings of a study group devoted to the philosophy of Edgar Cayce. In the following fieldnote, she describes an incident recounted by a member to the group:

> Dolores lost her purse and did not panic. She threw the white light around it and asked God to protect it. She also asked that no one be tempted to take her identification, credit cards, and money. The next day when she went to work, she asked the guard on duty if the purse had been turned in. Indeed it had, and nothing had been displaced.

The student initially interpreted this story as indicating an extremely "passive" approach to the problems of daily life:

> The moral of the story was to leave everything in God's hands. . . . To me visualizing the white light and talking to God are very passive ways of dealing with an emergency situation as opposed to going to the police or retracing one's steps.

Yet what the student initially thought of as nonactions—"casting the white light" and "talking to God"—did involve action when seen from within this particular religious worldview. Whether going to the police or retracing one's steps would have been more *effective* responses begs the issue; the member's account asserts that exactly *because of* her prayerful actions, the purse had been turned in, and nothing was taken. It is only by suspending her own beliefs that the ethnographer can begin to understand the beliefs and practices of a distinctive social group regarding the efficacy of action in everyday life.[1]

Fourth, fieldnote descriptions and memos may be framed in terms of a standard of what is "supposed to be" that derives from official rules or understandings that are held to govern action in some specific setting. For example, noting a discrepancy between an elder's account of the traditional meaning and sequences of a ritual and the actual performance of that ritual, an ethnographer might describe this ritual as "in decline" rather than as subject to adaptation and variation.[2] Similarly, an ethnographer might describe and analyze police action on the streets in terms of official regulations for the use of force; how actual police officers evaluate specific street situations and decide when and what kinds of force to use is thereby ignored.[3] In both instances, ethnographers implicitly determine whether actions should count as conforming to or departing from the "traditional" version or "official" regulations and, hence, whether these actions are "in fact" "authentic" ritual behavior or a "legitimate" use of force.

Fifth, the researcher may invoke a priori theoretical categories, often those sacred to the core of a particular discipline, to characterize events and settings. For example, an ethnographer would want to avoid *beginning* a study of the homeless by looking for their uses of "social capital" on the street because starting with such an exogenous concept prespecifies the salience of particular features and events and tends to marginalize members' understandings and use of relevant resources.

Likewise, in studies of traditional narrating, past researchers relied heavily upon the analytic categories of "myth," "legend," and "folktale" even in explaining non-Western traditions. Since these categories often impose Eurocentric notions, and, thus, misrepresent a people's storytelling traditions and practices, many contemporary folklorists now characterize storytelling with the indigenous terms and explanations of the group studied and describe how people use these terms in particular storytelling events.[4]

Indeed, a field researcher may implicitly impose such categories in asking exogenous questions rooted in an a priori research agenda or theoretical framework. Not only might a researcher impose ideas when questioning an "informant," but she might also impose an inappropriate form of expression whose constraints distort responses. For example, a field researcher who asks for a list of ingredients in cures or discrete steps in a ritual may get arbitrary lists intended to please the researcher. Or, when asked questions imposing external analysis and itemization, people may offer "nonanswers" such as "yes," "no," or "sometimes," especially if they usually describe these healing and ritual events by recounting the story of the experience.[5] In sound ethnographic research, in contrast, "both questions and answers must be discovered from informants" (Spradley 1979:84).[6]

Finally, describing local settings or actions in terms of dichotomized variables may involve an imposition of exogenous categories. For an ethnographer to describe those present in a bar as "regulars" and "nonregulars," particularly if these distinctions are based solely on the ethnographer's observations, rather than on members' references to these different types of bar patrons, may ignore a range of other, more variegated distinctions that bar patrons may draw between one another. In general, the reduction of ongoing social life to dichotomized variables tends to produce a radical decontextualizing and destruction of local meanings.

In all of these ways, ethnographers tend to produce fieldnotes that ignore, marginalize, and obscure indigenous understandings. In the following sections, we suggest alternative procedures for writing fieldnotes that avoid such impositions and that help develop descriptions and preliminary analyses that are sensitive to local concerns, meanings, and categories.

REPRESENTING MEMBERS' MEANINGS

A number of distinct moments in group life highlight how members express, orient to, and create local meaning. Ethnographers begin to construct members' meanings by looking closely at *what members say and do* during such moments, paying particular attention to the words, phrases, and categories that members use in their everyday interactions.

Members' Terms of Address and Greetings

The way members address and greet each other is one of the most immediately noticeable and revealing kinds of talk. Ethnographers often begin by noting and learning the proper terms of address, especially when working in a foreign language and culture. In many communities, the way people address one another reflects their relative statuses; consider, for example, the difference between first-name familiarity and the deference marked by formal titles such as "Dr." or "Mr." and "Ms." Furthermore, how people greet each other—both with words and body language—often indicates something about the closeness, respectfulness, deference, or hostility of that relationship.[7]

In Chokwe villages, for example, people address each other with kinship terms, such as *tata* (father), *mama* (mother), *yaya* (older sibling of the same sex as speaker), *mwakwethu* (younger sibling of the same sex as speaker), or *ndumbwami* (any sibling of the opposite sex of speaker) (Fretz 1987:58–65). Listening to other people call out to each other reveals their kinship relationship and helps the researcher learn local expectations for appropriate speech and behavior. For instance, Chokwe grandparents and their grandchildren may be publicly affectionate and joke together about sexual matters in ways deemed inappropriate for other relationships. In contrast, in-laws greet each other formally from a distance (the younger person must step off the path) and never eat together.

Similarly in American society, terms of address and greetings can reveal distinctive features of social relations. It may be significant in classroom and psychiatric settings, for example, whether students and clients address teachers and staff by first or last name. Anderson (1990:168–73) has observed that whether people exchange greetings with strangers encountered on urban streets, and how they do so, provides indications of locally significant ethnic affiliation and disaffiliation among African Americans. Similarly, Garot (2010:69–91) describes how inner-city gang members initiate street encounters with unknown youth by demanding "where you from." This begins a process of "hitting up" aimed at determining the other's gang affiliation and possibly leading to violence.

Everyday Questions and Answers

An astute ethnographer notices the kinds of questions local people frequently ask and the kinds of answers ordinarily given. For example, in many African societies, people greet and ask each other the appropriate, basic questions many times a day. The Chokwe, for instance, inquire about each other's well-being, including the entire extended family (*Kuci ku nzuwo?* [How is it at home?]); they also ask about their own and the family's health (*Unahindvuka, nyi?* [Are you well?]). These questions can open to conversations about health, work, money problems, quarrels in the family, births, deaths, eating well or searching for food, or celebrations. Thus, learning to appropriately ask and answer such questions can lead into conversations about issues that members consider vital to their everyday success or failure.[8]

In some settings, ethnographers encounter unexpected questions. For example, a Korean fieldworker studying a small Christian church in Los Angeles was surprised when a youth group member (an ethnic Korean from China), on first meeting her, asked her the year she was born: "She said she was born in 1984, and she could probably call me *unni* (meaning elder sister) since I was born in 1978." Youth group members not only commonly asked newcomers this question but also began their self-introductions in youth group meetings by announcing their birth years. This differed from the researcher's experiences in Korea, where, although asking a person's age is culturally permissible, people rarely asked about birth years directly: They instead ask animal years (although young people rarely do this these days) or the year of college entrance (as a proxy for the other party's age), or perhaps even directly ask another's age.

Ethnographers sensitive to members' experiences and views not only listen to members' questions; importantly, they also ask questions that are intentionally open-ended to allow members to use their own language and concepts in responding to them. In doing so, they orient such questions to topics that members find meaningful, that is, interesting, relevant to everyday concerns, and in keeping with the ways they act and talk. Similarly, by orienting questions to mutually observed actions and overheard speech, an ethnographer is more likely to ask questions that make sense to members; he might ask a question about an incident they both witnessed, about the member's explanation of a term he just used, or about a comment someone else made during a conversation. Such questions allow people to answer with familiar forms of expression, embedding responses in a context that makes sense to them, thereby revealing their concepts—their *members' orientation* to the "information."

Naturally Occurring Members' Descriptions

Ethnographers pay close attention to how members themselves characterize and describe particular activities, events, and groups. Recognizing that an event has no single, necessary, or invariant meaning, the field researcher does not assume that she knows what significance members attribute to the incidents and objects that make up their world. Rather, she attends closely to how members talk about and depict these matters at different times and in different situations.[9]

Members frequently provide naturally occurring descriptions of their setting when they introduce or orient outsiders. Such descriptions may be explicitly framed to highlight qualities that members consider special or unique. For example, in the following fieldnote, a HUD (Housing and Urban Development) caseworker describes his work to the researcher, emphasizing that he usually does not have the "luxury" of being able to make individualized contact with applicants for federally subsidized housing:

> "The larger a bureaucracy is, the less luxury a professional working within that bureaucracy has of making human contact. If I'm interviewing 20 or 25 people per day, I don't have time to break through. I have to do the job, and I

have to move on to the next. Sometimes, that's truly a case of numbers, why people in government jobs act the way they do. We're a small agency, we sometimes have that luxury. Other times we don't."

This description does more than orient the researcher to the setting; it also reveals the caseworker's views about his work, as he signals that he would like to make personal contact with clients but is frequently unable to do so as a practical matter because of "high numbers." In so doing, he also provides an "account" to an outsider about what he considers to be good work and a plausible reason for why he may be failing to live up to that standard.

Naturally occurring descriptions can also arise more informally in the course of ongoing talk about significant events in the setting. Here, for example, a field researcher may want to pay close attention to how any other newcomers are introduced to and taught about "how things are done." Since newcomers are learning the ins and outs of what to do, they often ask questions and make mistakes that reveal, through their own ignorance of them, the implicit knowledge, skills, and unwritten rules that most longtime members take for granted.

Since members often socialize and instruct researchers, just as they do any other newcomer (or their own children), the ethnographer may want to record in detailed fieldnotes how she learns to make her way into and through a setting. Indeed, in many situations, such socialization is unavoidable. For example, when first living in a Chokwe village, every move the fieldworker made as she learned to cook outdoors on a charcoal burner—down to exactly how to stir the pot—was subject to laughter, commentary, and correction by watching neighbor women. Since people regularly work together and freely tease each other about mistakes, they enjoyed the researcher's awkwardness and jokingly told her she seemed like a child. The fieldworker not only learned appropriate behavior but also was able to notice the kind of expressions—laughter, reprimands, and corrections—through which people socialize others.[10]

Special problems arise in eliciting members' descriptions of what incidents and events mean when a researcher has directly observed a particular event, since others in the setting could assume that because the researcher saw something happen, or is generally familiar with the setting, he now knows what it means. One option for dealing with this situation is to listen to how members talk about this event with others. Thus, a fieldworker who has observed a complaint-filing encounter between a district attorney and police detective can record fieldnotes detailing how the former recounted "what happened" to a colleague either in the moment or later over lunch. Alternatively, as noted earlier, it may be possible through indirect and cautious questioning to elicit members' descriptions and accounts of an observed event. Having observed a probation officer interview a delinquent youth and her parents, for example, a fieldworker might ask the probation officer what she found to be significant (and why), what statements or stances surprised her, or how this interview compared with other interviews. Such questions accentuate the member's expertise and experience and, conversely, play down the ethnographer's local knowledge. Similarly, the ethnographer can directly suggest his lack of knowledge of a particular matter by asking for relevant background information about an observed incident or event. Indeed, it is sometimes useful explicitly to fall back on the researcher's role, telling the other something like "I think I know what this means, but I want to be sure that I am getting it right. So could you walk me through what just happened?"

One important and distinctive type of members' description arises when people explicitly name, characterize, or summarize the meaning and import of some issue, event, or incident. Through such *formulations* (Garfinkel and Sacks 1970; Heritage 1984), people identify the "gist" of something that has been said or done, in this way characterizing and describing it in a distinctive way. For example, to say "you interrupted me" formulates the character and meaning of another's prior utterance in a way that asserts that the spate of talk that just occurred was, in fact, an "interruption" and implies that this is a matter of immediate importance and relevance in the conversation (Sacks 1992:637). Formulations thus assert particular meanings or understandings, shaping up the meaning of something that has occurred in a new and subtly different way. For example, in the continuation school staff meeting discussed earlier, the teacher recounted two occasions where students had openly used sexual terms in talk to her and others; she then formulated these two incidents (and the general problem they represented) as "sexual harassment"; this formulation transformed the meaning of what the two youths had said from playful obscenities to a known, legal form of abuse appropriately subject to punishment. In general, field researchers should note both when formulations are proffered and the work that they do in creating or shifting meanings on these occasions. Since any event may be formulated in a variety of different ways, a particular formulation reveals something about the concerns and relevancies of the person making it.

In everyday and institutional settings, it is important to appreciate formulations as social constructions rather than as simply the ethnographer's statements of unproblematic "facts." By way of example, consider the following fieldnote describing a probation officer's interview with Tom, a sixteen-year-old, white surfer enrolled in a special probation school. Having looked at a "progress report" from the special school the youth was attending, the researcher wrote the following fieldnote:

> Overall, his progress report has improved a little. But there was one day when Tom was sent home. Shelly asked him about this.

Here, the researcher offers "improved a little" as his own characterization of the youth's recent period of probation. In doing so, he is clearly repeating the view of the probation officer, since a bit later in the notes, the latter characterized the report in just these terms. But, in uncritically taking over a member's description in this way, the researcher treats "improved a little" as a fact, failing to appreciate its character as a formulation. He also neglects considering both how the probation officer interpreted "progress" and "improvement" and what "facts" or developments she attended to in making these determinations. Furthermore, treating "improved a little" as a "fact," rather than as a formulation, ignores the possibility that this meaning was constructed in a specific context for a particular reason; for example, the probation officer may have been sensitive to the youth's presence and, in order to keep up the latter's morale, offered this characterization to tone down a more negative evaluation.[11]

In general, it is particularly tempting to privilege descriptions provided by official documents, viewing them as a simple record of relevant "facts" recorded in transparent and unproblematic ways. But ethnographically, it is more useful to recognize that descriptions incorporated into such documents are both highly selective and rife with formulations. A probation report and recommendation, for example, is not a simple factual record of a youth's behavior but, rather, a highly selective summary and interpretation that reduces complex and often contested events to one particular form. Thus, rather than simply treating reports as objective records, an ethnographer should seek to understand how such documents are constructed, read, and interpreted by members. In practice, this requires looking closely at what members see as significant in a report, how they characterize its "gist" or "bottom line"; it also requires writing fieldnotes that recount both what is in the document (and, if possible, what gets left out) and how the member interprets and responds to it.[12]

Members' Stories

People may present extended descriptions of events they witnessed or directly experienced, or of the reported doings of others (e.g., "gossip"), organized by means of some narrative strategy into a personal story.[13] Such members' stories may provide insight into the people and events they describe. However, such stories are always partial, being told for many different reasons and adjusted to fit different relationships and situations. In this sense, they may provide insight into the teller's momentary concerns and circumstances. Consider, for example, this extended story told to a researcher by a probation officer:

> "You been missin' the action, man," Jim said to me. I replied, "What happened?" Jim walked over to the vending machine to get his staple snack. Then he started to tell me that parents of a twenty-one-year-old male called him today, and they wanted their son arrested. The son had just gotten out of the "house" [jail] and had evidently not shown up for his first appointment for probation. His father said he was already back on crack and "bingeing hard." Doing nothing all day except for smoking crack, he would stay in bed . . . only getting up to eat and go to the bathroom. And the father said in the phone conversation that his son should not be given the choice of jail or rehabilitation because he would always choose prison. (By choosing jail, the convict can be back on the streets smoking crack again in only a month.)
>
> Jim continued to tell me that he went over there to arrest him because he was "crashing." . . . When he arrived, he had the parent sign all the legal papers. And, when he opened the door to arrest him, Jim noticed "he had a strawberry with him" (a whore who sells her body for drugs, not money). He said that the arrest went smoothly because the son "was so out of it"; he was "in the house right now."

While this story is *about* a young man on probation, it *reveals* the probation officer's ordinary work practices and concerns and the distinctive perspectives and commitments that underlie them.[14] In this sense, ethnographers do not take a member's story as a factual account but, rather, as an expression of the speaker's experience and views at a particular moment in time before a specific audience that is intended to accomplish particular purposes. He values and documents these stories as revealing a member's experience and perspective.

Ethnographers should also look out for and record different stories told about the same events. These different versions might be grounded in some of the same details, but each account is likely to include details not present in the other, to order actions in slightly different ways, and to offer different interpretations of cause and responsibility. Thus, a teacher's account of a "disruptive" classroom fight told to a field researcher might sound very different from the version the teacher subsequently relates to his peers over lunch. In writing fieldnotes, the researcher should preserve these differences if she is fortunate enough to hear both versions.

Diverse versions provide insights into the ways different members construct and make meaning of the same event as well as the meanings that they hope the telling of the story will convey to others.[15] For example, in a study of personal experience stories about the Los Angeles riots that followed the acquittal of the police officers who beat Rodney King, an African American student researcher highlighted the diverse voices of African Americans talking about their similar experiences. In the following story, for example, the teller exults in the camaraderie between different races and the "sense of community" he felt with those helping each other "take the sh—, the stuff":

"I remember—hearing the verdicts were in, and—this was at school, and—uhmm, also being in a state of disbelief, that, uhmm, they came back not guilty, the cops.

"And, uhmm, I went home, and my friends were coming by, and I didn't know that they were about to go out. So, I went with them, and we went out into downtown, and—we started taking things.

"And I just remember that it was like a unified effort and everyone was in the streets. And people who were gangbangers and everything else were, like, helping you take the sh—, the stuff. Like, 'Oh you want that, man? Here, I'll get that for you.' And it was like, I felt, a, a, sense of community there, with different races. I mean, these were Hispanics and everything else, and we were all throwin' up the power sign and goin' in taking what we wanted. And, uhmm—basically, that's what went on after I had first heard."

Judy, a married, African American property-owning woman, talked about similar events and her own experiences in very different terms:

"I talked to a lot of the neighbors. And, I asked the, the Latinos, why is you stealin' all this stuff, you know. It's bad, you know, you know.

"And me and my husband, we went walkin'. We just went walkin', you know, we wasn't hurtin' nobody, 'cause you could easily walk up and down the streets and see what was goin' on.

"And, you know, the funniest thing, you know, one of the neighbors said, 'You know, my clothes is in the cleaners around there.' And so they started walkin' over there to see had they messed up the cleaners. And when they got around there—they was at the cleaners. And there was her clothes, one of the Mexican guys had them—And my husband told them to 'put that stuff back there.' And [the neighbor] said, 'You ain't gonna take my clothes. You ain't gonna take my clothes. You ain't gonna take my clothes.' 'Cause that was the main reason we went around the corner."

In the first story, the African American narrator identifies himself as an active participant in "taking stuff," along with "gangbangers," "Hispanics," and everyone else. He narrates the experience as a bonding between people, as a "sense of community there, with different races." In contrast, from the very beginning of the second story, another African American teller depicts the conflicting stances people took in the street activities: Some are out walking around just to look, while others are actively "stealing." She begins telling about watching and rebuking the Latinos for "stealin' all the stuff." Then, she continues by recounting her neighbor's experience as a near-victim of such stealing: The teller, her husband, and the neighbor go to check on the local cleaners and find "one of the Mexican guys" taking the neighbor's clothes; they insist that the man "put that stuff back there." The two stories reveal the narrators' strikingly different alignments toward the participants and, more implicitly, their different understandings of the nature and significance of the incidents. In writing about these stories, the ethnographer—herself an African American present during the riots—pointed out that this ethnic community did not respond as a homogeneous group but, rather, voiced a variety of views. In fact, though some called it a "riot," others referred to it as a "rebellion" to more emphatically express their political interpretation of the fires and looting. By carefully documenting multiple stories, this researcher was able to examine the different ways people make meaning of a collective event.

Members' Terms, Types, and Typologies

Ethnographers give close attention to the terms or phrases that members regularly use to characterize people and events. Many ethnographers are less concerned with the formal, technical terms that reflect the demands of bureaucracy, public relations, and front-stage civility than they are drawn to everyday, colloquial, and often evocative terms that may be graphic or earthy (e.g., "shit work" in Emerson and Pollner 1976; "assholes" in Van Maanen 1978) and that reflect and express practical, mundane concerns.

Consider some of the types recognized among those living in a residential facility for ex–mental patients (Shaw 1988:282–320). On the one hand, staff identified some residents as "together" or "movers," implying that they would benefit from therapy and eventually find a job and set up independent living situations. They contrasted this type with "losers"—chronic patients with minimal skills and resources who are deemed unlikely to ever get out of the system of mental health care. On the other hand, residents recognized distinctions based on whether one emphasized ties with some other residents or oriented toward developing ties and receiving favors from staff. The former included "gadflies," "therapists," "spiritualists," "nice guys," and those known to hang out with the "drug group." Residents called those peers who were oriented to staff and staff concerns the "old powerhouse" and "top dogs." Clearly, the differences between these various terms suggest important differences between the practical concerns of staff and different groupings of residents.

The ethnographer who hears such native terms should not assume that they have single, discrete meanings but, rather, should explore their various shades of meaning and differing import as well as the uses made of them by members positioned differently within the setting. For example, a student ethnographer observing in a cottage for delinquent girls at the Reyes Reform School heard both staff and inmates talk about "buzzes"—personal letters written by one inmate to another that were officially banned by staff as an expression of gang affiliation. In the following incident recorded in her field-notes, she presents an inmate's concern about staff searches for "buzzes":

> Then Kate started talking about how she was so excited that there wasn't a room search today because she remembered during 4th period that she had 7 illegal buzzes in her room.

But "buzzes" had very different significance for staff and inmates. Staff saw buzzes as a form of gang activity that might well escalate tensions between gang members. The girls described buzzes simply as "love letters" without implications for gang affiliations and activities. Consider, for example, these comments taken from an analytic memo written by the ethnographer:

> Three girls in the cottage described buzzes in the following ways:
>   Claudia: "It's like a regular letter . . . like a love letter we write to boys, or they write to us."
>   Kate: "Illegal letters—not passed through POs and we get 24s" [24 hour seclusion in their room].
>   Dani: "A small note that is passed to any other minor in the form of communication and if caught with one, you must suffer consequences, such as in a 24."

Not only do these descriptions lack any reference to gangs, but they also convey that buzzes are significant to the girls exactly because they comprise the focal point of the staff's stringent searches and expose those caught to a standard house punishment ("24s").

To explore and convey broader meanings, it is useful to pay attention to how a term's use compares with, and differs from, the uses of related terms. For example, the Chokwe have terms for several different kinds of "tellings."[16] They distinguish between these tellings by using various cognitive categories, which are marked by distinctive terms, expressive features such as diction and style, and social behaviors appropriate to different situations.[17] For example, *kuta pande* refers to informal talking and telling about recent personal experiences—usually in an exaggerated, dramatized manner—as people visit together in the late afternoons and evening. However, *kulweza sango* refers to telling about community news or events that people know to have happened; people tell such news often as a part of greetings or when visiting. In contrast, *kuta yishima* refers to telling traditional stories (and sometimes proverbs),[18] supposedly based on real events the ancestors experienced and reported to others long ago. People describe *kuta yishima* as "coming from the ancestors" and as "told to make us wise," but they recognize that these tellings are a sort of fictionalized truth often manipulated during the performances for persuasive purposes.

Indeed, ethnographers should attend to momentary and situational distinctions between terms as well as to more pervasive ones. Although these distinctions may not become evident during any one observation or interview, over time by writing fieldnotes and memos, such distinctions become increasingly evident to the researcher. By noticing members' distinctions between related terms, an ethnographer is less likely to impose her own ethnocentric distinctions. Paying close attention to the situated use of terms often reveals finer distinctions within the cognitive categories than the terms may at first appear to indicate.

Member Invoked Contexts and Contrasts

Ethnographers can effectively understand and represent members' meanings by being sensitive to the ways in which members invoke relevant contexts for particular actions and relevant contrasts for some feature or quality of their setting.

In terms of context, how members interpret an action and event is intricately tied to how they understand the context of that action or event

(Schegloff 1997). For example, how a person understands and interprets the statement "that's a nice one" depends upon what she takes to be the context of the remark (Heritage 1984:142); "that" acquires different meanings when the context is "a photograph in family album, a diamond ring in a jeweler's window, or a lettuce in a shop." Thus, what "that" refers to and the possible meanings and implications of "nice one" depend upon what is known or assumed to be the relevant context; such matters can "only be grasped by seeing who was speaking, or when, or where it was said, or by knowing what had been said just previously" (Heritage 1984:142–43).

While researchers generally recognize that the meaning of actions depends upon their social context, they often conceive of such a context as "a static set of influential circumstances—a set of variables that surround persons, actions or situations" (Holstein and Gubrium 2004:269). An ethnographic approach, in contrast, insists that context is "never fixed, but instead is actively brought to bear in the ongoing course of social life." In trying to identify and understand members' meanings, then, we need to understand how members determine the *relevant* context of particular actions and utterances; thus, the goal is to "look at how context is used by actors themselves" (Holstein and Gubrium 2004:269).

For example, for decision makers in institutional settings, who refers a case and under what circumstances often provides a relevant context for deciding how urgently that case will be handled. Thus a middle school mediator explained:

> "Priority comes by crisis." One time I was setting up a mediation, sending out call slips, had some students in the room already, and then I got a call from Mr. Garcia asking for a mediation right now! He said he had the girls in his office, and he didn't want to have to call the police, but they needed to be mediated immediately to de-escalate their problem because it resorted to physical fighting. . . . She looks at me and says, "If it's from an administrator, and especially if it's the principal, I will most likely have the mediation go through. Physical fighting involved is number one though." She adds, "It depends on the immediacy of the crisis. If it's between two good friends, I might let it take more time to get going."

Here, the mediator accords priority to cases on the basis of two contextual features: whether an administrator, especially the principal rather than a teacher or a student, refers the case and the "immediacy" or seriousness of the conflict, "fighting" needing a quicker and more serious response than problems or "squabbles" between "good friends."[19]

Similarly, in criminal and juvenile justice settings, assessments of the seriousness of an offense and the character of an offender are regularly shaped by the depiction of the relevant context of an offense. For example, in an interview with a student ethnographer, a usually tough-minded police officer depicted what he saw as the relevant context of an incident in which a youth had been arrested for bringing a knife to school:

> "Thirteen year old kid. Fat as a blimp, big round roly-poly guy, his hair is messy, can't fit his clothes. . . . Every day the other kids pick on him. Knock his books down. When he picks them up, they kick him in the butt. Every day he gets this kind of abuse so one day he decides he's gonna bring a knife to school . . . because he's tired of the abuse he's getting, tired of people hitting him, calling him fat, pushing him. So he brings a knife to school . . . I asked him, what were you gonna do with the knife, and he said I don't know, I just want them to leave me alone. . . . He's getting beat up every day Monday through Friday, he gets picked on for being a fat boy, and he is—what else can he do? He says he can't fight because he's too slow. . . . He has to equal the playing field and his reasoning is if I have a weapon, they'll leave me alone. That's where I would consider this a good kid just trying to do the right thing, but he gets picked on. That's when I would consider he's just a good kid.

This officer dramatically recounts what he sees—having accepted and honored the youth's explanation for the act—as the relevant context for possessing a dangerous weapon in a school: The youth is subject to constant teasing and abuse, "getting beat up every day Monday through Friday." This context (and background) neutralizes the offense and its possible dangerousness, allowing the officer to depict bringing a knife to school as a "stupid" reaction by a "good kid" who had been pushed to his "breaking point."

Significant members' meanings are revealed in another way through indigenous contrasts[20] that people offer to explain important differences in the situations they are now in compared to those they have previously experienced. These sorts of member-generated contrasts may provide useful insights into local perceptions and evaluations. For example, in talking to a student ethnographer, a probation officer compared the Reyes Reform School and its residents with several other juvenile halls and their residents:

> Having worked previously in detention halls for juveniles, she was struck by the differences at Reyes. At Reyes they are less stringent than in the halls. "The big thing here is buzzes, which are like nothing to me." In the halls, pens and pencils aren't allowed, but they are in Reyes. Metal isn't allowed in either;

she took a metal splint that she found in Kate's room for fear that it could be used as a weapon. . . .

She described Reyes as a "placement center" where the kids receive "treatment." "These kids aren't terribly sophisticated." The kids in the halls would hide things in Noxzema or baby powder, but that wasn't as big a concern here. In the halls, "potential danger's always present." Here, the girls mostly just want to talk to the boys.

Here, the researcher picks up on and writes in her fieldnotes about the contrast that a staff member draws between this reform school and juvenile hall. This indigenous contrast highlights several differences between these two work settings that are relevant to this staff member: less staff concern with danger, more relaxed forms of surveillance, and more effort to "help" the kids. On other occasions as well, local staff made similar comparisons between Reyes and juvenile hall, emphasizing the former's "leniency" relative to the latter.

Similarly, in police patrol work, officers frequently contrast those who "hustle a lot" to "burn outs" who are just "putting in their time." A student ethnographer elaborated this contrast in the following memo:

The term "hustling" is used by [sheriff's] deputies to refer to an officer who is always looking for crime, for a "good shake," for someone to take to jail. A "good shake" refers to someone whose search by the police will lead to a "good arrest." A "good arrest" typically refers to most felony arrests and some misdemeanor arrests (i.e., possession of a concealed weapon). One deputy described some recent good arrests: "The rapist I got yesterday was pretty fun. A couple of weeks ago, I got a biker with a 45 automatic. He also had a bulletproof vest and some drugs. That was a pretty good arrest." . . .

[In contrast], hustlers characterize burnouts as making "bullshit" arrests; that is, he arrests people for crimes not considered to be serious by hustlers but merely for the sake of "stats." "Stats" are a monthly record of which deputies at the station are making the most arrests. Burnouts are thought to be concerned merely with the quantity, not the quality, of their arrests. One deputy remarked that he didn't want to work with another deputy, Al, because he feels Al arrests people for "petty shit"—drunkenness and traffic warrants.

Drawing contrasts not only attributes meaning but may also serve micropolitical purposes that seek to advance the interests of one group in the setting over another. Here, patrol officers contrast two general orientations to patrol work—actively looking for serious crime and "good arrests" as opposed to making easy, "petty shit" arrests in order to build up monthly "stats." In that the former is clearly valued and the latter explicitly demeaned, this contrast is one-sided and partisan, drawing an "us"-versus-"them" distinction between types of officers. Such a contrast, then, tells us less about the differences between types of patrol offices and more about the particular concerns, perspectives, and priorities of the "hustlers" who provided the types.[21] "Burnout" may be completely an imposed category in that those so identified might not classify themselves as sharing a distinctive approach to patrol work. Furthermore, "burnouts" might characterize their work style as a product of experience and maturity in contrast to the violence-prone, "gung-ho" attitude of some younger, more aggressive officers.

Finally, members may invoke indigenous contrasts highlighting individual, personal changes over time. One such contrast involves drawing distinctions between the self someone used to have and the one they have now. Consider, for example, how an ex-prostitute and ex-addict who had been clean for some months described the problems she encountered from current contact with her family:

> Your mom came to visit you Sunday right? Noel replies, Yeah I was really upset because of that. She pauses and then continues, "Well I wasn't upset because of my mom it was my older sister . . ." She pauses and then says, "Also before when I'd see my mom I'd be high, and this was the first time I wasn't high." I nod my head, and Noel says, "My parents bug the shit out of me, and the way I'd deal with them was to get high, and now that I'm not high, I have to actually deal, and that's new to me."

This woman contrasts how she used to handle contact with her parents—by "getting high"—with what she has to do now that she is not high when she sees them—"actually deal" with the stresses she feels in their presence. She uses this contrast to mark her progress in working on her problems with drugs and related issues.

In sum, indigenous contrasts do not provide reliable ways of characterizing differences in settings, orientations, or people that the ethnographer should understand as representing what is "real," "true," or "the facts." Rather, such contrasts tend to offer distinctive insight into what a particular group or collection of people perceive and value as central to whom they are and what they do.

Members' Explanations and Theories

While earlier we recommended against imposing researchers' theoretical categories, an ethnographer should look for and seek to convey members' more complex *explanations* for when, why, or how particular things happen. In effect, the ethnographer puts aside his own inclinations to explain when and why particular events occur in order to highlight members' accounts of them. In this way, the ethnographer seeks to elicit or distill members' theories of the *causes* of particular happenings.

By way of illustration, consider a study of the door-to-door canvassing activities of the local chapter of a feminist political action committee. The committee sought contributions and signatures on petitions supporting state legislation on behalf of women. Canvassers were assigned to territories or "turfs" in crews of four to fourteen persons under the supervision of a field manager, and they were paid a percentage of the contributions they brought in above a preset minimum. Canvassers varied widely in the contributions they collected: Some worked a full shift and brought in little or nothing, while others working the same turf collected hundreds of dollars in an evening.

These variations might well have tempted the researcher to come up with her own explanation or theory for why canvassers differed so drastically in collecting contributions. Instead, she attempted to understand what issues were of most concern to those involved in the campaign. In asking this question, she noted that participants in the fund-raising effort were themselves deeply and practically interested in differences in canvasser performance and that the explanations offered varied depending upon one's position in the organization. *Canvassers* emphasized distinctions between "good turf" and "bad turf," contending that no one could raise significant amounts of money when going door-to-door in neighborhoods where most people were predisposed against their message. The researcher wrote of one incident:

> It had been a hard week canvassing in Beach City, and no one was making any money. The crew was vocally complaining and wanted to leave immediately because it was "bad" turf and was upset at management's unresponsiveness to their plight.

Supervisors supported different explanations, generally honing in on some failure in the canvasser's technique. For example, the researcher quoted one supervisor's comments on how to get canvassers to focus on improving a weak "money rap":

> "People want to attack and blame the turf because it is the most varying condition. This is the most natural reaction. But, we need to make them realize that there are other factors going on while one is canvassing that they can control. If a person has a lot of signatures and talked to a lot of people but got small contributions, then they are connecting with people, and it's just a matter of working on the money rap."

Supervisors and frontline canvassers came into recurrent conflict over exactly which theory was most accurate and, hence, what could be done to alleviate the problem. Management strategies for training supervisors, for example, emphasized practices that would prevent canvassers from "blaming the turf":

> A consultant advised a prospective field manager: "When someone has done shitty, get them away from blaming the turf even when they are emotional. Act as an emotional lightning rod, but hold firm."

> The officer manager urged her field managers: "When you pick all the canvassers up at night, you should do what are called 'trunk talks.' When you pull up to a person's pickup spot, pull a few feet away from them, and hop out to debrief them. If they did well, ask them what was going good for them that made the evening successful. If they did poorly, take a moment to look at their turf sheet and do a quick analysis of what went on out there. This trains them to analyze the evening instead of automatically blaming the turf."

In this instance, then, the ethnographer proceeded exactly by tracing out different "members' theories." As she made the differing nature and location of these working theories her analytic focus, she went on to explore their practical, interactional, and organizational uses.

Finally, the field researcher should realize that people may offer more than one explanation for an occurrence and, indeed, may express what appear to the researcher as "contradictory explanations." Particularly in multicultural and multilingual communities, people frequently shift between languages, cultural expectations, and differing frameworks for perceiving and assessing behavior. In contemporary Africa, this flexibility is not uncommon. For example, in Northwest Province of Zambia, the Lunda, Luvale, Chokwe, Luchazi, and Mbunda peoples intermingle and intermarry. In addition, many younger people have completed grammar school taught in the official national language, English. In this multilingual context, people regularly invoke contrasting cultural frameworks. For example, when talking about illnesses and deaths caused by *wanga* (sorcery/witchcraft), young people often shift between traditionally based views and biomedical explanations learned in school. Talking in Ki-Chokwe with the ethnographer and several other neighbors, a man reflected on a young woman friend's untimely death, concurring with the local diviner's claim that she had died from *wanga*. Later on, explaining details of her life to the ethnographer and one of his brothers in English, he talked about her long-term symptoms as characteristic of "TB" and "AIDS." Since he did not see these explanations as mutually exclusive, in foregrounding one, he did not negate the other one: *Wanga* was the cause of death, though TB or AIDS was the disease. Recognizing that, as their social identity, situation, or language shifts, human beings readily adjust their explanations, an ethnographer should carefully document in fieldnotes when, how, to whom, and, if possible, for what purposes people explain their crises.[22]

MEMBERS' CATEGORIES IN USE: PROCESSES AND PROBLEMS

Members' descriptions, stories, types, and theories, no matter how rich and evocative, provide only a starting point for ethnographic fieldnotes. Deeper, fuller memos and analyses in a final ethnography require examining not simply what terms members use but also when, where, and how they use them and how they *actually* categorize or classify events and objects in specific situations.

By way of illustration, consider the following fieldnote provided by a student ethnographer with extensive gymnastic experience, in which he identifies terms for those attending an "open gym night" at a local university campus:

> At open gym nights, there are different classes and subclasses of people attending. The major classes include the regulars, the visitors, and the walk-ins. Of these, there are many subclasses too. In the regulars' class, there are the novice, the ex-gymnasts (old-timers), and the advanced amateur. The novices are people that have never taken gymnastics, classes or lessons, and are people that just walked in one day due to interest. The advanced amateurs are people who were never on any gymnastics teams but have taken classes or lessons or used to be walk-ins. Finally, the old-timers are those who competed at either the high school or college level. . . . Walk-ins are students who have had a long-term interest in gymnastics and would like to learn from the old-timers.

This description provides a typology of those coming to the gym: "regulars" (subtyped into three further classes—"novices," "advanced amateurs," and "old-timers"), "visitors," and "walk-ins." But based on the notes, it appears that this typology identifies only categories recognized by the ethnographer; it is not clear that people in this setting actually apply these categories to others (and themselves) and, if they were to do so, when, where, and under what circumstances. Thus, the problem with this typology is twofold: We do not know whether or not members recognize and use terms such as "regular" and "walk-in"; and, more fundamentally, if they do use these terms, we do not know exactly how, when, and for what purposes they do so.

In insisting on considering members' actual situated use of specific terms or categories, the issue is not the "validity" or "reality" of these categories in a conventional sense. Rather, any object or event can be categorized in multiple ways (Heritage 1984:144–50); and the fact that some objects/events *might be* classed in one way or another (e.g., on the basis of having this or that trait or attribute in common) is not adequate grounds for recommending a particular classification, since we can always invoke or imagine other traits that would produce very different sorts of classifications.[23] Gym participants might indeed, *at some times for some purposes*, recognize "regulars," "visitors," and "walk-ins" as meaningful categories. But, we cannot tell from this description, since no effort is made to look at how members actually talk about and identify others on specific occasions; that is, the types are presented without interactional context as always and everywhere relevant. Rather, the ethnographer, alerted to possibly relevant local categories, should look closely at how *members actually classify events* on particular occasions and for particular purposes.

Ethnographic fieldnotes, then, should not simply report indigenous terms discoverable in a setting. Rather, fieldnotes should more fundamentally detail members' actual, situated uses of such terms. The following pages provide two extended examples of how field researchers can make their notes and other writings more sensitive to the interactional uses of member-recognized categories.

"Storytelling" as "Doing"

Stories, as noted above, are told for specific purposes. Indeed, people may tell a story to convey and support a particular interpretation of past events or to define current relations in order to shape future actions. Thus, what stories are "about" must consider the kind of speech, to whom the teller is speaking, and the stated or implicit purposes as well as other contextual influences.[24]

Consider the following incident that occurred in Zambia as Rachel Fretz was preparing to leave a Chokwe village in which she and a local assistant, Mwatushi, had been working for several weeks. Mwatushi's father called his wife, son, and the ethnographer into his house for a farewell discussion and well-wishes for travel:

We greeted each other and then chatted about our leaving. . . . He [the father and host] said that he was very pleased that I had come to stay here and that they did not know until yesterday that we were leaving today. Otherwise, they could have sent something with us. Now they only have sweet potatoes to send, and maybe when I come the next time, they can send something good, like a chicken, with me.

Then he started to narrate. His voice shifted into the rhythms of story-telling and speeded up. . . .

"There was a *chindele* (foreigner/white person) who had two servants, and when he went back to his country to get married, he left his house and all his things with his servants to watch over them until he came back. Now the *chindele* stayed longer than they expected, and so the one servant said, 'Let's leave, he's not coming back.' But the other servant said, 'No, he told us to stay here until he came.' The one servant left, and when the master came back, only one servant was there—"

He paused: "Ah no, I made a mistake. Both servants stayed until the *chindele* came. He came with his wife and he said, 'I am very pleased that you stayed here until I came, and because of that, I will give you each a small present. It is only a small present for you to take back to your village to your wives. It is small because I used all my money to get my wife, but please take these small bundles of grass as presents.' Then he gave each one a very small bundle of grass.

"Halfway home, the one man said, 'Ah we have much grass at home and here I am carrying this small bundle. No, I will not carry it. I'll throw it away.' But the other man said, 'No, I am carrying mine to the village.' So they went.

"When they arrived in their village, the one man gave his wife the bundle of grass and said, 'It is a small present from the *chindele* because I stayed until he came back. Here, put it in the house.' So she saved it. Then later that day it began to rain, and it came through the holes in the roof, so the man took his grass and repaired his roof. That night they slept well.

"In the morning, the other man—the one who threw his grass away—got up and looked out his window. He called his wife and said, 'Come see the house of our relative, the one who repaired his roof with the *chindele's* grass.'

"They saw a large house with a tin roof and windows and many rooms. In the yard, they saw two vehicles, one for the man and one for the woman, who just then came out wearing good clothes.

"Then the man who threw his grass away said, 'Wife, let's go back on the road to where I threw the grass away so that we can bring the grass and have a fine house, too.' But when they got to the place where he had thrown the grass, they found that the bundle was scattered and all the grass broken."

The father (narrator) continued, "Thus even though we do not have much to give you—we have no chicken to send with you—we give you these small words to keep and not throw away: May God bless you and carry you well on your journey. May He keep you where you are (live)."

Then he said, "It is good that you are taking our son with you. He should do everything you tell him. If you call him to come with you, he will come. If you tell him to stay, he will stay. Whatever you tell him, he should do."

Together with the sweet potatoes, this story is a gift presented to the ethnographer in lieu of a chicken. The father implies that this seemingly small gift, like the grass in the story, may turn out to be of exceptional value if one has the sense to receive it properly.

Furthermore, the story is a *misende* (parable) through which people address each other indirectly (Fretz 1994) and which here provides a context within which to hear the subsequent conversation. The father uses the parable to introduce a conversation about reciprocal relations: Mwatushi, his son, will not only work very well for the researcher and follow her directions exactly, but the ethnographer must become his family in the distant village where she lives:

> "So it is for you to keep him. . . . It is for you to advise him so that he lives well. Because he is alone over there [without relatives in the village where the researcher lives and works], you are now his mother, his father, you are his grandmother and his grandfather. You are his brother and his sister. It is for you to keep him."

The parable provides connotations for the word "servant," suggesting that someone who stays with the *chindele* will (and should) be rewarded like the servant in the story who exactly followed the directions of the master. But in the subsequent conversation, the father suggests that Mwatushi as "family" will be even more closely allied and loyal to the researcher than a "servant" would be, perhaps traveling a great distance with her. Having established these relationships, the father then asks for a gift that the ethnographer might bring in the future should she return from America to Zambia. According to the Chokwe, people in a close relationship not only give each other gifts, but they respectfully ask each other for gifts and favors in order to establish and solidify a good relationship. As a respectful form of speech, the parable graciously created an opening for his comments and requests.

In sum, the parable—heard in context—subtly reinforces and extends through connotation the father's courteous remarks and questions about reciprocal relationships. His story is not only an immediate gift and blessing for the road, but it also connotes an ongoing relationship. The father's creation of family ties with the ethnographer would, indeed, have long-term benefits to her. But, only by recognizing the storytelling as a *misende* through which the father addressed her indirectly could this ethnographer truly hear what he was saying.

Members' Terms in Everyday Interaction

Through experience in commission sales, student ethnographers have found that salespersons in some contexts who regularly or blatantly "steal customers" are termed "snakes" or "sharks" by coworkers and are generally subject to a variety of pressures, rebukes, and sanctions for their behavior. It is tempting for a field researcher to simply accept these definitions of particular salespersons as "snakes" and then to draw contrasts between how they work the floor or deal with customers and how those not categorized as "snakes" do so. But ethnographers who proceed in this way will produce truncated, rather than complex and nuanced, descriptions and analyses of relations among workers in these settings. Specifically, they will fail to fully appreciate and document the micro-political, interactional processes through which some workers determine that others are "snakes" and attempt to convince coworkers that this is, indeed, the case. And they will fail to fully trace out the intricate *local knowledge* (Geertz 1983) that underlines any competent use of members' terms in specific situations.

To illustrate the depth and complexity that can be added by looking closely at how members actually use indigenous categories, consider the following fieldnote written by a salesperson/researcher who worked in an expensive, high fashion women's clothing store and who herself played a major role in the workplace dispute she describes:

> I was helping a woman who was shopping with her husband, and I had taken her to the back dressing room where she was trying on a lot of clothes. Whenever a customer is trying on a lot of clothes, all the salesgirls notice the cus-

tomer and who is helping her. While I was fitting her in the dressing room, the husband . . . asked Ellen at the counter about a pretty sweater hanging above the cash drawer. It was a $710 Iceberg sweater with a beaded picture of Tweety and Sylvester on it. He quickly told Ellen that he wanted to buy it as a present for his wife and to wrap it before she came out of the dressing room. As soon as I came out, I saw Ellen writing up this sale. I was furious. I was helping the wife, and they were a unit. If I am helping her, then I am helping him also. Ellen said that she didn't know that I was helping his wife in the back when I asked her why she didn't get me to help him. I didn't believe her. The sale was too big and easy for her to pass up. So when the wife came out with about $500 worth of clothes to buy, Pat and Jane, watching over the counter, gave me eyes like they can't believe what Ellen had just done. . . . Ellen had snaked my customer, and we all knew it.

I confronted Ellen and said that what she did was wrong, implying that she was a snake. She became very defensive. She said, "Hear me out, and then I'll listen to you." After I heard her out, I started to talk but she cut me off in the middle of my sentence and said, "Let's see Sammie" [the manager]. Meanwhile, Pat and Jane both told me that I should have the whole sale. I went upstairs to speak to Sammie alone first, and she asked me if I wanted the whole sale or half of the sale. I said that I believe I deserve the whole sale, but I will split it if she understands what she did wrong. Sammie then told Ellen that she must split the sale with me. When I went up to Ellen to say that it was not fair that she cut me off earlier, she cut me off again saying, "It's over!"

Initially, note the explicit one-sidedness of this fieldnote account; its author does not take the stance of a neutral, uninvolved party but clearly presents herself as one of the story's two major protagonists. The account is explicitly political in that it is "making the case" that Ellen "snaked my customer." The accusation appears at least partially contested by Ellen, who is indirectly quoted as saying she did not know "I was helping his wife in the back" and who clearly refused to relinquish her claim to the commission.[25] The author ignores these possibilities in laying out specific grounds for her claim: any competent salesperson should "know" that a husband and wife are a "unit" and would notice a promising customer trying on a lot of clothes; other parties in the setting interpreted the event in the same way as the author; and the local authority figure actually settled the conflict in a way that confirmed the author's version.

The circumstances described in this fieldnote account also direct attention toward the interactional work that took place to get this incident defined and treated as "snaking." While this incident ends up being treated interactionally by others in the setting as an instance of "stealing a customer," this result is not predictable in advance. Rather, it emerges as the inter-action unfolds with the various parties advancing their respective claims and accounts in order to appeal to, and elicit support from, coworkers. In general, it is important for ethnographers to look beyond the simple use of such members' terms to appreciate the underlying micro-political charac-ter of these processes. In the case of "snaking," this author, as a careful eth-nographer, pushed beyond the mere claim that another "stole a customer" to look at *how* salespeople establish claims to specific customers, when and how such claims are ignored or bypassed, how they reassert and sustain these claims, and how conflicting claims and interpretations are presented and resolved.

Furthermore, this account points the way toward appreciating the ex-tensive, local knowledge required to make convincing accusations of "snak-ing." Specifically, the claim that another salesperson "stole my customer" presumes knowledge of a whole set of local practices for "claiming custom-ers." Elsewhere, the student researcher began to sketch these practices in the following terms:

> Having asked a customer if she would like any help, you stand nearby; if any other salesgirl makes a move toward the customer, then we can say that per-son's name out loud. When she looks over, we can point to the customer, sig-naling that we have already asked them if they would like any help and im-plying that they are "my" customer. This is how we preserve our claim to the average customer who walks in off the street.

"Stealing a customer" thus assumes that a salesperson specifically ignored this sort of asserted claim. Indeed, the account of the Iceberg sweater inci-dent underlines how the accused culprit "must have known" that the cus-tomer had been tagged: "Whenever a customer is trying on a lot of clothes, all the salesgirls notice the customer and who is helping her." In this sense, a members' term presupposes and encodes specific local knowledge and prac-tice that the ethnographer wants to identify and describe.

As ethnographers pay close attention to members' meanings, they begin to appreciate how much interactional and political "work" it takes for people to create their meanings. In so doing, the careful ethnographer learns to explore the knowledge that undergirds the implicit claims that people make about events. These often unstated purposes and claims make it clear, however, that field researchers cannot fully determine members' meanings through interviews or informal questioning. Ethnographers must discern local knowledge, not simply on the basis of people's talk, but, rather, through their "talk-in-interaction," that is, they must notice what people do in relation to others in order to produce specific, situated meanings.

RACE, GENDER, CLASS, AND MEMBERS' MEANINGS

Because they are committed to members' meanings and experience, ethnographers treat the relevance of gender, race, or class (as well as other consequential characteristics, e.g., age, sexual orientation, disabilities, etc.) for everyday life in ways that differ significantly from common theoretical approaches. Often, such approaches slight or obscure members meanings by setting forth a priori assumptions and definitions about the significance and meaning of these background characteristics for members' lives. Even though, like such theorists, the ethnographer may assume from the start that these are significant matters that should always be attended to in understanding social life, she places priority on how people themselves socially construct and deal with gender, ethnicity, and class within the dynamics of specific interactions, situations, and social conditions.

This ethnographic stance toward issues of gender, ethnicity, and class has been criticized on several counts. One line of criticism insists that ethnographic research is uninformed by theories that might enable the fieldworker to transcend the limited view of specific events and members' understandings of them to allow her to write about more generally significant and sometimes unrecognized social forces. Another line of criticism holds that ethnographic treatments of gender, ethnicity, or class are narrowly restricted to empirical observations: That is, ethnographies describe specific locales and situations as isolated from the broader social structures and forces that critically determine specific events and individual lives.

Certainly, both criticisms highlight areas in which an ethnographic approach to gender, ethnicity, and class differs from more encompassing theoretical approaches. Committed to members' meanings and experiences, ethnographers are more attracted by what Geertz (1983) termed "experience-near," as opposed to "experience-distant," concepts; thus, they generally give priority to these meanings over a priori, received theories and researchers' assumptions about the salience and import of these background characteristics. Valuing the local and the specific, field researchers look in a focused way at daily life rather than in a broad and sweeping manner at general patterns. Ethnographers certainly prefer to see the direct influence of social structures rather than to assume their relevance and effects at the outset. At first glance, this "experience-near" approach seems to create tensions between ethnography and theories about the effects of broader social structures. However, some of these apparent tensions lessen, and perhaps even disappear, by looking closely at several ways that ethnographers can and should bridge their commitment to members' meanings with their concerns for gender, ethnicity, and class.

At the most basic level, the ethnographer with strong interests in gender, race/ethnicity, and/or class should carefully select a site for field research where he expects one or more of these processes to be particularly salient. In choosing such a site, the researcher should look for a setting where gender, ethnic, or class diversity not only seems clearly highlighted but also where these issues concern the members. Examples would include police forces with increasing numbers of women or ethnic recruits or schools with ethnically diverse student populations. In addition, a researcher might choose to study events in which members directly address these issues. For example, an ethnographer interested in gender issues in traditional societies might study occasions in which elders teach the next generation how to behave in appropriately gendered ways. In many societies, for example, initiation ceremonies explicitly focus on instructing youth about gender roles and responsibilities. Among the Chokwe in Zambia, such rituals as *mwadi* for girls after they begin menstruating and *mukanda* when boys are circumcised are central village events that provide explicit information about gender construction.

Indeed, an ethnographer not only can select a setting and events that focus directly on gender, ethnicity, or class, but she might also design a field research project exactly for its relevance to a theoretical issue derived from these concerns. To study class, racial, and gender differences in child-rearing practices, for example, Lareau (2003) carried out intensive observations of the daily lives of six black and six white families with third-grade children focused on the differences between poor, working-class, and middle-class families. Frohmann (1991, 1997) compared the prosecution of sexual assault cases in district attorneys' offices in a middle-class white community and a low-income, minority area; while cases in the former typically involved "date rape," and in the latter drug dealing, prostitution, or gang activities, prosecutors in both offices processed cases in a very similar fashion, keying on assessments of victim credibility and constructing convincing accounts of the offense to be presented to juries.

Once in a setting, the ethnographer's first concern should be to explore the significance of gender, race/ethnicity, or class matters for those studied.

A first step in this direction requires paying close attention to any occasion upon which people *explicitly invoke* race, gender, and/or class as a relevant context for talking about and/or acting toward each other. For example, rather than assuming that ethnicity is invariably a causal factor producing a behavior or event, the ethnographer seeks to describe, in detail, any interaction in which ethnic identification becomes a matter of attention. In the following fieldnote, a student ethnographer describes what happened when an African American high school teacher opened a discussion of white-black relations in an African American history class:

> Ms. B picked Dapo next. Dapo said that he had just moved to the Valley, Southland Hills. This comment drew a couple of "woo's." Dapo grinned. He said the area he moved to is a "white neighborhood." One time he was walking down the street by his house and passed a white child playing there. The child's parents saw Dapo and grabbed the kid and dragged it inside. Dapo was kind of laughing as he said this. He said he wanted to tell the people, "I'm black, but I'm not going to kill you." Some classmates burst into laughter and talked among themselves. Dapo continued, "My parents are Creole. . . . They're all (lowers voice to an aside) 'you're not really black.' My cousins have blue eyes and blonde hair and all that. . . ." He continues, his voice firming up, "I'm black. I'm a black person. . . . I'm proud to be black."

This account conveys a number of dimensions and contradictions of ethnic identity that are meaningful to a high school student. For example, we see the complex tensions that exist between who his parents tell him he is ("You're not really black") and who he is to those in this neighborhood and for this class ("I'm black").

However, the significance that people attribute to gender, race, or class may often be difficult for ethnographers to document because people are not always aware of or do not always directly reference them. On some occasions, an ethnographer may feel that people regularly act toward one another in "classed" or "gendered" ways; yet, they may not be able to pinpoint how this is so or to record specific scenes or actions in which members explicitly allude to these features. It may thus be extremely difficult to identify and tease out these matters in writing fieldnotes. In other situations, a researcher might expect gender, race, or class to be important but find that members fail to acknowledge, or may even deny, these factors. In such instances, the ethnographer must push beyond explicit use of relevant terms to make more systematic observations to identify patterns of activities that reflect the relevance of gender, ethnicity, or class.

For example, in her study of storytelling in a Chokwe village, Fretz was consistently told that "anyone may tell *yishima*." And, indeed, in most villages, men and women, adults and children told stories around the family firesides. But in her own research in the village of the highest chief, after one initial evening in which a woman narrated in the *chota* (the chief's pavilion), she could not get any woman to tell a story. With continued observation and reflection, she eventually realized that not only did the chief consistently dominate the storytelling, but he also requested that all storytelling take place in his pavilion, a locale where men meet to talk and where women, if invited, participated by responding and singing. Thus, questions about women's roles in storytelling did not reveal the status and gender impact of "storytelling rights" in the pavilion because the answers to these questions were not linked to storytelling but, rather, to other relational and situational factors. Only repeated observation and comparison between similar situations finally led to an understanding of the complex web of situational, gender, and status influences working in this context.[26]

On other occasions, specific talk by members will provide a useful starting place for further inquiry to trace out the relevance of race/ethnicity, gender, or class in wider realms of local life. For example, when a group of students set out to study relations between students in an ethnically diverse high school, one of the group members came back with the following talk about different "groups" on campus:

Around the lunch table today, a bunch of guys who hang around together were talking. I thought they could help me understand the different groups at Central. They used a lot of terms I'd heard before to describe the kids. One guy talked about "trendy people" and how I could recognize a trendy person if I saw one. Someone else said there's "ballers," which are people who play basketball, and then there's "footballers," people who play football and then people who "kick" [hang around with] all the groups. And then there's "posses." They said a posse is a group of students who hang around together, kick it together, and they do it because it gives them a sense of belonging. One black guy goes, "It's just a coincidence that all the people in my posse are black." We were all laughing so hard. He goes, "No, no, we all come from the same neighborhood. Some of them are interracial." Then, there's the "swim team," those are the druggies because they use so many drugs that their eyes are always bloodshot so it's like they were swimming. Then there's the "GCP," the Green Card Posse, they go, "Oh, the Wetbacks." A "cool" person wears nice clothes. I asked, What if you don't have money for nice clothes, does that mean you're not cool? They said, If you have a good personality. But if your personality is the same way you dress, then forget it. "This place is a fashion show."

Here, we see that students invoke a range of local categories in distinguishing and categorizing one another. Some of these categories make direct and explicit reference to ethnicity, for example, "the Green Card Posse." Ethnicity is also directly mentioned with reference to "posses." But specifically how it is relevant appears more open: One speaker identified his posse as all black; and another claimed that some posses are neighborhood based and, hence, "interracial." In contrast, another speaker minimizes ethnicity as the basis for group formation. Finally, most of the categories are not explicitly identified with any particular ethnicity, for example, "ballers," "druggies," and "cool" people. An ethnographer in this setting would want to follow up and seek to establish the ethnicities of students identified as belonging to each of these various categories. This inquiry would be primarily a matter of observing the ethnic status of students identified with each category, then perhaps talking to students about observed ethnic patterns.

An ethnographer could also use this incident as a starting place for tracing out connections between these student categories and gender or class. It appears that this talk about groupings occurs among, and is about, boys; but the field researcher would want to find out specifically if any of these categories include girls and to ask further questions about similar or different groupings among girl students at the school. Here, in particular, the ethnographer should trace out gendered patterns of segregation and difference, as well as of integration and overlap, among students and their activities.

Handling issues of social class may be even more complex depending on the cultural context in which the ethnographer conducts her study. Compared to gender and race/ethnicity, class in American society is often an "experience-distant," rather than an "experience-near," concept (Geertz 1983). As a result, ethnographers rarely encounter members explicitly talking about "class" per se. But people employ a number of terms that refer to elements or components of the concept of social class. For example, identifying "cool people" as those who have nice clothes directly involves a kind of naturally occurring "ranking" of persons that mirrors one concern of the social class concept. Furthermore, these students discuss "money," "nice clothes," and the school as a "fashion show," suggesting that parental income and conspicuous consumption might bear on how one is categorized within the school. Thus, the field researcher might further question and observe these matters in order to describe what students consider "nice clothes," the care they take to display them, where these clothes and the money needed to purchase them come from, and the differences these make in shaping social relations within the school.

Ethnographers have long been concerned with the significance of the researcher's own race/ethnic, gender, or class background for what he can learn and write about members' meanings in a setting.[27] Some hold that differences in background characteristics of the researcher and those they study are barriers that limit rapport and trust, leading the latter to control or censor what they allow the ethnographer to see and understand (Riessman 1987). Such "outsider" research—university researchers studying poor or working-class people, white researchers studying people of color, or male ethnographers trying to find out about women's lives—has also been criticized on political grounds for advancing the careers of researchers while distorting, and some would say exploiting, the lives of those under study, and sometimes for exposing illicit activities key to the survival of some such groups (Andersen 1993; Baca Zinn 2001; Duneier 1999; Gearing 1970; Young 2008). Such concerns have led to recommendations that research on society's marginalized groups should be conducted only by members of those groups; this "matching strategy" would increase access and enhance trust and ongoing insight into the nuances of behavior and meanings that could be written about in these social worlds (Bhopal 2001; Papadopoulos and Lees 2002).

Yet, ethnographers have found this approach to be troubling as well as advantageous (Gunaratnam 2003). Myerhoff (1978), for example, in studying an elderly Jewish retirement community, felt plagued with guilt about the privileges in her life as a young, educated Jewish woman that were not enjoyed by those in the setting, and she experienced a strong emotional burden to provide an adequate portrait of their lives. In her study of marital relations among Latino families, Baca Zinn (2001) found that her Latina identity failed to provide access to working-class mothers who were initially distant and distrustful, becoming more open only when they discovered she lacked sewing skills that they felt every Mexican woman should have and took her on as their student. And Zavella (1996), while sharing ethnic identity and working-class background with the women farm workers she studied, still encountered profound differences and distrust based on her education, university position, and strong feminist commitments. Hence, matching backgrounds can, in some instances, be grounds for exclusion rather than greater access to important aspects of members' lives. Moreover, researchers, like those they study, are multidimensional, and matching on only one characteristic may not be sufficient to apprehend and write about members' ways of life (Aitken and Burman 1999; Riessman 1987). Finally, race, class, and gender are not static, self-evident attributes whose influence on interaction can be known beforehand (Ahmed 2000). Rather, they are qualities and attributes that are mutually constructed and negotiated. The meaning, salience, and value given to one background characteristic may differ between the researcher and members and between different members in the setting over time and in different circumstances.

Indeed, rather than enhancing access and ongoing understanding of what may be written about, matching backgrounds may result in researchers overlooking issues because they are familiar and taken-for-granted aspects of life shared between themselves and those they study; or just as members may be reluctant to reveal aspects of their lives with outsiders, they also may not talk about topics about which they expect the researcher who is a member of their community to be familiar. In the following memo, Linda Shaw reflects upon the complexities of trying to get direct access to members' meanings using the matching strategy in a study of ethnic relations among newly immigrated Taiwanese and longtime Latino and Anglo members of the community:

> In some cases, our strategy of matching researcher backgrounds seemed to work well, as when Anglo members of the community conversed easily with us at city council meetings. Yet, in other cases, our strategy of matching researcher backgrounds to those of members of the community took unexpected turns. We hoped, for example, that as a Taiwanese immigrant, Yen might learn how members of that community responded to the immigrant experience. So freely did she appear to move about and talk to them that we were perplexed when they refused her repeated requests to talk about experiences as newcomers, instead offering her advice about how to become a good American while maintaining her Chinese identity. At first thinking our efforts to achieve trust and rapport by matching ethnic backgrounds had failed, only later did we understand that in refusing to talk to Yen *about* their experiences as new immigrants, they were, in fact, instructing her about the ways of being a good American. We realized that members of the Chinese community had, indeed, opened themselves to her based on ethnicity. But they had done so indirectly by invoking cultural practices for incorporation of newly immigrated Chinese to American society that precluded talking directly about difficulties they had encountered.

These reactions suggest the possibility of moving beyond treating class, ethnic, or gender differences simply as barriers to be minimized or overcome; rather, ethnographers can focus on what social traits or attributes people consider most salient in their relations with the ethnographer and on what can be learned from their responses to both these differences and similarities. For example, researchers from diverse class or racial/ethnic backgrounds who are welcomed into settings may learn about the resources—either material or social—that they bring that those in the setting value. Or efforts—whether successful or not—to gain acceptance or to engage members in conversation about particular topics may reveal unspoken rules governing membership, gatekeeping, and authority within the group. And, finally, in keeping with our interactionist perspective, it is important for ethnographers to remember that race, class, and gender (and their meanings)—both of researchers and those they study—are not static, fixed categories; rather, they are constructed through interaction and may vary over time as circumstances and characters change within the setting (Morris 2007).

In sum, many ethnographers now recognize that they "are almost always simultaneously insiders and outsiders" (Zavella 1996:141). Race/ethnicity, class, and gender similarities and differences do not neatly and predictably determine access to writing about members' meanings as "fieldwork relations, in fact, involve whole persons, socially constituted as bundles of situationally relevant traits" (Emerson 2001:122–23). As a result, ethnographers should not orient simply to differences or similarities in these matters but, rather, to "the social location of the ethnographer and informants" and the ongoing negotiations of differences and similarities between them (Zavella 1996:140–41). This has lead Gunaratnam to argue for the value of a move from an emphasis on "commonality" to the ways in which "connectivity" is established between the researcher and members of settings (2003:97). Similarly, Duneier (1999, 2004)—a white, Jewish, upper-middle-class ethnographer—believes that race, class, and religious differences such as those between himself and the African American street vendors he studied can never be overcome. Nonetheless, he was able to develop a practical, working rapport with many of these vendors: While they suspected his motives as a white Jewish researcher, they nonetheless, *for their own reasons and purposes, accepted his presence* and, in so doing, provided access, although inevitably partial, to patterned routines and goings-on of their everyday lives. The goal, then, is to try to understand and write about how "a different social position can have a serious effect on one's work" (Duneier 1999:354).

Finally, white, middle-class researchers concerned with gender, race/ethnic, and class inequality can also pursue a very different strategy: They can "study up" (Nader 1969), focusing fieldwork on dominant, rather than marginalized, groups. Katz (2001b:367–70), for example, identifies "getting behind the scenes" of the "social worlds of the elite and the admired," challenging the distance created "by respectability and a privileged insularity," as one of the distinctive warrants for ethnographic fieldwork. In this way, ethnographers may examine the ways that institutional actors or members of dominant groups produce, perpetuate, and challenge gender, race/ethnic, or class relations in daily interactions.

LOCAL EVENTS AND SOCIAL FORCES

Field researchers can employ a number of different strategies to try to link the import of more distant social settings as well as general trends and patterns, such as inequality related to race/ethnicity, gender, and class, to local events and specific outcomes. Katz (1988b), for example, argues that it is critical to first understand the interactional and phenomenal realities that provide the "foreground" for various kinds of criminal acts, only then taking up the relevance and impact of "background" factors such as ethnicity, class, and gender. And while ethnography itself cannot provide direct access to large-scale structural forces, ethnographers can see patterns of race, class, and gender inequality, for example, as part of the "terrain on which interaction unfolds" (DeVault 1995) and aim to write fieldnotes that show how structural patterns involving race, class, or gender are socially constructed and produced in daily life. To accomplish this requires that the ethnographer avoid viewing gender, ethnicity/race, and class as reified variables or forces that act upon people and social settings to "cause" outcomes such as social inequality. Rather, we encourage ethnographers to write about the "doing" of gender (West and Zimmerman 1987), ethnicity/race, and class and to examine how large-scale patterns related to gender, race, and class are "enacted," that is, produced, reproduced, maintained, and challenged in and through social interaction.

To accomplish this initially requires that the ethnographer look for specific connections within the setting to outside social influences.[28] The ethnographer should write about how the people involved talk about and understand their connections with these outside entities and forces, but he would not be limited to these member-recognized understandings. Field research on the homeless, for example, might well begin by recording how people living on the street understand and cope with the conditions of their daily existence on a day-to-day basis, including how they see their relationship to the wider society (e.g., Snow and Anderson 1993). But the researcher would also observe relations between homeless people and the various persons, agents, and institutions with whom they have recurrent contact: for example, missions, hotels, and other places that provide occasional residence; regular feeding lines and informal arrangements with restaurants as sources of food; relations with police patrol officers and jailers; and caretaker agencies and welfare/relief workers. Then, a researcher (or other researchers) might move out to examine these institutions and agents and their conditions of existence.[29]

Ethnography can also explore links to broader social processes by observing people and settings as they change *over time*. Long-term, continuous field research is necessary, for example, in order to understand how working-class youth react to, and are affected by, their contacts with schools. Introducing a longitudinal component to field research, while practically difficult, allows the researcher to describe different life chances and to understand how these chances are shaped and determined. Field researchers, for example, often examine particular "institutional careers" (Goffman 1961) and the factors that shape them, whether these involve moving through schools to different outcomes or through processing by the police or courts to different fates. The limited "breadth" of many ethnographies can be improved through observations that span longer time periods, recording changes that are not evident in atemporal renderings that that provide a mere snapshot of social life.

REFLECTIONS: USING FIELDNOTES TO DISCOVER/CREATE MEMBERS' MEANINGS

In this chapter, we have proposed strategies for writing ethnographic fieldnotes that collect and represent members' meanings in a rigorous, grounded manner. These strategies require the ethnographer to bracket preconceptions about what is important in order to attend to people's indigenous ways of ordering and interpreting their worlds. In so doing, ethnographers assume that members' meanings are *consequential* and that how people act is based on their understandings of their local social worlds. In pursuing members' meanings, ethnographers begin by looking at how members describe and categorize people and events; they try to discern *their* terms, phrasings, classifications, and theories. But indigenous categories provide only a starting point; the ethnographer's task is not simply to identify member-recognized terms and categories but also to *specify the conditions under which people actually invoke and apply such terms in interaction with others*. No term or category is self-applying to actual situations, and its relevance to specific circumstances cannot be determined in advance. Hence, the ethnographer should not describe social scenes by applying member-recognized terms and categories to situations independently of members' actual applications.

Several implications flow from recognizing that the ethnographer who writes fieldnotes about indigenous meanings should specify the conditions under which members' meanings are invoked and applied. First, such fieldnotes must incorporate not words and phrases abstracted out of context but, rather, the actual interactional occasions in which these members' terms are used. Fieldnotes useful to appreciating members' meanings, then, will be interactionally, rather than cognitively, focused in order to document how members *construct meaning* through interactions with other members of the group and how they actually interpret and organize their own and others' actions.

Some methodological implications follow. Many ethnographers seem to assume that the pursuit of members' meanings is equivalent to interviewing people about what is important to them. But ethnographers collect materials relevant to members' meanings by focusing, not on members' decontextualized talk, but, rather, on naturally occurring, situated *interaction* in which local meanings are created and sustained. Writing ethnographic fieldnotes that are sensitive to members' meanings is not primarily a matter of asking but, rather, of inferring what people are concerned with from the specific ways in which they talk and act in a variety of natural settings. Thus, interviewing, especially asking members directly what terms mean to them or what is important or significant to them, is not the primary tool for getting at members' meanings. Rather, the distinctive procedure is to observe and record naturally occurring talk and interaction. It may, indeed, be useful or essential to interview members about the use and meaning of specific local terms and phrases, but the researcher's deeper concern lies in the actual, situated use of those terms in ordinary interaction.[30]

Finally, focusing on interactionally situated uses of indigenous terms heightens the ethnographer's sensitivity to the intricate processes of situated judgment and skilled interpretation that characterize members' use of local categories. Members' categorizations are not invariant and transcendent but, rather, are tied to specific situations and used for varying purposes. Extensive local knowledge and judgment-making skill are necessarily involved in their use. In the gym, for example, those about to undertake a particular gymnastic routine requiring a "spotter" may have a practical interest in recognizing and distinguishing between the experience and skill level of others present. Indeed, experienced gymnasts can see at a glance how much training another has had on the basis of her performance and actions. In general, a deeper appreciation of indigenous meanings requires learning when and how members actually make such assessments and what knowledge they rely on in so doing.

6

Processing Fieldnotes: Coding and Memoing

At some point—after weeks or perhaps months of writing notes—the ethnographer needs to draw back from the field and to cease actively writing notes. He must shift gears and turn to the written record he has produced with an eye to transforming this collection of materials into writings that speak to wider, outside audiences. Efforts to analyze now become intense, concentrated, and comprehensive: The fieldworker begins to sift systematically through the many pages of fieldnote accounts and initial in-process memos, looking to identify threads that can be woven together to tell a story (or a number of stories) about the observed social world. The ultimate goal is to produce coherent, focused analyses of aspects of the social life that have been observed and recorded, analyses that are comprehensible to readers who are not directly acquainted with the social world at issue.[1]

The prospect of creating coherent, focused analyses from a mass of materials (fieldnotes now several hundred pages and in-process memos several dozen) overwhelms many students. But fieldworkers have found that the task can be handled effectively by recognizing several distinct practices involved in carrying out analysis.

Initially, writing fieldnotes gives way to *reading* them. First, the ethnographer reads through all fieldnotes as a complete corpus, taking in the entire record of the field experience as it has evolved over time. She begins to elaborate and refine earlier insights and lines of analysis by subjecting this broader collection of fieldnotes to close, intensive reflection and analysis.

Second, the researcher combines this close reading with procedures for *analytically coding* fieldnotes. Ethnographic coding involves line-by-line categorization of specific notes. In this process, the researcher's stance toward the notes changes: The notes, and the persons and events they recount, become textual objects (although linked to personal memories and intuitions) to be considered and examined with a series of analytic and presentational possibilities in mind.

Qualitative analytic coding usually proceeds in two different phases. In *open coding,* the ethnographer reads fieldnotes line-by-line to identify and formulate any and all ideas, themes, or issues they suggest, no matter how varied and disparate. In *focused coding,* the fieldworker subjects fieldnotes to fine-grained, line-by-line analysis on the basis of topics that have been identified as being of particular interest. Here, the ethnographer uses a smaller set of promising ideas and categories to provide the major topic and themes for the final ethnography.

Reading through and coding fieldnotes on a line-by-line basis inundates the ethnographer with new ideas, insights, and connections. While continuing to code and review initial memos, she elaborates these insights by writing more systematic theoretical *code memos* (Strauss and Corbin 1990). These memos are generated by, and are closely tied to, phenomena, topics, and categories created by rereading and closely coding fieldnotes. Later, as the fieldworker develops a clearer sense of the ideas or themes she wants to pursue, memos take on a more focused character; they relate or integrate what were previously separate pieces of data and analytic points. These *integrative memos* seek to clarify and link analytic themes and categories.[2]

We present analytic practices that parallel methods developed by sociologists taking the *grounded theory* approach to analyzing qualitative data.[3] Grounded theorists give priority to deriving "analytic categories directly from the data, not from preconceived concepts or hypotheses" (Charmaz 2001:336–37). They maintain that if the researcher minimizes commitment to received and preconceived theory, he is more likely to develop new analytic categories and original theories from his data. By making frequent comparisons across the data, the researcher can formulate, modify, and extend theoretical propositions so that they fit the data. At the actual working level, the researcher begins by coding data in close, systematic ways so that he can generate analytic categories. He further elaborates, extends, and integrates the properties and dimensions of these categories by writing theo-retical memos.

The earliest versions of the grounded theory approach depicted anal-ysis as a clear cut, almost autonomous activity with the researcher "dis-covering" theory in fieldnotes and other qualitative data. This approach seemed to imply that concepts and analytic categories lurked in fieldnote data, waiting to emerge and be discovered by the field researcher. But con-temporary grounded theory practitioners, while remaining strongly com-mitted to inductive procedures, no longer emphasize the "discovery" of theory (Charmaz 2001:335); rather, they recognize that analysis pervades all phases of the research enterprise—as the researcher makes observations, writes fieldnotes, codes these notes in analytic categories, and finally devel-ops explicit theoretical propositions. In this sense, then, analysis is more ac-curately described as both inductive and deductive, what some have termed "retroductive" (Bulmer 1979; Katz 1988a). The process is like someone who is simultaneously creating and solving a puzzle or like a carpenter alternately changing the shape of a door and then the shape of the door frame to obtain a better fit (Baldamus 1972:295).

In this chapter, we develop an approach to analyzing fieldnotes based on these ideas. Initially, we suggest ways to begin the analysis of fieldnotes: close reading, open coding, and writing memos that formulate and clarify the ideas and insights that such coding produces. We then consider proce-dures that are helpful in carrying out more specific, fine-grained analyses: focused coding and writing integrative memos. While we discuss reading, coding, and memoing as discrete steps in analytically processing fieldnotes, we want to emphasize that the researcher is not rigidly confined to one pro-cedure at a time or to undertaking them in any particular order. Rather, she moves from a general reading to a close coding to writing intensive analyses and then back again. Said another way, from reading comes coding and writ-ten memos that direct and redirect attention to issues and possibilities that require further reading of the same or additional fieldnotes.

READING FIELDNOTES AS A DATA SET

The ethnographer begins concentrated analysis and writing by reading his fieldnotes in a new manner, looking closely and systematically at what has been observed and recorded. In so doing, he treats the fieldnotes as a data set, reviewing, reexperiencing, and reexamining everything that has been written down, while self-consciously seeking to identify themes, patterns, and variations within this record.

We strongly recommend reading line by line through as many pages of fieldnotes as possible, at least until coding seems to generate no new ideas, themes, or issues. Reading notes as a whole, and in the order they were written, confers a number of benefits. First, the fieldworker can perceive changes in her relations with those in the field over time. The gradual movement from distance to rapport, for example, may only become apparent when reading in a matter of hours a record of events that took place over weeks and months. Second, the ethnographer gains fresh insights as she changes her own understanding and interpretation of people and events by reviewing the completed set of notes. Based upon what has subsequently been learned, initial interpretations and commentaries now reencountered may seem naive or erroneous. This contrast between initial and later understanding is often striking when working in a totally unfamiliar culture and language. The fieldworker may come to feel that foreign concepts and terms have no equivalent in English. And patterns and tendencies recognized when reading all of the notes may suggest alternative interpretations of actions or talk previously understood in another way. Finally, working with a corpus of fieldnotes allows the ethnographer to take in, for the first time in a relatively concentrated time stretch, everything that she has been able to observe and record. Reading notes as a whole also encourages recognizing patterns and making comparisons. She begins to notice how an incident is like others in previously reviewed notes. Conversely, she also begins to note important differences between incidents previously seen as similar.

To undertake an analytically motivated reading of one's fieldnotes requires the ethnographer to approach his notes as if they had been written by a stranger. Indeed, many fieldworkers find it difficult to achieve the sort of emotional distance required to subject to analysis those with whom he has been deeply immersed. Some fieldworkers report discomfort at "examining under a microscope" the lives of people with whom they have become deeply involved and, in many cases, care about. For some, analysis comes close to an act of betrayal; many fieldworkers report having taken several weeks or months after they stopped writing fieldnotes before they could begin their analyses. Some researchers resolve this internal conflict by working collaboratively with people in the setting, even occasionally coauthoring their writing with a local assistant.

Although the deliberate and self-conscious analysis ethnography entails may contribute to feelings of estrangement, it may be helpful to remember that making sense of "what's going on" is an activity that members of the setting engage in and that it is one of the usual and expected activities of social life. And it is also sometimes helpful to remember that while our analysis of patterns of social life in the field site is ordinarily for audiences and purposes outside of it, we seek to convey an appreciative understanding of the world and lives of persons under study.

OPEN CODING

While subjecting fieldnotes to a careful, minute reading, the ethnographer begins to sift through and categorize small segments of the fieldnote record by writing words and phrases that identify and name specific analytic dimensions and categories. Such codings can be written in the margin next to the pertinent fieldnote, on a separate sheet of paper (with some marking of the location of the relevant fieldnote), or in a "comment" field in a word-processing program or a keyword field in a text database. In such line-by-line coding, the ethnographer entertains all analytic possibilities; she attempts to capture as many ideas and themes as time allows but always stays close to what has been written down in the fieldnote. She does so without regard for how or whether ideas and categories will ultimately be used, whether other relevant observations have been made, or how they will fit together.

Coding fieldnotes in this way differs fundamentally from coding in quantitative research. In quantitative coding, the researcher proceeds deductively by constructing questionnaires with categories derived from theory. He fits people's responses to the questionnaire into the already established categories in order to determine the frequencies of events within those categories. By contrast, qualitative coding does not start from preestablished or fixed analytic categories but, rather, proceeds inductively by creating analytic categories that reflect the significance of events and experiences to those in the setting.[4] Qualitative coding is a way of opening up avenues of inquiry: The researcher identifies and develops concepts and analytic insights through close examination of, and reflection on, fieldnote data. Such coding is not fundamentally directed at putting labels on bits and pieces of data so that what "goes together" can be collected in a single category; rather, the ethnographer is indeed interested in categories but less as a way to sort data than as a way to name, distinguish, and identify the conceptual import and significance of particular observations. In contrast to quantitative coding, then, in qualitative coding we ask questions of data in order to develop, identify, elaborate, and refine analytic categories and insights.

In some situations, ethnographers may benefit from using one of the increasingly sophisticated computer-assisted qualitative data analysis software (CAQDAS) programs as a tool to help manage, code, and analyze their data. If the ethnographer has accumulated hundreds of pages of fieldnotes and interview transcripts, code-and-retrieve software provides useful and efficient ways to organize and manage field data. With such a program, the field researcher categorizes or labels "passages of the data according to what they are about or other content of interest in them (coding or indexing)" and can then collect or retrieve passages labeled in the same way (Richards and Richards 1994:446). Sorting field data into general, coherent categories is essential when working with large, qualitative data sets. Field researchers can also use more elaborate theory-building programs (Fielding 2001; Kelle 2004; Weitzman and Miles 1995) that do not simply sort categorized data but also facilitate the logic and application of actual analytic coding. These programs enable the fieldworker to place very specific and detailed codes on particular segments of fieldnotes and interviews, to link these codes to other codes and categories, and to retrieve all data recorded under any code. Theory-building programs also allow the field researcher to assemble and integrate all data, codes, memos, and more finished analyses in one file.[5]

Despite their attractions and potential advantages (Corbin and Strauss 2008; Fielding 2001; Kelle 2004), computer-assisted qualitative analysis programs also have a number of limitations. First, there are often heavy start-up costs as time and effort is required to put field data into appropriate formats and to develop and review emerging code categories. Hence, these programs are not usually helpful to students collecting limited amounts of data for research classes; in these cases, it is easier to use a standard word-processing program to sort data by simply creating new files using highlight and copy functions and to enter code categories as marginal comments. Second, it is difficult, even in theory-building programs, to modify codes once applied to specific pieces of data, even though such modification is an important process. Third, these programs may entice the researcher into a superficial, "fit-it-in-a-category" sorting-oriented coding procedure; this facile categorizing shifts the ethnographer's attention away from the essential task of creating new codes and categories that requires actively reading and rereading notes on a sentence-by-sentence basis and repeatedly rethinking and refining prior codes and categories. Corbin warns against this danger in the following terms, "Computers can be used to do coding, but the analyst must be very careful not to fall into the trap of just fixing labels on a piece of paper, then putting pile of 'raw' data under that label. If a researcher does just this, he or she will end up with a series of concepts with nothing reflective said about what the data are indicating. Even with computers, the researcher must take the time to reflect on data and write memos" (Corbin and Strauss 2008:163). Despite the power of the computer, only the ethnographer creates, changes, and reconceptualizes interpretations and analyses.

Whether carried out by hand or by computer entries, open coding begins with the ethnographer mentally asking questions of specific pieces of fieldnote data. In asking such questions, the ethnographer draws on a wide variety of resources, including direct experience of life and events in the setting; sensitivity toward the concerns and orientations of members; memory of other specific incidents described elsewhere in one's notes; the leads and insights developed in in-process commentaries and memos; one's own prior experience and insights gained in other settings; and the concepts and orientation provided by one's profession or discipline. Nothing is out of bounds!

But the secret of coding lies in turning the answers to these questions into a distinctive kind of writing—a word or short phrase that captures and signals what is going on in a piece of data in a way that links it to some more general analytic issue. Such writing is integrally linked to the processes of thinking and interpreting, whereby the ethnographer "comes up with" a code to write down. In turn, writing down codes—putting an idea or intuition into a concrete, relatively concise word or phrase—helps stimulate, shape, and constrain the fieldworker's thinking and reflection. This mutually necessary relationship between reflection and writing is expressed in John Forester's (n.d.) apt phrase, "thinking with your fingers."

We have found the following sorts of questions useful in beginning to examine specific fieldnotes:

- What are people doing? What are they trying to accomplish?
- How, exactly, do they do this? What specific means and/or strategies do they use?
- How do members talk about, characterize, and understand what is going on? What assumptions are they making?
- What do I see going on here? What did I learn from these notes? Why did I include them?
- How is what is going on here similar to, or different from, other incidents or events recorded elsewhere in the fieldnotes?
- What is the broader import or significance of this incident or event? What is it a case of?

Such questions reflect and advance several specific concerns linked to our approach to ethnography and writing fieldnotes. First, these questions give priority to *processes* rather than to "causes" or internal psychological "motives." Specifically, this priority means asking questions that identify what is occurring and in what order, rather than "why" questions that ask what is causing or producing some outcomes. In this sense, we view open coding as a means for developing interpretations or analytic themes rather than specific causal explanations.

Second, these questions reflect a sensitivity to the *practical* concerns, conditions, and constraints that actors confront and deal with in their everyday lives and actions. This concern with the practical or the pragmatic requires paying attention to mundane, ordinary, and taken-for-granted routines and ways of life, rather than looking only, or primarily, at the dramatic or exceptional action or event.

Third, these questions can help specify the meanings and points of view of those under study. We try to frame questions that get at how members see and experience events, at what they view as important and significant, and at how they describe, classify, analyze, and evaluate their own and others' situations and activities. Yet, to get at these matters, it is initially crucial to clarify what the ethnographer felt was significant about what occurred by asking: "Why did I include this item in my fieldnotes?" It is then important to ask whether or not, and on what basis, members seem to attribute this same significance to events or incidents. These procedures keep the ethnographer aware of the complexities involved in pursuing members' meanings; in other words, they remind the ethnographer that she always writes her *interpretation* of what she feels is meaningful and important to members.

Finally, these questions provide ways of moving beyond a particular event or situation recounted in the fieldnotes to identify more general theoretical dimensions or issues. As noted earlier, such analysis is not a matter of trying to fit observations into preestablished analytic categories. Rather, the ethnographer engages in an active analytic process in which he seeks to identify general patterns or categories suggested by events described in the notes themselves. One useful way of proceeding here is by asking how some current observation or incident relates to other observations and incidents. Close *comparison* of such incidents and processes, attending to both similarities and variations, can often suggest key features or dimensions in detailed, specific ways. This process leads to identifying or naming broader categories within which this specific instance stands as a "case," in this way helping to build more generalized analyses.

Such questions will lead to codes that the ethnographer writes in the margins of her fieldnotes. The following example, from a student whose ethnography examined her work as an usher, illustrates these processes:

customer types: late arrivals	Dance audiences do tend to come right at curtain, so we have to hold many out. Tonight was no different. I'd say we had about 50 people waiting in
holding out audience members	the lobby through the first number. . . . One man we held out was irate. He had already been in but
waiters: irate	had come out for some reason. When we closed the door, he began yelling at the door attendant. He said
latecomer claims exception	he was already in—not like these other people who were "LATE." He was not late and shouldn't be
mgr intervenes	treated like them! The house manager came over and smiled and told him in a quiet voice why he
passing the buck	was being held out—that it was requested by the dancers. He calmed down but was still angry. He waited without another word, except when I came
calming latecomers *keeping occupied* *distracting*	around. I went around giving out programs so they could read something and so the ushers wouldn't have to waste time doing that when these people charged their doors. I also asked people if I could tell them which aisle to go to so as to alleviate confusion for the door attendant. When I got to this man and asked him if he wanted me to tell him which door to enter through, he said in a huff that he had already been in and knew where to go.
smiling *minimizing the wait*	Other people were just as irritated. I just smiled and told them it would just be a few minutes. I think that calmed them a little because the exasperated look left their faces.

This student ethnographer focused on the practical situation of ushers, implicitly asking how ushers understood and made sense of behavior and events and how they interacted with one another and with customers to manage difficult situations. Specifically, the codes "holding out audience members" and "calming latecomers" identify specific processes for dealing with and managing latecomers as practical work problems. The ethnographer then asked herself *how* these activities were actually done by ushers which led to a series of more specific codes for "calming," for example, "keeping occupied," "distracting," "smiling," and "minimizing the wait."

These codes begin to identify and elaborate a variety of analytic distinctions. For example, the code "late arrivals" names a particular "type of customer"; in framing "late arrivals" as a "type," she asserts that coming late is a normal, routine event in this setting and that "late arrivals" are one among a range of customer types. In identifying one customer type, this code raises the possibility that other customer types exist and, hence, opens the question of just what these other "customer types" might be. That is, the process here is a dialectical one that consists of asking, "What is this a case of?" or "Of what more general category is this an instance?" In answering this question, the field researcher may draw upon a wide variety of experiences and different sorts of knowledge: her own experience as an usher, her awareness that dealing with people who come late is a practical matter that ushers must routinely confront, her experiences as someone who has come late to a performance, and her familiarity with sociological thinking about waiting as a key to power differences (e.g., Schwartz 1975).

But while latecomers are expected at dance performances, the code "irate waiters" distinguishes a particular audience type, a latecomer who is a source of trouble and special concern. The code "latecomer claims exception" identifies both the responses with which ushers have to deal and the categories and distinctions advanced by this particular latecomer. The next codes—"mgr intervenes," "passing the buck," "keeping occupied," and "distracting"—identify additional forms of "backup" responses. These responses include the manager's efforts to placate the disgruntled patron and the writer's attempts to take waiting audience members' minds off the delay.

Codes, then, take a specific event, incident, or feature and relate it to other events, incidents, or features, implicitly comparing and distinguishing this one from others. By comparing this event with "like" others, one can begin to identify more general analytic *dimensions* or categories. One can do this by asking what more general category this event belongs to or by thinking about specific *contrasts* to the current event. For example, the response of "holding out" customers would stimulate a concern with the reverse situation (e.g., "taking latecomers in during a performance") and, hence, would suggest looking for observations describing how this would have to be managed.

While many of the codes used here involve members' concerns and terms, we also see attention to members' meanings in the code "latecomer claims exemption." This code tries to capture the actual distinction that this audience member advances in trying to get back in to see the performance—that some people arrived after the show had begun, but he had arrived before, had left temporarily, and was now trying to reenter, and, therefore, was "not late" and should be treated differently than those in the first category. In the staff response, we see the practical irrelevance of this distinction; to the staff, what presumably matters are not considerations of justice and fairness (such that "real latecomers" should be treated differently from those who had to leave momentarily and, hence, were returning) but the disruption that would be caused by anyone entering at this time.

Through an initial line-by-line reading of her fieldnotes, this student began to clarify the socially ordered work activities of an usher for dance audiences. As she continues through her notes, asking the question, "What are the processes by which the ushers accomplish their work?" she will generate more codes; some will be further instances or elaborations of earlier codes, while others will suggest entirely different themes and lines of analysis. Having a code "waiters: irate," for example, implies that becoming irate is only one response in the general category of audience responses and suggests the possibility of looking for others. She could also wonder: This goes on here, but does it always to on? What are the conditions under which it occurs?

Similarly, the student may identify an order or natural sequence of events or stages that make up the larger activity. She can further develop themes along these lines by continuing to look for expected or routine events that are problematic at each stage and the kinds of skills and practices used to respond to them. For example, the strategies noted in the codes—"keeping [customers] occupied," "distracting," and "smiling"—suggest that she look for further instances to illustrate the general issue of ways that ushers manage, respond, control, or cope with different types of audience members.

In conclusion, this illustration reveals some of the distinctive qualities of open coding. While quantitative coding aims for reliability—different coders should categorize the same data in the same ways—different ethnographers will code the same set of fieldnotes differently. Disciplinary background and interests, in particular, will exert a deep influence on analytic coding: Anthropologists working with the concept of culture, for example, might formulate different analytic categories than folklorists interested in performance and the dynamics of performer-audience interaction. Theoretical differences within a discipline may produce almost as marked variations in coding. For example, two sociological field researchers studying households might well write and code their fieldnotes quite differently (even, we would argue, were they to carry out their studies in the same setting); one might focus her coding on household relations and the division of labor occurring in the context of particular economic policies, while the other might examine women's invisible work in families. In sum, there is no single, correct way to code fieldnotes inasmuch as ethnographers ultimately decide which, among a number of possible patterns and ideas, including member concerns and interests, to choose as a focus.

Open Coding as Process

While it is often useful to begin coding by focusing on a term in the notes—whether the fieldworker's or a member's—the fieldworker seeks to transform that term so that it references a more general category. Yet, at the other extreme, it is not useful to use overly general categories as codes. For example, it would not be helpful to code as "social control" staff procedures for searching residents' rooms for "buzzes" and other contraband in a reform school. This category is too general and without specific connection to the events and practices described in the notes. But, a code like "staff control—room searches" would categorize these staff activities as a specific kind of control and perhaps stimulate the field researcher to think about and identify other forms of "staff control."

In open coding, the ethnographer also seeks to generate as many codes as possible, at least initially, without considering possible relevance either to established concepts in one's discipline or to a primary theoretical focus for analyzing and organizing them. In particular, code categories should not be avoided because they do not fit with the fieldworker's initial "focus"; this focus will change as he moves through the notes. Rather, all ideas and concepts that can be linked to, or generated from, specific fieldnotes should be treated as being of possible interest and should be framed and expressed as clearly and explicitly as possible. Hence, any particular code category need not necessarily connect with other codings or with other field data; integrating categories can come later, and one should not ignore or disregard codings because they suggest no obvious prospects for integration within a major focus or with other emerging categories.

To illustrate these processes, consider the following open coding of an incident from a support group for those taking care of family members afflicted with Alzheimer's disease:

trouble: memory loss;	Lucie says her husband is in good health, but his
bad driving	symptoms include memory loss and poor and dan-
dr does not "help"	gerous driving. The doctor does nothing to stop
asks advice	him from driving. She asks, "What does everyone
	else think?" Some other members say, "Change

fam pressures dr

med test → no results

doctors." Lucie explains the doctor is a friend of the family. Her son has stressed to the doctor that his father's driving is dangerous, and they could be legally involved. The doctor has done a catscan, but there is no direction from that.

advice: be active
cger to DMV

no med dx prevents action

Pat, the group leader, recommends, "Take it into your own hands." She suggests that Lucie go to the DMV. Lou says she thinks there is a new law that states anyone with a mental deficiency, including Alzheimer's disease, is not supposed to drive. Lucie says, "But I don't have a name on it—that's what hinders action. I am so frustrated."

advice: coalition w/dr

practical remedy: deception

proposed remedy will not work

"talking to"

Vie says, "Isn't it important for the doctor to tell him not to drive?" Lucie says, "Why won't he do that? Maybe he's too close, and he doesn't want to get involved." Lou: "What about Nicholson? He's a geriatric psychiatrist." Others suggest that she hide the car keys. Joey says, "You need to lie to him." Lucie says, "I must say, I have been doing that." Joey says, "We all have." . . . Lucie says in terms of the car keys, he knows there is a second set. Another woman says she talked with her husband, and he doesn't drive anymore. "I've done this. It is not working." Someone says, "You need a good diagnosis from a medical doctor." Lucie: "That's what I think." Others in the group agree.

Through these marginal codes, the fieldworker has identified a variety of loosely related (or even unrelated) issues:

- driving by Alzheimer's patients may be dangerous; family caregivers may have to actively manage those who insist on continuing to drive;
- medical diagnoses may play a critical role in caregivers' efforts to manage patient activities;
- caregivers may experience frustration with doctors who fail to be sensitive to and support family concerns;
- support group members may suggest ways of getting around obstacles presented by doctors; and
- support group members may recommend various practical responses that will prevent the person with Alzheimer's from driving.

Some of these codes reflect issues that the field researcher was interested in from the start: practical "troubles" and how people respond to or "remedy" such troubles (see Emerson 2008; Emerson and Messinger 1977). But many of these codes elaborate or specify a prior concept in original and unanticipated ways, for example, "hiding the keys" as a practical response to prevent dangerous driving. Other codes identify issues that are entirely unexpected, for example, doctors as both barriers and possible allies in handling unfit drivers.

By the time the ethnographer finishes reading the complete set of field-notes, her categories and themes will have fundamentally changed. And many of those initial categories will be dropped, in turn, as the researcher becomes more focused and aware of other, more interesting and recurrent, issues. Furthermore, the process of generating codes may help to clarify the meaning or import of previous as well as upcoming notes, for coding shapes and may alter the fieldworker's sense of what the notes "contained" in the first place. As one student commented: "You feel you know your notes because you wrote them, but the thing is, you wrote them so long ago that it doesn't click."

Many students report that the evolving, seemingly unending character of coding initially proved discouraging and upsetting:

> The coding process, it happened once, and then it happened again. I ended up coding again and again and again. . . . I had to get over the fact that I would do it the wrong way, or I wouldn't really find any good categories or things wouldn't relate to one another. I had to get over the fear of thinking that there was nothing there.

Coding is indeed uncertain, since it is a matter, not simply of "discovering" what is in the data, but, more creatively, of linking up specific events and observations to more general analytic categories and issues. Although researchers inevitably draw on concepts from their particular disciplines to develop linkages, coding keeps them focused on, and anchored in, their data. This often means that the researcher is already familiar with the key concepts and interests of her discipline and quickly sees how a given piece of data is relevant to them; but at other times, the researcher may have to turn to specific writings that she has not previously read to find pertinent concepts. With time, practice, and wider exposure within a discipline, the researcher gains confidence that she can make analytic connections, and coding becomes less threatening and uncertain.

This open-ended approach can lead to anxiety on several different levels, and some students fear they may never come up with a specific focus for a paper. Others, finding line-by-line coding time consuming and tedious, want to focus on a smaller number of themes in order to move ahead quickly without a lot of "wasted" effort. Still others express concern over a procedure that, in seeking to generate so many different codes, contradicts what they have been taught about "logical" (i.e., carefully planned in advance) thinking and writing. Consider the comments of two students:

> I didn't have any categories before I began. I just was looking at the notes and jotting down codes, but it didn't seem that I was going about it in a very logical way.

> I went through two or three sets of notes and there were so many random, recurring themes and not anything that was organized.

But the fact that fieldnotes seem unwieldy, with codings leading in many different directions, is actually a good thing at this stage; such codings will suggest a myriad of possible issues and directions. Especially early on in the process of open coding, we recommend resisting these inclinations to focus only on specific themes and topics while continuing to go through the fieldnote record and generating additional codes.

Yet, we have also found that continuous open coding can generate a great deal of frustration as ideas begin to coalesce; continuous open coding may actually discourage developing a specific focus when it would be possible and useful to do so. Thus, a strategy of *selective* open coding, in which the fieldworker uses these procedures at different times and with discrete sets of fieldnotes, may therefore be advisable. For example, one may begin with systematic open coding but then, after going through a significant portion of their fieldnotes, code remaining notes and recode previously coded notes selectively, focusing on "key," "rich," or "revealing" incidents.

WRITING CODE MEMOS

Inspired by coding fieldnotes and by rereading in-process memos, the fieldworker begins to develop, preserve, and elaborate these ideas by writing theoretical *code memos* (Strauss and Corbin 1990). While the fieldworker should try to read and code all fieldnotes, he may turn from the coding to writing memos at any time, seeking to get ideas and insights down on paper when they occur. He may also reread in-process memos, abandoning some, while revising and elaborating others in light of subsequent observations and the insights generated by coding. We encourage writing memos about as many ideas, issues, and leads as possible. While some of these ideas reflect concerns and insights that the fieldworker brings to the reading, others grow out of reengaging the scenes and events described in the fieldnotes.

One use of a code memo is to identify and write about core processes that characterize talk and interaction in a particular setting. In the following memo, a fieldworker in a residential treatment program for ex-prostitutes gradually realized that the women involved usually characterized their problem, not as prostitution, but, rather, as drug addiction. She then organized this memo around talk by one resident that illustrated this typical priority placed on overcoming drug problems:

> Admission to the program rests on the women's outside identities as street prostitutes; however, the identity that is presented at the foreground of their recovery program is that of drug addicts. When discussing the bad behavior and the deviant identities that resulted in their placement at the house, the women present their addictions, that is, their identity as addicts, at the forefront. The following interaction is between Melinda, a twenty-one year old resident, and me, the ethnographer.
>
>> I nod my head in response and Melinda says, "I'm glad to be sober, I'm happy now, and I don't want to use anymore. But for me, the first thirty days were easier than the second seem to be." She looks down at the floor and says, "I used to wake up and be pissed off and depressed and need to use. I'd use just so that I could get through the day, through the shit . . . just to get through a day at work." She laughs and says with a grimace, "I used to want to get high so bad that I'd make excuses to my pimp, I used to tell him that it was a slow day, just so I could get high."
>
> Melinda expresses her gratitude for the program by expressing a positive opinion of sobriety, and, indirectly, proposes that her role as a prostitute was secondary to her desire to acquire and use drugs. Melinda places the primacy of the drug problem over prostitution when she says, "I used to want to get high so bad that I'd make excuses to my pimp." We see here how Melinda mentions prostitution as a behavior secondary to her desire to use. In this way, Melinda situates her identity as an addict at the forefront of her previous lifestyle. She also states, "Before, when I'd see my mom, I'd be high, and this was the first time I wasn't high." Her roles as daughter and as prostitute are placed secondary to her identity as an addict.
>
> Also, Melinda's current identity at the house revolves around her participation in the role of an addict. She states: "I'm glad to be sober . . . But for me

the first thirty days were easier than the second seem to be." We see here how her time at the house, or time "in recovery," is not relative to when she stopped hooking (which we will find out had ceased a month earlier than her drug dependency); rather, it is based on her "days sober." . . .

Finally, Melinda continues to identify herself as an addict, or that drugs are still problematic, when she says, "the first thirty days were easier than the second seem to be." She is in her second month of "recovery" and is therefore emphasizing that her addiction to drugs is a continuing struggle. Therefore, we see that the identity of an addict is built and presented as the most important and problematic character "defect" the women in the house are struggling with.

Note the limited intent of this analytic memo: It looks in detail at one piece of talk to establish the various ways in which a resident emphasizes her identity as an addict rather than as a prostitute. Although the ethnographer presents this as a common pattern among residents of the program, she makes no effort here to provide evidence for this general claim, to examine "exceptions," namely, women who do identify as having been prostitutes, special circumstances in which women will emphasize prostitution rather than drug use, and so on. Furthermore, she makes no effort to locate either general reasons for why this preference for addict rather than hooker identity occurs, or its broader implications for outcomes and resident fates in this or other programs.

Ethnographers also write initial memos to try to identify and explore a general pattern or theme that cuts across a number of disparate incidents or events. Along these lines, consider the following memo from a study of support and interaction among courtroom personnel (clerks, recorder, bailiff) that explores patterns of "sustaining community and insideness" in courtroom proceedings:

Examples of "sustaining community and insideness" tend to occur during dead time (recess) on easy days with little business and also after session ends for the day. . . . For example, after today's session, all of the participants except the judge, who always leaves, were actively looking for interactions. Their methods included making eye contact with each other, walking toward each other, making jokes, and interrupting conversations. In this way, information could be shared, and opinions could be aired.

This category can be distinguished from idle chatter during recess by the involvement of the participants in the events. High involvement equals community and insideness; low involvement, which is evidenced by briefness of interaction and lack of emotion and eye contact, equals idle chatter.

Here, the field researcher identifies a regular pattern of more intense, animated talk and action between courtroom workers that she contrasts with other occasions of less engaging interaction ("idle chatter"). In her memo, she offers some initial observations on *when* this pattern of relating occurs (during recesses, on slow court days, etc.) as well as on *what* it involves (actively seeking out others, joking, etc.).

In sum, initial coding and memoing require the ethnographer to step back from the field setting to identify, develop, and modify broader analytic themes and arguments. Early on, these efforts should remain flexible and open as the ethnographer reads, codes, and analyzes fieldnotes to foster a wide range of new ideas, linkages, and connections. Eventually, however, the ethnographer will move beyond these open, inclusive procedures to pursue focused, analytic themes more intensively. Initially, this narrowing and focusing process involves selecting a small number of core themes that the researcher will subsequently pursue through focused coding and integrative memoing.

SELECTING THEMES

Through initial coding and memoing, the ethnographer identifies many more ideas and themes than he will actually be able to pursue in one paper or monograph. Hence, he must decide which ideas to explore further and which to put on the back burner, at least for the moment.

Field researchers have different ways of selecting core themes. The ethnographer might begin by coding fieldnotes for themes and topics that she has already identified and begun to develop in writing in-process memos. During open coding, the ethnographer can elaborate, deepen, and refine or discard themes developed at earlier points in time. But, because she is not bound by previous preliminary analysis, open coding provides the opportunity for developing new themes and insights as she views the entire corpus of her notes through fresh eyes. One consideration is to give priority to topics for which a substantial amount of data has been collected and which reflect recurrent or underlying patterns of activities in the setting under study. Fieldworkers might also give priority to what seems significant to members, whether it is what they think is key, what looks to be practically important, or what engages a lot of their time and energy. For example, one student who wrote fieldnotes while an intern at a county probation office described the following process:

> I was going through [the notes] and kept thinking of things like we have all this paperwork to do, and people have to sign this, and I started to get the sense of this larger issue—how is the department dealing with so much paperwork? And as I went through it, I found, "Oh, well, a lot of times we help each other out." One probation officer will say, I saw your client yesterday on the Commons; that will count as a collateral contact (a kind of contact that must be noted in the paperwork) for you because I saw him. There are shortcuts that way. There are summary reports called "quarterlies" that summarize basically three or four months' worth of work into one sheet. So three or four things like that are subtopics of this larger issue.

In going through her notes, this student began to notice the different tasks that probation officers must accomplish with a sensitivity to the conditions and constraints that accompany the work. Looking at what probation officers actually did amid the practical constraints and opportunities offered by other agencies—police, clinics, and so on—provided a frame for drawing together what had initially seemed like discrete tasks. Discovering additional themes of this sort provided a guide to reading and coding the rest of her notes.

The fieldworker must also consider how a selected theme can be related to other apparent themes. A theme that allows the researcher to make linkages to other issues noted in the data is particularly promising. Finding new ways of linking themes together allows for the possibility that some of the themes that might have been seen as unrelated and possibly dropped can, in fact, be reincorporated as "subthemes" under more general thematic categories.

In the process of identifying promising themes and trying to work out possible linkages, the fieldworker might, for the moment, lose a sense of focus and have to rework ideas until she can reclarify matters. A student who studied the band at a public high school started coding with a good sense of what her paper would be about only to find her direction changed. She reflected on these processes in an interview:

> I first thought I would explain how, in the face of budget cuts, somebody could keep a program, an extracurricular program like this, going. And then in listing the ways that the teacher does that, I came across the idea that he has to do things to get all of these kids to be friends together. And then I thought, wait a minute, that could be a whole topic of its own. There's so many things going on. How do I explain in my paper the different social cliques with 110 kids—there's so many social cliques? And then I just started looking at the relationships that students have with each other inside band and outside. It

was just the weirdest thing—I lost my paper! The more I coded, the more I lost my paper.

Eventually, this student shifted her focus from the many differences between social cliques to how the teacher kept the program going, both in the face of budgetary cuts and the divisive tendencies of these different cliques. What she initially reported negatively as "having lost her paper" really indicates an openness to new issues and ways of putting things together.

Students engaged in this process often talk about a particular theme "jumping out at them" or, alternatively, of the "focus" for the ethnography "disappearing." This experience is so strong and pervasive that it is important to recall two closely related issues that were touched on previously. First, while the ethnographer often experiences "something going on in the notes," neither the fieldnotes nor their meanings are something "out there" to be engaged after they are written. Rather, as creator of the notes in the first place, the ethnographer has been creating and discovering the meaning of and in the notes all along. Particular sensitivities led to writing about some topics rather than others; these sensitivities may derive from personal commitments and feelings as well as from insights gained from one's discipline and its literature and/or the course instructor. Second, when an ethnographer thinks he has "a substantial amount of data" on a topic, it is not so much because of something inherent in the data; rather, it is because the ethnographer has interpreted, organized, and brought a significant body of data to bear on the topic in particular ways.

Once the ethnographer has identified a set of core themes for further analysis, he might find it useful to sort fieldnotes on the basis of these themes. Here, the fieldworker breaks down the corpus of fieldnotes into smaller, more manageable sets, collecting together, in one place, all those pieces that bear on each core issue. This sorting or retrieving procedure involves physically grouping segments of the data on a theme in order to more easily explore their meanings. Sorting into one place or pile facilitates analysis by concentrating fieldnotes relevant to an emerging issue.[6]

In sorting fieldnotes, it is advisable to use themes that are inclusive, allowing for notes that may have been identified with different but related codes to be grouped together. For example, in the study of family caregiving for persons with Alzheimer's disease, the researcher decided upon *management practices* as a core theme based on her extensive open coding. Management practices included any actions that caregivers took to manage and control the patients' circumstances and behaviors. This category was intentionally inclusive, and it allowed the researcher to incorporate fieldnotes given widely varying codes, including incessant monitoring of the patient; warning or "talking to" the patient; and deliberately deceiving the patient in order to manage troublesome behavior. The analysis at this stage is still preliminary, and the meaning and significance of any fieldnote is open to further specification and even fundamental reinterpretation. For this reason, the ethnographer should feel free to include any particular fieldnote excerpt in multiple categories.

Sorting requires physical movement of data excerpts in ways that alter the narrative sequence of the fieldnotes. In the past, fieldworkers often cut up a copy of their fieldnotes and sorted the pieces into piles that would then be repeatedly rearranged as the analysis proceeded. Word processing and programs specifically designed for processing qualitative data can now perform the sort function very quickly and efficiently, although some fieldworkers still prefer the flexibility that an overview of fieldnotes spread out on a table or the floor affords. We strongly recommend that in using either method, the ethnographer keep a computer copy, (with a backup) and possibly an intact, hard copy, of the original notes for later reference.

FOCUSED CODING

Having decided on core themes, and perhaps having sorted the fieldnotes accordingly, the ethnographer next turns to focused coding that is a fine-grained, line-by-line analysis of selected notes. This involves building up and, in some cases, further elaborating analytically interesting themes, both by connecting data that initially may not have appeared to go together and by further delineating subthemes and subtopics that distinguish differences and variations within the broader topic.

As an example, the fieldworker whose research focused on caregivers looking after family members with Alzheimer's disease became aware of the *stigma* frequently attached to the latter's condition and behavior. Sorting all fieldnotes on stigma (broadly conceived) into one long document, she then reread and recoded all these materials, and, in the process developed a series of subthemes of stigma. For example, she distinguished "passing" (efforts to prevent the stigma from becoming publicly visible) from "covering" (efforts to cover up, normalize, or distract attention from visible stigmatizing behavior). She also recognized and coded for situations in which the caregiver cooperated with the person with Alzheimer's to manage stigma and for situations in which the caregiver entered into some kind of "collusion" with others to apologize for or manage the stigmatizing incident and its social effects.[7] In focused coding, the researcher constantly makes comparisons between incidents, identifying examples that are comparable on one dimension or that differ on some dimension and, hence, constitute contrasting cases or variations. When the ethnographer identifies such variation, he asks how the instance differs and attempts to identify the conditions under which these variations occur.

By breaking down fieldnotes even more finely into *subcodes*, the ethnographer discovers new themes and topics and new relationships between them. The same openness to new ways to understand and fit pieces of data together that we encouraged earlier applies to focused coding as well. In some cases, this process generates new issues or opens up new topics that carry the analysis in an entirely different direction and may even require a rethinking and regrouping of the fieldnotes. One student ethnographer engaged in this process reported:

> You're both discovering and creating the pattern as you create the pieces— the initial codes—and these begin to structure and frame what the other pieces are going to be and how they will fit together. You have one note and you say to yourself, "Oh, this note seems to fit and be similar to the first note, but it's slightly different, and that's what I mean by variation. But somehow, they seem to follow one another." Then you continue and read, and maybe 15 pages later, there's something that seems like it follows or fits. You begin to find pieces that fit together in some kind of way. Don't worry how they all fit in the total paper, just keep fitting them together even if you don't have the connections between them. The aim is to identify what is going on irrespective of whether you will use it later on.

Another student, initially overwhelmed by the number of preliminary codes, said, "I felt that there were so many codes that it wasn't very logical." But she persevered until she could begin to see that there was more to discover in the notes: "I did see that within the more general codes I could see how that once I cut them up, I could separate them out into smaller subgroups. What I need to do is do them again." Through the process of focused coding, the ethnographer begins to recognize a pattern in what initially looks like a mass of confusing data. With focused coding, the ethnographer may also begin to envision possible ways of making an argument or telling a story about some aspect of the lives of people in the setting.

Students often express concern when they have only one example of a particular kind of incident or issue. They are concerned that writing about just one instance may distort their analysis if it reflects the response of only a few of those in the setting. Finding only one example would be a problem if the field researcher's purpose were to make claims about frequency or representativeness. But frequency is only one dimension for analysis. While the researcher delights in numerous examples of a theme or topic, the goal in ethnographic analysis is not representativeness. Rather, the ethnographer seeks to identify patterns and variations in relationships and in the ways that members understand and respond to conditions and contingencies in the social setting. That there is "only one case" often does not matter.[8] But, when the ethnographer is fortunate enough to find more than one instance, it is important to note how they are the same and how they vary. Useful questions to keep in mind at this point include the following: What are the similarities and differences between these instances? What were the conditions under which differences and variations occurred?

INTEGRATIVE MEMOS

As the ethnographer turns increasingly from data gathering to the analysis of fieldnotes, writing integrative memos that elaborate ideas and begin to link or tie codes and bits of data together becomes absolutely critical. One approach to writing integrative memos is to explore relationships between coded fieldnotes that link together a variety of discrete observations to provide a more sustained examination of a theme or issue. Alternatively, the ethnographer may reorganize and revise previously written in-process and code memos, identifying a theme or issue that cuts across a number of these memos and pulling together relevant materials.

At this point, many ethnographers continue to write primarily for themselves, focusing on putting the flow of their thoughts on paper and maintaining the loose, "note this" and "observe that" style characteristic of several of the memos we have considered to this point. Others, however, find it useful to begin to write with future audiences explicitly in mind. For these researchers, integrative memos provide a first occasion to begin to explicate contextual and background information that a reader who is unfamiliar with the setting would need to know in order to follow the key ideas and claims. Imagining this future readership within a particular discipline spurs the ethnographer to write in a more public voice, that is, to word ideas in concepts and language that approximate the analytic writing in a final text. This becomes a first attempt to formulate a cohesive idea in ways that would organize a section of the final ethnography (see the discussion in chapter 7). Thus, such memos sound more polished than earlier memos.

Substantively, integrative memos may move through a series of fieldnote incidents, linking these incidents by connecting sentences. We examine the following extended memo on "remedial covering" by family members caring for persons with Alzheimer's disease to illustrate these processes:

> Remedial covering involves attempts to correct the troublesome behavior once it has occurred. Caregivers take it upon themselves to watch over the family member and attempt to "smooth over things" in a variety of public places. For example, Laura explains what she does in the presence of friends:
>
>> He may take the cup off the saucer and just put it somewhere else on the table. And I'll say, "I think you'd probably get that cup back over here because it'll get tipped over, and it's easier if you have it close to you like that." . . . I try to smooth over these things.
>
> In a similar case, Carol recounts how Ned embarrasses her by removing his dentures in a restaurant and how she handles this:
>
>> I got up real quick and stood in front of him and said, "Get your teeth in your mouth." Then she explains to me, "I felt I had to protect him. What if the waitress came?"

In this first segment, the ethnographer links two separate incidents occurring in restaurants through the themes of "watching over" and "smoothing over things." In doing so, differences between the incidents—for example, in the first instance, that something untoward is prevented from happening, while in the second, the untoward action has occurred but is literally "covered" and then corrected—are subordinated to these commonalities.

The researcher then takes up a further dimension of remedial covering, specifying the contrast between covering that relies upon the cooperation of the person with Alzheimer's and covering that is carried out directly by the caregiver:

> Remedial covering involves having to negotiate the individual's cooperation when he or she is capable of doing so. For example, Laura describes her husband in a local restaurant, how she instructs and physically maneuvers him through various eating tasks ("puppeteering," Pollner and McDonald-Wikler 1985) and how he responds. Her description of their interaction gives a real flavor of the minute detail to which the caregiver must attend:

> I'll say, "Now turn around some more so that your legs are under the table, and then move over so that you're in front of the placemat." . . . Then he would set the beer out very perilously near the edge, and I'd move it back. . . . And then I'd have to arrange things . . . he picked up the tortilla, and it wasn't appropriate. And if anybody were watching, they'd say, "Tsk tsk."

While Laura suggests remedial practices to William in the above example, Tess in her situation takes over and attempts to remedy the situation on her own. She describes going to a buffet restaurant with some of her coworkers, where she tries to cover her father's mistakes so the coworkers are less likely to notice:

> Him and I go to buffets all the time . . . and I watch him. I make him go ahead of me so I can fix everything he screws up. He like takes the spoon, puts some cheese on his salad, puts the spoon on his plate. . . . And I grab the spoon and put it back . . . all the employees that I work with are behind me.

Here, the ethnographer sets up a contrast between two different responses to the problematic acts of a person with Alzheimer's. First, she notes Laura's handling of her husband by means of orders; in so doing, she sees and marks a parallel with the concept of "puppeteering" developed in an article she is familiar with.[9] Second, she examines Tess's ways of managing her father by directly "taking over." She then continues by considering the conditions under which one or the other form of remedial covering is likely:

> As the person with Alzheimer's is less and less able to cooperate with the caregiver in these covering practices, the caregiver is forced to take more control of the situation. For example, Carol states, "I'm more ready to be the ultimate authority. . . . This is the way it's going to be done. In other words, take total control."

In composing this memo, then, the writer outlines a progression from milder to more active and restrictive forms of remedial covering that are likely to occur as the disease progresses. She ends by arguing that this progression fundamentally involves increasing control over the behavior of the person with Alzheimer's disease; she quotes a caregiver who talks openly of her need to now "take total control."

In writing analytic, integrative memos of this sort, the central task is to develop theoretical connections between fieldnote excerpts and the conceptual categories they imply. In so doing, the ethnographer confronts difficult analytic choices. One major issue is deciding which theme to make the primary focus, which to include as subthemes, and which to exclude entirely. Let's return to the dilemma of the student who "lost her paper" while focusing and sorting her notes: One strategy was to divide the paper up into different sections, such that the issues of the teacher's strategies for managing the band and of the students' grouping themselves into cliques would be analyzed as topics unto themselves. Another possibility was to see these strategies as different aspects of the more general theme. Here, the paper would have focused on how the teacher managed to keep an extracurricular program going in the face of overwhelming odds—declining resources and a large and heterogeneous group of students. Specific subtopics would have included how he tried to motivate kids to spend extra time on weekends or extra time during the week and how he managed the tensions and different interests between the various student cliques.

Deciding how to frame an analysis often requires taking a step back from the particulars of the analysis in order to answer the question, What is the larger, more encompassing question I am responding to? One student who studied an alternative school, for example, was able, once she clarified the story she wanted to tell, to incorporate themes from the following incident involving negotiations over the use of a chair at an all-school meeting:

> The chair was just sitting there, and I was sitting behind a group of guys who were saving chairs, and this girl took this chair and started to put her feet on it, and the guy says, "Hey, someone's sitting there." She said, "Well, can't I just use it until he comes back?" Then a student teacher comes along, and you can see him eyeing the chair, and he says, "Can I use your foot rest?" She said, "Someone's sitting there." He said, "Well, I'll just use it until he comes back," and then he sits down. But the first guy says, "Excuse me, someone is sitting there." He says, "Well, I'll give it back when he gets back." The student [whose chair it is] comes back and the teacher just got up and left.

The ethnographer saw in this fieldnote ways that the students at the school negotiated with one another and with a student teacher over seating. But, while she found the incident and several like it to be of interest with regard to relations between students and between students and teachers, she struggled with how to link such incidents to a variety of other themes. She decided at this point to step back and attempt to relate the incident more broadly to what she knew and found interesting about the school. She thought, for example, about the pride that both students and teachers at the alternative public school took in the ethic of "democratic decision making" and "shared power." She contrasted this with many more traditional schools where teachers readily exert authority. With the more general issue of this contrast in mind, the student saw that, on some occasions, teachers in the alternative school may not hold or choose to exercise authority but, rather, negotiate or defer to student claims to space. This led the student to see that she could tie negotiating for space to a range of other incidents that were decided in nonauthoritarian ways. She also began to look for contrasts in this theme and, specifically, for examples of matters that were closed to negotiation. By pursuing this line of analysis, the student saw that what initially might have seemed to be an isolated, mundane incident was related to larger questions of power and authority. More fundamentally, finding a frame for this incident helped her not to take teacher and student claims to "democracy" and "power sharing" at face value or as givens but, rather, as achievements that were variously honored in the setting.

Again, there is no single, correct way to organize themes and subthemes. Part of the decision about which course to take depends on the kind of data that has been recorded. In the study of the high school band, very rich and detailed notes on types of students in the school would allow focusing on student cliques. But, if such observations are lacking, cliques must move from the center of the picture and become part of the context or background with something else in the foreground. It is usual for ethnographers to try on, modify, discard, and reconsider several possibilities before deciding which tells the best story. As was the case when writing fieldnotes in the first place, organizational decisions will be influenced by factors that range from how inclusive an organizational scheme is to how well it highlights particular theoretical and substantive interests and preferences.

REFLECTIONS: CREATING THEORY FROM FIELDNOTES

This chapter has developed a grounded, open-ended approach to ethnographic analysis, an approach keyed to the close, systematic consideration of fieldnote data aimed at generating as many ideas, issues, topics, and themes as possible. Rather than proceeding deductively with a theory that explains phenomena and attempting to find instances in the data that illustrate or disprove it, this form of ethnographic analysis shifts through and pieces together fieldnotes into a series of themes and more sustained analytic writings, at all times attending "closely to what happens in the empirical world he or she studies" (Charmaz 2001:337) and to the everyday meanings, underlying assumptions, and practical concerns of those who live and act in these worlds. As analyst, the ethnographer remains open to the varied and sometimes unexpected possibilities, processes, and issues that become apparent as one immerses oneself in the written data.

But this open-ended process does not mean that the fieldworker completely ignores existing theory or has no theoretical commitments prior to reading through the notes. It does suggest, however, that for the ethnographer, theory does not simply await refinement as he tests concepts one by one against events in the social world; nor do data stand apart as independent measures of theoretical adequacy. Rather, the ethnographer's assumptions, interests, and theoretical commitments enter into every phase of writing an ethnography; these commitments influence decisions ranging from which events to write about to which member's perspective to privilege. The process is thus one of reflexive or dialectical interplay between theory and data, whereby theory enters in at every point, shaping not only analysis but also how social events come to be perceived and written up as data in the first place.

Indeed, it is misleading to dichotomize data and theory as two separate and distinct entities, as data are never pure but, rather, are imbued with, and structured by, concepts in the first place. Fieldwork is continuously analytic in character, as fieldnotes are always products of prior interpretive and conceptual decisions and, hence, are ripe with meanings and analytic implications. Thus, the analysis of fieldnotes is not just a matter of finding what the data contain; rather, the ethnographer further selects out some incidents and events from the corpus of fieldnote materials, gives them priority, and comes to understand them in relationship to others. Sometimes these insights seem to "emerge" as the ethnographer reviews her accounts of local events and actions as part of a larger whole. But often ethnographers struggle to find meaningful, coherent analytic themes in their data, only with difficulty coming to take on a more active "ethnographic voice." As one student reflected on her experience:

> At first, I wanted the paper to emerge through the notes in the sense that it had its own story, and I was supposed to tell its story. But I had to make the shift from just wanting to talk about what was in the notes to making something solid out of them—my ideas, instead of thinking that it's hidden somewhere in the notes.

Rather than simply tracing out what the data tell, the fieldworker renders the data meaningful. Analysis is less a matter of something emerging from the data, of simply finding what is there; rather, it is, more fundamentally, a process of creating what is there by constantly thinking about the import of previously recorded events and meanings.

In sum, in many instances of poring over fieldnotes, the ethnographer may experience coming up with theory as a process of "discovery." But theory only *seems* to jump out of the data and hit the researcher in the face. This flash of insight occurs only because of the researcher's prior analytic commitments built into the notes, the theoretical concerns and commitments she brings to the reading, and the connections she made with other "similar events" that were observed and written about. Thus, it is more accurate to say that the ethnographer creates, rather than discovers, theory. She does so, not simply in the culminating moment of reading and reflecting on what she has seen and written about previously, but also throughout that prior process of seeing as she writes fieldnotes.

7

Writing an Ethnography

In moving from fieldnotes to writing ethnographic texts, the ethnographer turns away from local scenes and their participants, from relations formed and personal debts incurred in the field. Now an author working at her desk, she reviews her recordings of members' everyday experiences and reorients to her fieldnotes as texts to be analyzed, interpreted, and selected for inclusion in a document intended for wider audiences. Thus, the dual awareness of members and outside audiences, inherent but often muted in the participant observer role in the field, becomes overt and insistent in writing a polished ethnographic text.

While field researchers may envision different outside audiences, most write for other scholars.[1] Having been trained in a particular discipline (such as sociology, anthropology, or folklore), the field researcher draws upon and develops ideas that make sense within the conceptual language of that discipline. While disciplinary concerns will already have shaped many fieldnote entries, in actually composing ethnographic texts, the researcher self-consciously makes his observations and experiences of particular local scenes speak to the concepts and traditions of a scholarly discipline. The ethnographer as author must *represent* the particular world he has studied (or some slice or quality of it) for readers who lack direct acquaintance with it. To do so, he moves back and forth between specific events recounted in his fieldnotes and more general concepts of interest to his discipline. An excessive concern for a scholarly framework and general concepts would distort and obscure the nuances of everyday life; but to simply present members' categories exclusively in their terms would produce texts devoid of relevance and interest to scholarly audiences.

In this chapter, we present an approach to writing finished ethnographies that seeks to use and balance this tension between analytic propositions and local meanings. Rather than composing a tightly organized analytic argument in which each idea leads logically and exclusively to the next, we advocate writing ethnographies as narrative "tales" (Richardson 1990; Van Maanen 1988). Ethnographies are tales or stories, not in the sense that they are fictional, but in that the writer uses standard literary conventions (Atkinson 1990) to construct from fieldnotes a narrative that will interest an outside audience. Such tales weave specific analyses of discrete pieces of fieldnote data into an overall story. This story is analytically thematized but often in relatively loose ways; it is also fieldnote-centered, that is, constructed out of a series of thematically organized units of fieldnote excerpts and analytic commentary.

We begin the chapter by examining the distinctive sort of ethnographic story we seek to produce—what we call a "thematic narrative." Thematic narratives incorporate several analytic themes or concepts linked by a common topic.[2] We then discuss a series of steps that move progressively toward creating a thematic narrative that is fieldnote-centered. These steps include writing out initial statements of analytic themes, then selecting, explicating, sequencing, and editing fieldnote excerpts in order to build up a series of thematically organized units of excerpts and analytic commentary. Finally, we discuss the writing of introductions and conclusions necessary to produce the completed ethnographic manuscript.[3]

DEVELOPING A THEMATIC NARRATIVE

In coding and memo writing, the ethnographer has started to create and elaborate analytic themes. In writing an ethnographic text, the writer organizes some of these themes into a coherent "story" about life and events in the setting studied. Such a narrative requires selecting only small portions of the total set of fieldnotes and then linking them into a coherent text representing some aspect or slice of the world studied.

Writing a thematic narrative differs fundamentally from writing an analytic argument, both in the process of putting that text together and in the structure of the final text. Structurally, in a text that presents a logical argument, the author sets forth a formal thesis or proposition in the introduction as a stance to be argued, then develops each analytic point with evidence logically following from and clearly supporting the propositional thesis.[4] In contrast, an ethnographic story proceeds through an intellectual examination of evidence to eventually reach its contributing central idea. While a thematic narrative begins by stating a main idea or thesis, it progresses toward fuller elaboration of this idea throughout the paper. Indeed, the more precise, fuller statement of the thesis is often most effectively presented at the end of the story in a conclusion to the paper.

In addition, the structure of an ethnographic story results from an ordered progression of fieldnote excerpts. The details in the fieldnotes stand as the essential kernels of the story. That is, thematic narratives use fieldnotes, not as illustrations and examples of points that have already been made, but, rather, as building blocks for constructing and telling the story in the first place. In this sense, the main idea grows out of the process of coding and selecting excerpts rather than prefiguring the choice of fieldnotes to include. The excerpts in an ethnographic story are not so much evidence for analytic points as they are the core of the story.

In terms of writing processes, developing a thematic narrative requires constant movement back and forth between specific fieldnote incidents and progressively more focused and precise analysis. To facilitate this process, we do not recommend beginning with a tentative thesis or working hypothesis. Instead, we urge the writer to hold off formulating an explicit thesis until the paper is finished, so that even in the process of writing, she will make discoveries about data and continue to balance her analytic insights with the demands of sticking close to indigenous views. We suggest that the ethnographer begin developing a thematic narrative by writing out a statement of a general *topic* or *question*. A topic ties a broad analytic concern or sensitivity to the events that occurred in the setting. For example, "ethnicity as social construction in a high school" and "parental involvement in juvenile court hearings" provide such topic statements.[5] At this early stage, topic statements point to a concern or phenomenon, but they do not pose a specific problem or question or propose a formal thesis or explanation. Rather, a topic or question identifies a more general focus and helps the author to begin tying fieldnotes together into a coherent whole.

In general, the topic of the ethnographic story will incorporate several more specific analytic themes, namely, claims about key patterns, processes, or regularities within the setting. Hence one way to develop a topic is to review earlier codings and memos, identifying a number of the more interesting or relevant themes in one's fieldnotes. At this point, we advise that one write out phrases stating possible themes clearly and explicitly. Initially, the researcher need not be concerned with deciding how these themes relate to one another or with how they might be tied together; the writing is intended simply to clarify and specify themes of possible interest. But once several promising themes have been identified, the ethnographer looks for ways of relating some of these themes to one topic and then decides to drop those themes that cannot be tied to this topic.

Alternatively, the ethnographer may come away from his coding and memo writing with a clear sense of an interesting and unifying general topic. He should write out this topic as explicitly as possible and then attempt to specify more particular themes that might develop that topic by reviewing his codings, memos, and original fieldnotes. For example, having written the phrase, "I will show that parents become involved in court decisions," the student ethnographer studying juvenile court then asked in what different ways parents might become involved in these hearings. On reviewing his codings, he found two distinct patterns, one in which the judge used parents as a source of information about youth and another in which the judge sought to help parents control their children. He then wrote out these two more specific themes: "The judge sometimes uses parental information against the minor in order to sentence him" and "the judge also might support the parents in disciplining the minor and, therefore, threaten punishment."

In either case, the ethnographer will move back and forth between topic and themes, writing an overview statement that relates themes to a topic and to one another and/or develops explicit phrasings for each identified topic. The relations between themes need not be tight and closely reasoned; in thematic narratives, the themes can be loosely integrated. Relating and ordering themes will usually require changes in wording and conceptualization. Clearly, some themes may not "fit" with others, even on these terms, and may have to be dropped. In fact, even after developing an overall plan for a first draft, it is quite common to revise both the specific thematic statements and their interconnections a number of times as work progresses and the ethnographic story begins to take shape.

Consider how one student began to develop a thematic narrative around the general topic "ethnicity as social construction" in a public high school. First, he wrote out an elaboration of his topic: "Through people's interactions 'ethnicity' is constantly being recreated and modified within a situation." Then, he wrote out a number of specific themes or issues that he wanted to deal with. Finally, to present these themes, he worked out the following order for five specific sections of the text—each centered on one theme:

- An overview of some different ways ethnicity is used in schools
- Students refer to and recognize different social and ethnic groups, but the composition of the groups varies
- The use of black ethnicity and the ways black social groups maintain ethnic boundaries
- People who use ethnic aesthetics of other people (whites' use of black styles), in terms of boundary definitions
- Ethnic conflict as a process of generating cultural distinctions

In developing these themes, the ethnographer does more than name different situations; more fundamentally, he points out distinctions and interconnections between related phenomena. For example, the theme of how students talk about and identify "different social and ethnic groups" not only considers a range of ethnic (and social) groups but also deals with the ethnic identities assigned to others. In contrast, the theme addressing how "black social groups maintain ethnic boundaries" will involve examining how group members establish their own ethnic identity. Yet he also suggests important linkages between these phenomena; for example, exploring "whites' uses of black styles" suggests a concern with the blurring and crossing of ethnic boundaries that will elaborate and extend his interest in the maintenance of black ethnic boundaries.

To pick a topic and specific themes, the ethnographer must make choices. Fieldworkers regularly find that they have many more themes than they are able to include in any particular manuscript. The process of developing a story is essentially one of selecting some themes that resonate with personal or disciplinary concerns and that recur in a number of specific fieldnotes. In selecting these themes and the data they make relevant, the ethnographer inevitably ignores other themes and data, at least for this particular manuscript.

In developing a topic and then assembling themes into a story, the ethnographer should make every effort to incorporate multiple voices and perspectives. To do so often requires giving special attention to selecting and framing the topic and subsequent interrelated themes, for how a topic or theme is named and developed can implicitly privilege some voices and perspectives and exclude others. For example, one student studying the relations between domestic workers and their employers initially identified "hiring" as one topic in her ethnography. But "hiring" frames events from the point of view of the employer, highlighting and privileging her concerns with finding a worker who is "reliable" and "trustworthy." "Hiring" implicitly neglects the domestic worker and her practices for "getting hired" or "finding work." A more relational framing—for example, "the hiring situation"—would incorporate the perspectives of both employer and domestic worker.

In the following sections, we present ways of turning fieldnotes into ethnographic texts. While recognizing that the initial commitment to a general topic and several initial themes informs this process, we emphasize how the ethnographer elaborates, specifies, and excerpts fieldnotes—which may be only loosely associated with a common theme—in order to develop a finished ethnographic story.

TRANSPOSING FIELDNOTES INTO ETHNOGRAPHIC TEXT

Atkinson (1990:103) argues that the "persuasive force" of an ethnographic text derives from the "interplay of concrete exemplification and discursive commentary." We are explicitly concerned with producing such *fieldnote-centered texts*—stories that stay close to, and are highly saturated with, bits and pieces of fieldnotes. To create such a text, the ethnographer must conceptualize the relevance of local happenings so that they relate to analytic issues; but simultaneously, the ethnographer must remain sensitive to how these reframings might distort the meaning of member categories.

To begin this process, the fieldworker must return to the fieldnotes that inspired the story to look for potential excerpts that could develop a story line. The ethnographer first identifies pieces of fieldnote data and then writes interpretive commentary about these excerpts; she also edits each excerpt and commentary unit so that the analysis elaborates and highlights the fieldnotes that are the kernels of the story. Finally, the researcher must organize these excerpt-commentary segments into coherent sections of the ethnography; that is, she orders them in a sequence that creates a compelling story line that leads readers to an ever fuller understanding of the people and issues addressed.

Selecting Fieldnote Excerpts

With a topic involving a number of themes in mind, the field researcher can return to the set of coded fieldnotes to identify the particular ones most relevant to key issues. He returns to these sorted notes, creating fieldnote *excerpts* that will comprise the building blocks of the emerging ethnographic story. We suggest several guidelines for deciding which fieldnotes to excerpt.

Selecting fieldnote excerpts is not a simple matter of "picking the most interesting examples." Rather, the ethnographer has a variety of reasons for deciding which fieldnotes to include in the final text. In introducing a setting, for example, a field researcher may select fieldnotes because they aptly illustrate recurring patterns of behavior or typical situations in that setting. Similarly, a field researcher may choose fieldnotes recounting commonplace happenings or concerns. These excerpts may introduce more specific analytic themes or identify significant variations from what is usual.

The ethnographer also selects fieldnotes for their evocative and persuasive qualities. An excerpt may appeal because it portrays a rare or moving moment—someone expressing deep anguish or two people in a poignant exchange. Or a fieldnote description may seem likely to engage and persuade readers by enabling them to envision scenes, hear voices, and identify momentarily with the ethnographer's perspective on the action. In general, excerpts that contain close-up, vivid descriptions that portray actions and voices will situate readers in the scene; such excerpts will often enable readers to imagine and vicariously experience what the researcher observed. In contrast, a "skimpy" excerpt lacking vivid details fails to persuade because it relies more on the author's interpretation than on sights and sounds readers can visualize or hear. In addition, excerpts that report naturally occurring dialogue often persuasively reveal members' concerns. Through hearing people respond to each other in a conversation, readers can infer their interpretations of each other's words. Through such a dialogue excerpt, an ethnographer presents the negotiated quality of interactions—hence revealing a process rather than just an outcome. A perceptive author, therefore, looks for excerpts—especially those rich in talk and action—that reveal members' different views and concerns as well as consequential moments in interactions.

In selecting evocative excerpts, the ethnographer does not need to have a precise analytic idea in mind. But in most cases, she will come to discern analytic significance in such excerpts. An ethnographer trusts her own intuitive sense that a particular written account is revealing, even if, at the moment, she cannot clearly articulate why this might be so. Continuing reflection on how and why an excerpt is evocative, moving, or telling may ultimately lead to a new appreciation and a deeper, more insightful story.

When constructing a thematic narrative, the ethnographer also specifi-cally seeks excerpts that illustrate concepts and suggest ways of elaborating or specifying these concepts. Finding and selecting excerpts clarifies and gives content to the emerging story. As ethnographers find and review new excerpts, they further clarify ideas, and, in turn, consider additional excerpts they had initially ignored. Often, these insights happen spontaneously: As they clarify a theme or concept, a related instance recorded elsewhere in the fieldnotes comes to mind ("I remember another instance of that!") because it ties in analytically. And on finding and reviewing that data, the ethnogra-pher may further modify the core idea. He looks again in his fieldnotes and memos for other excerpts that he may now see as relevant.[6]

A critical starting place, then, may lie in those fieldnote bits that touched off particular codings and memo writing on themes of current interest. It is important to review these previously thematized fieldnote accounts (and to related coding and memos) and to revise and excerpt those that are relevant. For example, a research project on women applying for domestic violence restraining orders focused on the role of a friend or supporter in facilitating this process. The following fieldnote played a pivotal role in helping the eth-nographer to recognize key dimensions in this process:

> Julie Peters was my fifth client. She was a 24-year-old Caucasian, married to a Caucasian cop. He had never hit her but held a gun to her face and strangled her at one point and constantly abused her verbally. Julie had brought in her friend, Tina, who did most of the talking for her. I could tell that Julie was very quiet and preoccupied. Tina said that Julie was really "messed up" and was los-ing her hair, literally.
>
>> Julie: I just don't want my husband to lose his job. He's a cop, you know.
>> Interviewer: I know you're worried about him, but let's worry about him later. First, let's take care of you.
>> Julie: I know, you're right.
>> Tina: It took a lot for her to come in. I had to drag her in. She called me this morning, crying, and I said, "That's it, we're going in."

This friend's account of getting the wife to come in for a restraining order against her husband typified a process whereby a supporter pushed a "vic-tim" to seek legal remedy. Resonating with fieldnotes related to friends' ac-tive participation in the application for the restraining order, this fieldnote crystallized an appreciation of "third-person support" in legal and other bu-reaucratic encounters.

In general, an excerpt may jog the memory, suggesting other "similar" instances or events and, hence, provide a starting place for collecting a body of excerpts bearing on a common theme. Or, the ethnographer may begin to systematically review codings and fieldnotes, looking for excerpts of that "same thing." One might then note a common pattern or regularity captured in the mass of fieldnote data. In a study of probation progress hearings in juvenile court, for example, a field researcher observed that judges regularly solicited parents' views about their children's behavior, as in the following instance:

> Judge Smith answers [the minor] with a quiet but sharp tone: "I told you to get good grades. . . . You haven't been getting good grades. . . . I also told you to be obedient to your mother." He then asks the mother: "Has he been obedient or disobedient?" "Disobedient. He doesn't go to school when I tell him to go . . ." she answers while looking at her son.

By collecting a number of such instances, the ethnographer can see nuances within a theme and refine his interpretations of particular excerpts.

To do so, an ethnographer may begin to address issues of the *differences* between instances she has observed and written about. In the first place, she can look for *variations within the theme or pattern* seen in different fieldnotes. For example, in studying the role of friends and supporters in interviews applying for a domestic violence restraining order, one might first look for instances in which the supporter becomes actively involved in the interview and, second, in which the supporter says little and plays a secondary role. Similarly, one might look for excerpts showing differences in how parents respond to judges' questions about their children's misconduct. Thus, the ethnographer could juxtapose the excerpt in which the youth's mother reported that her son had been "disobedient" to the following one in which the mother supports her daughter—at least to some degree—by minimizing reports of misconduct:

> A young girl sits down to the left of her attorney. The mother sits down in the back of the room in a chair closest to the entrance. Judge Smith asks the mother directly how the girl is doing. She comments that she has no problem at home "with her" but that school is "a problem."

Considering variations within a context of similarity helps the field researcher pursue further comparisons and, thus, make additional excerpts relevant.

In the second place, the ethnographer can select additional excerpts that involve more profound differences. Here, he looks for instances that *contrast with the previously discovered pattern.* In juvenile court probation hearings, for example, an ethnographer might select an excerpt in which the judge does *not* ask the parent for her view of her offspring's misconduct. Such excerpts begin to reveal the circumstances that shape and limit the previously noted pattern of interaction in the first place. In the juvenile court setting, this may occur in cases in which the parent has been discredited in some way or when incarcerating the youth is a foregone conclusion.

In this process, the ethnographer should actually write out all of the key dimensions, patterns, or distinctions. While the phrase or word that coded an excerpt implies an idea, an author's thinking often remains fuzzy until she actually writes it out in a sentence. In writing out ideas, she continues mulling over her interpretations. Ultimately, she will hone tentative ideas into more clearly articulated propositions in a final paper. But at this stage, she tries to fully explore variations in, and exceptions to, the theme she is investigating. She aims for textured richness and flow, rather than logical tightness, and leaves precise formulations and wordings to be worked out later.

Throughout this process, an ethnographer continually refines her overall sense of the emerging ethnographic paper. Often, a main idea for the ethnography becomes clear to her quite early—while determining a topic or identifying themes during coding. Other ethnographers clarify the main ideas while selecting excerpts. For still others, the central idea comes into focus with the start of writing commentaries on the selected excerpts. And many ethnographers only finally settle on the exact focus and wording of a thesis statement when writing an introduction. In the meantime, by writing out a tentative statement of the central idea, the ethnographer begins to shape the paper's overall focus and sense of what this ethnographic story will tell. But this tentative, central idea—not yet a controlling thesis statement—often changes during the process of explicating fieldnotes and revising sections of the paper. Some beginning ethnographers are uncomfortable with this ambiguous, shifting nature of deciding on the central focus of the ethnography. But, it is important to know that this uncertainty is an important, even necessary, aspect of the analytic process, and that with persistence, the ethnographer will clarify the focus of her paper.

Options for Explicating Fieldnotes

With a story in mind and a series of fieldnote excerpts and memos in hand, the ethnographer next begins composing more elaborated analytic commentaries that explicate each excerpt and link it to others. Proceeding in this manner—producing a series of written segments combining analytic interpretation with fieldnote excerpts—builds up, piece by piece, a coherent, fieldnote-centered story.

Ethnographers use two different textual strategies for creating and presenting units of fieldnote excerpts and interpretive commentary. An *integrative strategy* weaves together interpretation and excerpt; it produces a text with minimal spatial markings—such as indentation or single spacing of fieldnotes—to indicate where the fieldnote ends and interpretation begins. As an example, consider the following account of one way in which amateur pyrotechnists—people who illegally construct and set off homemade fireworks and related devices—acquire their working materials:

> A second category of high-yield explosives that are obtained primarily by the core pyrotechnist includes such things as dynamite and various liquid and plastic explosives used for both military and industrial purposes. In certain areas, dynamite is reportedly very simple to acquire. I was informed that in a neighboring state, anyone over eighteen years of age with a "respectable purpose" could make an over-the-counter purchase of dynamite. During the study, Arnold, Russell, and Hank made an excursion to that state to buy, among other things, eight sticks of the explosive. As Arnold remarked: "We just said we had a mine south of—that we were working, and the only purpose we had in mind was to set it [the dynamite] off, just like anyone who uses firecrackers—just for the entertainment of it." He further reported that he and the others proceeded to detonate the dynamite in a remote spot to avoid the risk of transporting the explosive across state lines back to their home state.

Here, the ethnographer employs fieldnotes as illustrations or "exemplars" (Atkinson 1990) of a claimed pattern, selecting and reworking them to explicate and document those claims. As a result, fieldnotes and ideas are merged into a single, flowing text written in a single voice. The writer does not mark differences between fieldnotes recorded in the past and present interpretations through textual devices but, rather, indicates this shift through such transitional phrases as "for example" or "a telling episode."

In contrast, an *excerpt strategy* visually marks fieldnote excerpts off from accompanying commentary and interpretation, usually by indenting and/or italicizing the fieldnotes. Consider the following paragraph from an ethnographic section on "the difficulties which autistic clients experience as they attempt to integrate into the community." The author begins the paragraph with the analytic point that neighbors frequently treat them in a "stigmatizing manner." Then, she provides an excerpt to illustrate the point she is making:

> At times, people in the community respond more inclusively to clients, although in a stigmatizing manner. At a local bowling alley, a bartender attempted to accommodate John but patronized him instead:
>
>> I went with John to the bowling alley to get his coffee. John asked the man behind the bar if he could have a "very large coffee." The man gave him a cup of coffee and then, when John went to pay for it, the man handed back the dollar bill and said, "I forgot your birthday last year, Happy Birthday." John put the dollar back into his pocket and said, "Thank you," to the man. When we got back into the car, John said, "It's just my birthday. I'm going to get some things to open up." John continued to repeat these phrases (to "perseverate") until another situation redirected him.
>
> Although the bartender gives John positive social reinforcement, he too treats him in a discriminatory way. John in trying to "fit in" in his community receives a response showing that he remains locked out. The bartender's "special treatment" of John reveals that he views him as "special"—different—deserving of or in need of a break. In the bartender's attempt to do a good deed, he further stigmatizes a person who already has to work hard to attain the minimal entrance he receives into his own community.

Here, the particularized instance clarifies the more analytic statement the author sets forth as the topic sentence. The fieldnote description inclines the reader to be persuaded by her analysis. Then, through analytic commentary following the excerpt, this ethnographer extends her initial point by considering several features of the interaction found in the fieldnote: John's trying to fit in, the bartender's positive reinforcement, and the subtly stigmatizing effect of special treatment.

The fieldnote is easily recognized as an excerpt since it is indented. This visual layout enhances the discursive contrast between descriptive and analytic writing. It also produces distinctly dialogic text since the ethnographer speaks in two different voices—as fieldworker describing the experience depicted in the excerpt and as author now explaining those events to readers.

Furthermore, by visually separating excerpts from commentary, this mode of presentation frames fieldnote excerpts as accounts composed in the past, close to events in the field. In this sense, excerpting shapes up fieldnote bits as "evidence," as what was "originally recorded," standing in contrast to subsequent interpretation. Indeed, through clear-cut excerpts, the ethnographer adopts a stance toward the reader that says, "Here is what I heard and observed, and then here is the sense that I *now* make of it."

Many ethnographers develop a preference for one or the other option and employ it consistently throughout a given text.[7] But it is also possible to use both integrative and excerpt strategies at different places and for different writing purposes. The integrative style promotes a smoother, more thematically focused presentation of field data. It allows the author to convey many ideas in a concise, focused manner, since the writer heavily edits portions of the original fieldnotes that are not germane to the issue or argument at hand. Moreover, an integrative style is particularly suited for presenting longer, continuous fieldnotes: Long, direct quotes from interviews or extended episodes with complicated background circumstances can be recounted as one continuing story.[8] For this reason, this strategy facilitates consistent use of the first person and, hence, encourages more flexible and reflective narrative accounts. Finally, the integrative strategy is also useful for bringing together observations and occurrences scattered in different places in the fieldnote record to create a coherent overview of an issue or pattern.

In contrast, the excerpt strategy preserves earlier descriptions and details without extensive editing, in some sense letting readers see for themselves the "grounds" for analytic and interpretive claims. By textually distinguishing fieldnote and analysis, the excerpt style invites the reader to assess the underpinnings, construction, and authenticity of the interpretations offered. Clearly, this strategy relies heavily upon the rhetorical impact of presenting fieldnote excerpts as "evidence" collected prior to, and perhaps independently of, the eventual interpretation. Finally, the excerpt strategy allows for maximum presentation of unexplicated details and qualities of events observed in the field. For ethnographers need not, and in practice do not, explicate every aspect of the fieldnote excerpts they incorporate into the text. Rather, they often allow the scenes to speak for themselves. Containing more than the ethnographer chooses to discuss and analyze, such excerpts give depth and texture to ethnographic texts. In fact, these unexamined qualities or details contribute to readers' tacit understanding of the scenes or events being described and analyzed. In this strategy, the excerpts evoke as well as convince and, thus, stand out as striking, central, key writing in the ethnographic story.

Despite stylistic and other differences, integrative and excerpt textual strategies share the common goal of interweaving portions of fieldnotes with analytic commentary. In this sense, both involve writing coherent units combining analysis with fieldnote data. We now address the specific writing processes involved in creating excerpt-commentary units.

Creating Excerpt-Commentary Units

To maximize the interplay between analytic idea and excerpt, a fieldnote-centered analytic commentary does a number of things. It focuses attention through an *analytic point,* illustrates and persuades through a *descriptive excerpt* introduced by relevant *orienting information,* and explores and develops ideas through *commentary grounded in the details of the excerpt.* We use the term *excerpt-commentary unit* to characterize this basic component of ethnographic writing. While in some instances all these components can be combined into a single paragraph built around a particular piece of fieldnote data, in others, full explication of the excerpt may require a number of paragraphs. We examine how ethnographers write such units using an excerpt strategy; we would point out, however, that the integrative strategy generally involves only minor variations in the procedure.

Consider the following complete excerpt-commentary unit from an ethnography of a storefront continuation high school for gay and lesbian students. Following a paragraph introducing the theme of the section—students subtly undermine teachers' power and role by "sexualizing" exchanges—the author has presented and interpreted a typical incident of "sexualizing." He then moves to this unit:

analytic point	Furthermore, students sometimes position themselves as more powerful than the staff members by sexualizing the staff members' instructional comments. The
orienting information	following excerpt is between Michael, the tutor, and Mark, a student:
Excerpt	Soon after Michael had left the room, after his exchange with Chris, he came back and looked at Mark and said, "Come with me, Mark." Mark, who at this point was putting some of his belongings in his back pack, had his back turned to Michael and said, "I don't want to come with you." While he said this, he looked up slightly toward Chris and smiled. The others [all students] laughed
analytic commentary	There are several aspects of this excerpt which are of particular importance. First is the sequence in which

the comments occur. The teacher's command, "Come with me," is a function of his authority as a staff member, and Mark's subsequent sexualization is a challenge to this authority. Second, Mark not only refuses his authority command but also, by treating Michael's comment as a sexual proposition which he then turns down, further enhances his status. In essence, Mark had positioned himself as the more powerful of the two "potential partners" by refusing the staff member's "advance." Finally, the fact that this was done in front of the other students greatly affects the consequences of the interaction. When the other students laugh at Mark's comment, they are acknowledging the sexual component of his remark to the point that Michael cannot simply overlook the sexual aspect as he could if they were alone. In other words, the students' laughter makes the sexual component of Mark's comment real and consequential for Michael's role as staff member.

The author begins the segment with his *analytic point*—that students may sexualize staff orders as a way of redefining and resisting them. This statement not only links back to ideas in preceding paragraphs, thus contributing to the theme of the section and to the overall story of the ethnography; it also "instructs" the reader in how the writer intends for him to read and interpret that excerpt by directing attention to certain of its features.

Following the analytic point, the author provides orienting information by writing a short sentence that acts as a bridge to the excerpt. This information identifies the major characters in the scene by name and role. Since the author has already described the physical structure and daily routines of this small school, he can assume that the reader understands that the action takes place in a classroom. He also assumes that the reader can understand the significance of the events that are about to transpire without knowing exactly when during the day this incident occurred or exactly what was involved in the unspecified encounter between the tutor and another student, Chris. In many circumstances, however, the author needs to orient readers explicitly to the context and previous actions of about-to-be-recounted events. Following this orienting sentence, the author presents his *excerpt* in indented form.

Finally, the ethnographer discusses the interaction described in the excerpt in more extended *analytic commentary*, raising three issues relevant to his theme: first, that Mark's remark represented a challenge to the teacher's authority; second, that Mark pulled off this challenge by interactionally reframing the instructor's command as a sexual proposition, playfully transforming their respective roles; and, finally, that other students made up an audience to this exchange, their laughing response confirming and dramatizing the sexualized meaning Mark had offered and making this incident a consequential challenge to Michael's authority.

In analytic commentaries, then, ethnographers tell readers what they want them to see in the fieldnote. It is generally helpful when writing analytic commentaries to consider such questions as the following: What are the implications of the events or talk recounted in the excerpt? What nuances can be teased out and explored? What import does this scene have for the analytic issues addressed in the paper? Indeed, ethnographic writers often develop such commentary by exploring the tension set up between the focused idea and the more textured and complex fieldnote. Rather than just considering outcomes, for example, the writer might examine the negotiated quality of the interactions that lead to a particular outcome (e.g., transforming an order into a sexual proposition; examining the role of other students as audience).

Although ethnographers may have written their fieldnotes in either past or present tense, they usually write their analytic points in the "ethnographic present." This convention portrays the incident recounted in the excerpt as temporal and historical, whereas it presents the analytic commentary as ahistorical and generalizable.[9] Indeed, analysis inevitably generalizes specific individuals, unique interactions, and local events—at least to some extent. But these abstractions never veer too far when commentary stays grounded in fieldnote excerpts. The specificity and interactional dynamics, so vividly clear in the excerpt, temper the generalizability of abstract insights.

In writing an excerpt-commentary unit, the ethnographer must closely examine his writing strategies to check whether idea and description reinforce each other. In a fieldnote-centered ethnography, a creative tension exists between analytic points and illustrative excerpts; the ethnographer tells the story through both excerpt and commentary, and, thus, ideas and descriptive details must support each other. An excerpt should not only further a theme or concept; it should also *convince* the reader that the ethnographer's specific interpretation and more general story are justified. Conversely, the ethnographer should also ensure that the analytic point highlights the details of the excerpt. Often in checking the fit of fieldnote and commentary, the ethnographer must revise the latter to bring it closer to the excerpt. In some instances, this revision so changes the analytic commentary that it becomes irrelevant to the theme of the section; consequently, the entire excerpt-commentary unit may have to be deleted or moved—at least for the moment—until its relevance becomes clear.

A discrepancy between idea and descriptive detail might also arise from tensions between the implicit point of view in the excerpt and that implied by the analytic claim. To be convincing, the perspectives of the analytic point and the description must conform. For example, a student-ethnographer studying a juvenile detention hall wished to focus his ethnographic story on juveniles' responses to staff authority. Yet, consider the following excerpt and the perspective it presents:

> The boys sitting in the dayroom had expressionless faces. One Hispanic boy rested his feet on one of the plastic chairs, and L told him to take his feet off. He took his feet off of the chair, and then L walked down the hallway. When she came back to the control room a few minutes later, she noticed that the boy's feet were back on the chair, and she called him to the control room. He walked in with a grin on his face. She asked why he put his feet back on the chair, and he shrugged and looked at the ground. She then told him that when she tells him what to do, he had better do it. She told him to go and sit down in the dayroom.

Despite an initial focus on "the boys sitting in the dayroom," this excerpt quickly shifts from the point of view of an anonymous observer of the boys' activities to that of the adult probation officer charged with maintaining control in this setting. This staff point of view conflicts with an analytic focus on the activities of the boys and their responses to adult authority.[10]

The fit between fieldnote excerpt and analytic point should be seen as part of the progression of the whole ethnographic story. The author should think not only about writing an analytic point that develops the theme of this section but also about how this excerpt and accompanying commentary will convince through the interplay of fieldnote details and ideas and, therefore, move the story along. In writing excerpt-commentary units, the analytic point does not so much govern the excerpt as it highlights its features; the excerpt itself—as previously constructed—constrains what analytic points the author can now make and how to angle them. In a sense, a thematic narrative progresses through incremental repetition. Each unit both repeats the theme but also, through small increments, adds some further ideas and glimpses of people. The repeated look at the section theme from different angles deepens the reader's understanding.

Finally, the ethnographer should consider the implications of excerpt-commentaries already included in the ethnographic story for any additional such units that might be developed. Indeed, Katz (1988a:142) argues that well-crafted ethnographies possess a "weblike character," allowing readers to use data offered in support of one idea to confirm or disconfirm other ideas. The ethnographic author, aware of these confirming and disconfirming possibilities, should be sensitive to the import of unexamined features of other fieldnote excerpts and analytic commentaries for current theoretical claims.

In sum, the ethnographer does not allow a preexisting theory or thesis to overly determine how fieldnote excerpts are analyzed. Rather, she works back and forth between coding, potential excerpts, and analytic points so that, together, they move the story along. This process implants a creative tension between excerpts and analysis which enhances the story and deepens the reader's understanding of the world it represents.

Editing Excerpts

In writing an excerpt-commentary unit, the ethnographer reconstructs the relevant excerpt. The researcher begins by reviewing the original fieldnote to decide which portions to highlight and move to create a working excerpt. This decision involves making an initial determination about exactly where to start and where to end that excerpt. Generally, leaving in, rather than cutting, a longer fieldnote segment is a prudent policy in making these first cuts since the author can later eliminate portions that prove extraneous.

The ethnographer continues to review and edit these initial excerpts as she elaborates an interpretive commentary. As this process continues, we recommend thoroughly editing an excerpt as part of the process of writing an excerpt-commentary unit. Since the author is immersed in the details of the excerpt and its various analytic possibilities, this moment is an opportune time for assessing which portions of the fieldnote are pertinent to these issues and which are irrelevant. Such close reflection concerning the excerpt may push the researcher to new insights and analytic refinements. In building a complete excerpt-commentary unit, the author often decides to modify his decision about the point at which the excerpt begins and ends, often deciding to make his point more economically by shortening the excerpt and providing background details as orienting information in the prior text.

These editing decisions depend both upon the purposes for including an excerpt (e.g., providing vivid detail) and upon the issues pursued in the analytic commentary. But in editing excerpts, ethnographers also consider a number of more general criteria, including *length, relevance, readability, comprehensibility*, and *anonymity of informants*.

An excerpt should be held to an *appropriate length*. An excerpt should not ramble on endlessly just because the description or talk might be interesting; readers find it difficult to sustain attention and interest through long stretches—that is, pages—of unbroken fieldnotes. If deleting material is not advisable, the ethnographer can break up the initial excerpt into a series of smaller, separate units and write interpretive commentary for each one.

Relevance provides a primary concern in editing fieldnote excerpts. In deciding relevance, the field-worker must weigh both what qualities are vital to the descriptions provided and what qualities contribute to the theme of the section or analytic point of the unit. Thus, an ethnographer begins by marking those features that are core to the interaction and that reveal the point made. Then, she can review the intervening material and reflect on which portions can be deleted and which need to be retained to provide narrative continuity or to evoke a sense of scene and context. Following the editing conventions for elisions in a quotation, she then replaces the deleted portions with ellipses. Ethnographers should take special care in editing interview dialogue not to delete their own questions. Since these questions shape the answers given, they should be preserved as the context for the responses of the person interviewed.

Consider the decisions Rachel Fretz made in excerpting and editing fieldnotes to include in an analysis of Chokwe telling historical accounts (*kulweza sango*) in Northwest Province of Zambia (1995b). She was interested in the ways in which conventions common in narrating traditional stories were also employed in telling historical accounts about events that occurred in the recent past.[11] She focused on one instance of Chokwe storytelling about an aspiring political figure, Mushala, who, failing to win legitimate power, became an outlaw leading a band of soldiers who terrorized the community. Eventually, the government soldiers came to the area to search for Mushala and to free the community from his raids. Several listeners had witnessed these events, and others had heard many reports of them; they occasionally offered their remarks and insights during the narration. The fieldworker tape-recorded the narration and audience comments; in her fieldnotes, she wrote primarily about the circumstances of the storytelling, the family members present, and what their reactions were afterward that evening and the next day. She began to work on her analysis by listening to the tape and by rereading the following extended fieldnote:

We asked Uncle John if he knew anything about the events connected with Mushala. He paused and answered, "Yes, I know it very well." He began talking slowly, in serious tone of voice. He narrated about the way Mushala hunted and chased the Chokwe and Lunda peoples of this area: about the burning of villages, the slaughter of farm animals, about the villagers escaping into the bush to live there. He narrated for about one hour and a half. During the entire time, the family sat there very still. Uncle Don joined the group, but sat to the side with his own charcoal burner: Jerald, his nephew, went over to join him. Only occasionally did someone comment. [Listen to tape.] I noticed that it was a very traditional scene there by the fireside: a grandfather, two maternal uncles, and their nephews. Except for Joe's wife, Kianze, a young girl traveling with me, and myself, it was all men. [Most of the women were sitting by a fire in the kitchen house nearby and were also listening attentively.]

Before the evening was over the women, Nyalona and Kalombo, went home across the road. And Nyakalombo, the grandmother, went inside to sleep. Mwatavumbi (grandfather) was dozing and when he woke up, he went to bed too. And still Uncle John narrated: as I sat there, I noticed that he used the dramatic effects and dialogue conventions of storytelling and built his plot to peak and end with the killing of Mushala.

When he ended, everyone sat still for a while. I said, "Thank you," and then they started talking—Frank, Chester, and Uncle Don talked, each adding their personal knowledge of events. Don asked his brother John a question and he narrated more: his own father had known Mushala. He also talked about Chilombo, a neighbor, who was involved in these events. (Chilombo is the well-dressed man—in suit and tie who came by one day to talk in KiChokwe to me near the *chisambwe* [the pavilion where the men and guests sit]. He asked me if I would come to his village because he had stories to tell. I said I would come some time. Now today, Jerald said that he met him in town and that he asked him why I had not come and that I had promised. Jerald said that he—Chilombo—had waited for me. Next time!)

At the end of taping the narration, Mwatushi asked everyone to say his or her name. Even after the recorder was off, people just sat there and talked a while longer, rather spellbound by the shocking events. **As we crossed the road to return to our village, Mwatushi, Uncle John, Chester, Jerald, Kianze, and I kept talking about it. They told me (and demonstrated) how the villagers would cross the road backward, so that their footprints would seem to be going in the opposite direction so as to confuse the soldiers.**

It took me a long time to fall asleep—in my mind, I kept hearing the song, "*Kanda uliya mwana, kanda uliya. Kaakwiza akuloze.*" ["Don't cry my child, don't cry; they'll come to shoot you." It's a song composed by contemporary Chokwe who crossed the river to escape from the war in Angola—our earlier topic of conversation that evening.] I felt as though there were people hiding in the bush from the soldiers. We all slept a long time the next morning.

Today at lunch, Mwatushi said that it was Mushala's wife who betrayed him to the soldiers because she saw that eventually he would kill her family and her whole village. When she was near childbirth, they called a midwife to come stay with her in the bush. After the birth, one day when Mushala was away, she decided to leave with the midwife, and then they ran into four soldiers. **She told them who she was and that she would tell them where he was hiding. She also told them his charms and that they would be protected against them if they were naked, but they were ashamed, so she took off all her clothes, and they all walked naked on the path. Then they came to a pool of water, and she said you must wash here so that he cannot see you coming. Then they heard Mushala coming, and they stepped back into the bush. He came carrying his gun on his shoulder. He passed the first soldier who was shaking with fear and could not move. He passed the second soldier who also was shaking with fear and could not move. Then the third soldier shot him right in the eye and then in the chest. Mushala tried to walk on, but could not. He fell down. Then they all came and hit him with their bayonets. And that is how he died.** Thus, Mwatushi told the story of those events.

In reflecting on this extended fieldnote, the author came to see analytic issues in the two highlighted passages. The first suggested the possibility that, as part of their response to storytelling, people might reenact certain actions; such associations are most likely when a detail in the present landscape reminds them of traumatic events that had occurred there in the past.[12] The story of Mushala had evoked in listeners the memory of the abandoned villages, the surrounding bush where they hid, and the road that people had to cross as they sneaked back to their village occasionally to get supplies. To develop an excerpt-commentary unit, the author selected out and edited this brief account of the reenactment of walking backward to trick Mushala's soldiers:

> As we crossed the road to return to our village, . . . [we] kept on talking about it. They told me (and demonstrated) how the villagers would cross the road backward, so that their footprints would seem to be going to the opposite direction so as to confuse [Mushala's] soldiers.

She introduced the excerpt by saying that people were going home in the evening after hearing the tale. Thus, she did not need to include that information in the excerpt. She also deleted specific names of speakers but kept the real name of Mushala because he was a public figure—a common convention in excerpted fieldnotes; she also clarified in a bracket that it was

Mushala's soldiers, not the government soldiers, who were persecuting the people and from whom they were hiding their comings and goings.

The second passage suggested the idea that people recount and shape events to fit conventional story patterns. In the more casual conversation the next day, Mwatushi drew on familiar narrating conventions to recount how Mushala died: the use of charms to make oneself invisible (and invulnerable) and the repetition of three attempts to kill the villain with only the last effort succeeding.

> She told them [the government soldiers] about his [Mushala's] charms and that they would be protected against them if they were naked, but they were ashamed, so she took off all her clothes, and they all walked naked on the path. Then they came to a pool of water, and she said you must wash here so that he cannot see you coming. Then they heard Mushala coming, and they stepped back into the bush. He came carrying his gun on his shoulder. He passed the first soldier who was shaking with fear and could not move. He passed the second soldier who also was shaking with fear and could not move. Then the third soldier shot him right in the eye and then in the chest. Mushala tried to walk on but could not. He fell down. Then they all came and hit him with their bayonets. And that is how he died.

In editing this passage, the author did not include the wife's reasons for betraying Mushala since they were not directly relevant to a discussion of these narrative conventions. She also avoided making any editorial changes in the wording of this account; she wanted to maintain as much of the sequence and details of Mwatushi's retelling as she could even though it is not verbatim dialogue. She added clarification in brackets and determined what background information she could most efficiently provide in sentences leading into the excerpts.

Thus, when preparing a fieldnote for a final text, the ethnographer usually must do more than simply leave out portions of a longer fieldnote; rather, she sometimes refocuses and sharpens details in her editing. Consider the decisions that Linda Shaw (1988) made when describing borrowing and lending patterns among residents of a psychiatric board-and-care home. Her original fieldnote is not only longer, but is also more detailed, than the edited fieldnote.

Original Fieldnote:
I went into the dining room to see what the snacks were and came upon Marie angrily talking to Michelle about the fact that Michelle told Reid not to lend

her money. Michelle replied that she didn't tell Reid not to lend Marie money, but that he shouldn't lend anyone money, that he should keep his money for himself. Marie wanted to know who Michelle thought she was telling people not to lend to her, that she wasn't bumming but always paid her friends back. The argument went on this way for a little while, seeming to escalate as Marie charged Michelle with trying to cause her trouble and Michelle defending herself, saying that she hadn't done anything to Marie. Then Mic, the only other member sitting at the table, said something—can't exactly remember what— that seemed intended to lighten the conversation but had the effect of getting Marie off onto talking about Patsey being Mic's girlfriend and how could he have such a fat girlfriend. Mic defended himself, saying Patsey wasn't so fat, and they had only dated anyway.

In the midst of this diversion, Michelle got up and left the dining room. Marie then turned to me and asked if everyone at Vista didn't bum money. I agreed that it was done by quite a lot of people. She said that Michelle was new, had only been there a month, what right did she have going around telling people not to loan to her when that's what everyone here does. She said again, "Michelle is new. Just wait until she is here for a while. She'll be doing it too." Marie went on to say that she helps her friends out when they need it. She spoke about having given Earl and Kara her entire rebate check last month because they were out of money, and she felt sorry for them.

Edited Fieldnote:

In the dining room after dinner, I came upon Marie angrily accusing Michelle, a new resident, of having told Reid, another resident, not to lend her money. Michelle insisted she had urged Reid to keep his money for himself and not to lend *anyone* money, never mentioning Marie. Marie demanded to know just who Michelle thought she was, telling people not to lend to her; she wasn't bumming but always paid her friends back. Eventually Michelle got up and left the dining room. Marie then turned to me, asking if everyone at Vista didn't borrow. I agreed. She noted that Michelle was new, having only been at Vista a month; what right did she have going around telling people not to loan to her when that's what everyone here does? She continued, "Michelle is new. Just wait until she is here for a while. She'll be doing it, too." She added that she always helps her friends out when they need it; she gave Earl and Kara her entire rebate check last month because they were out of money and she felt sorry for them.

The author included this fieldnote in a section of her ethnography devoted to the broad theme of interdependence and cooperation among those living in the home. The fieldnote was chosen specifically to illustrate the point that because residents have little money and few sources of support, they count on being able to ask others at the home for small amounts of money and other needed items when they run short. In this excerpt, we see how intensely those in the home may feel when these sources are threatened. In editing this excerpt, the author preserved indirect speech in the original form and in the same order. She retained those parts of the fieldnote that revealed the grounds for participating in the system of exchange and edited out sentences and phrases describing actions that were unrelated to these issues (Mic and his girlfriend). She included aspects of Marie's talk that described those aspects of her participation that, in her view, demonstrated that she had entered into the exchange system (giving to others) in ways that entitled her to ask of them in return. Finally, she included Marie's explanation that only an outsider who had not fully experienced the need to call upon others would have questioned participation in the system of exchange. Hence, the author edited the fieldnote, dropping some of the description but preserving those sentences and phrases that bore most directly on that point. In the end, editing involves the delicate balance between efforts to preserve the essence of what members say and do while focusing the reader's attention on those bits of talk and action that most clearly and economically support the story the ethnographer is attempting to tell.

Thus, the process of editing is not a straightforward, simple task. On the one hand, shortening and editing for clarity forwards the smooth flow of the overall ethnographic story: Excerpts that are too long bog the reader down in extraneous details. On the other hand, there is always the risk in any condensation or selective quotation that the author will leave out details that might present people and their actions more convincingly, as one always loses some of the vividness and complexity of the original fieldnotes in the editing process.

At times, field-workers encounter problems because an excerpt is especially "rich" and contains materials that bear on several different themes. Simply duplicating the fieldnote in several sections of the final text does not work. Because readers quickly tire of unnecessary repetition, ethnographers should avoid using the same fieldnote excerpt more than one time. Rather, the solution lies in clearly identifying the different analytic themes in the excerpt and then using these themes either to split the excerpt into independent units or, if that is not possible, to discuss the various aspects of the excerpt sequentially. Consider an example from a study of domestic workers and their employers in which the following excerpt was initially used to illustrate workers' moral evaluations of their employers' own housekeeping practices:

"She never cleans her bathroom, and I couldn't get the scum off the—she had one of these tiled showers? And we used a good product, but I told her, 'you leave that on overnight.' 'Cause it was so filthy. . . . In fact, when I left that lady (hah hah) I said, 'I'm gonna leave it like this' [leave a paste of Comet on the sink], and *she* had to rinse it off the next day."

On reviewing this excerpt, the ethnographer decided to cut the worker's last statement—about how she maneuvered to make her employer finish cleaning up this mess herself—out of the excerpt and to use it instead in a subsequent section on house-cleaners' ways of resisting and turning the tables on their employers.

Ethnographers generally delete the reflective commentary they incorporated into the original fieldnote. Rather than retain these initial thoughts in the version of the fieldnote that appears in the finished ethnography, she can incorporate any useful insights into the analytic discussion that follows the excerpt. Frequently, however, the researcher will have elaborated and specified analytic issues to such an extent that earlier commentary seems more simplistic or undeveloped and, thus, of minimal use. Furthermore, because the author writes, selects, edits, and organizes excerpts, she already has a privileged voice. Excerpts dominated by the fieldworker's explanations sound contrived and become truly redundant in a final ethnography.[13]

The ethnographic writer edits to make excerpts *readable* by using standard conventions for punctuation, spelling, and grammar. For the sake of clarity, he should take particular care to revise unclear sentences and to correct confusing tense shifts in portions of the excerpts that are not direct quotations. The author, however, should be very conservative in editing direct quotations, carefully balancing the reader's need for clarity against a commitment to providing an accurate rendering of people's actual use of words. Ethnographers take special care to preserve and convey speakers' dialect, idiom, and speech rhythms. Even individual speech disfluencies—false starts, pauses, and repetitions—should be treated carefully. For many purposes, producing readable dialogue (especially from tape-recorded transcripts) requires editing out many such disfluencies.[14] But in some circumstances, the author may specifically want to preserve such speech in order to indicate the speaker's emotional state or mood. For example, retaining the "and- and- and-" in the following excerpt reveals the speaker's disturbed hesitancy as he talks about his "mental illness" to the researcher:

"I'm telepathic. I can actually hear thought in other people's heads. . . ." He said he wished he could tell people but . . . "they'll just increase my medication. . . . No matter how drugged I am, nothing can take away my telepathy. And- and- and- it's not because of me. It's because Jesus wills it for me."

Furthermore, editing should make excerpts *comprehensible* to readers. The author must clarify any *allusions*—such as names, places, procedures— which depend on references external to the fieldnote. She can do so when orienting the reader to the excerpt or for briefer, less central matters by embedding a brief explanation in brackets within the text. For example, an author might identify the locally relevant status of people named in the excerpt, such as "the others [all students]" or clarify the meaning of direct speech that might not be clear in context, for example, "the only purpose we had in mind was to set it [the dynamite] off." At this time, the ethnographer must once again verify that all details are accurate; misrepresentation of factual information or of local terms very quickly tells readers that this ethnographer is not reliable. Indeed, a few mistakes can undermine the credibility of the whole story.

Finally, in most cases, an excerpt should protect the people, institutions, and communities studied by providing *anonymity*.[15] Therefore, in completing the editing, an ethnographer changes all names and identifying markers such as personally distinctive details in descriptions. Authors provide pseudonyms, generally echoing qualities evoked (e.g., ethnic identity) by the original name. We do not recommend using initials to indicate different characters, since this minimal identification makes gender difficult to remember, lacks evocative qualities, and makes it difficult for a reader to recognize that person in other excerpts.

Ordering Excerpt-Commentary Units within a Section

With the overall framework as a guideline, ethnographers usually organize their ethnographies into sections set off by titled headings. Each section generally presents one theme, perhaps divided further into several subthemes. A section is built from a series of excerpt-commentary units. For example, the section of the ethnography on the gay and lesbian high school entitled "Sexualization of Conversation" is constructed of the following units:

First Unit
analytic point: "Sexual innuendos" are a common means by which students sexualized talk to and about teaching staff.

excerpt: On finding out that a teacher's age is twenty-seven, a student comments: "I've had sex with someone who was twenty-eight—it was gross."

Second Unit

analytic point: Students sexualize their responses specifically to staff instructions.

excerpt: A student responds to staff command to "come with me" as a sexual proposition.

Third Unit

analytic point: In some situations, staff do not let the challenge implicit in student's sexualizing comments pass but themselves respond in ways that reassert their position.

excerpt: Staff responds to a student who quipped "search my tongue" when asked to throw away his gum: "I don't want to—I'm sure many people already have."

Fourth Unit

analytic point: In some instances, staff members themselves use sexual talk in ways that implicitly maintain their authority.

excerpt: As a student turns down the researcher's offer to help with math, staff member comments: "Go ahead, you were asking about him earlier."

Within a section, the ethnographer organizes units to develop a progression of ideas in ways that increasingly reveal the complexities of fieldnote data and analysis so that the story progresses to a deeper understanding of the theme. In the above example, the first two units focus on students' sexualizing talk, the third introduces the added complication of how teaching staff respond to such talk, and the last looks at the more subtle issues involved when staff initiate such talk.

To aid the reader in following the progression of ideas from one unit to the next, the author should provide a clear *transition* that links the main idea of the current paragraph to those of preceding paragraphs. In some cases, constructing a transition is a relatively straightforward matter of writing an introductory sentence to the paragraph beginning a new unit. For example, the author of the "sexualization of conversation" section provides this transition sentence into his third unit:

Although, as in the previous excerpt, the staff members sometimes don't respond to the students' sexualizing comments, this is not always the case. . . .

This transition refers back to the prior excerpt, noting one feature not commented on at the time: Staff did not explicitly respond to students' sexualizing talk. This retroactively noted feature is then used to introduce, by contrast, the focus of the current unit: how staff did respond to such talk.

In other instances, when the analytic point in a subsequent unit raises a significantly different issue than that of the preceding one, the author should not rely simply on an introductory transitional sentence. Rather, she should also revise the *preceding unit* and explicitly anticipate the idea of the later one. For example, the transition to the second unit of the "sexualization of conversation" section reads:

> Furthermore, the students sometimes position themselves as more powerful than the staff members by sexualizing the staff members' instructional commands. . . .

This sentence focuses on student sexualizing as a response specifically to staff "instructional commands." However, in the first unit, the author had not considered the specific forms of staff-student interaction within which sexualizing comments occurred. To now learn that such comments are made in response to commands may leave the reader feeling slightly confused: Do students respond in sexualized ways to other sorts of staff talk such as polite requests or general questions? Thus, the author should have revised the discussion in the first unit to provide more context for this upcoming distinction.

In addition to deciding on the ordering of units, the author must also write an introduction and conclusion to the section. The introduction should connect the theme of the section to the overall theme of the ethnography, and it should discuss any general features of that theme needed to understand and appreciate the ideas of the different units that follow. The author introduced the "sexualization of conversation" section, for example, with a paragraph observing that students commonly sexualized conversations in this setting and that "the sexualization is consequential to the power relations between staff member and student." In this way, the author linked the section back to the major theme of the paper. In the next paragraph, he argued that "sexual innuendos" provide one form of sexualizing, a form that is "particularly useful for students since they are ambiguous [and] indirect," allowing denial of sexual intent.

Finally, in a conclusion to the section, the author tries to draw together the implications of the excerpts and analytic commentary for the core theme

of the section. He may also suggest how these issues tie in with the theme of
the section to follow.

PRODUCING A COMPLETED ETHNOGRAPHIC DOCUMENT

Depending upon the time available, the ethnographer might rework units
and sections a number of times, replacing initially selected excerpts with
new ones, refining analytic commentary and transitions, reordering units
within a section, and/or rearranging sections within the overall ethnography. Although she sees still further possible changes and refinements, at
some point, she must stop revising and take up a series of final writing tasks
required to turn the now substantial body of text into a completed ethnographic document. These projects include titling the ethnography, writing
an introduction linking the topic and major theme to other research, describing the setting and methods, and providing an overall conclusion to
the ethnography.

Introducing the Ethnography

The title and introduction to an ethnography provide readers with their first
means of orienting to the text. The title and introduction not only tell readers what they can expect the ethnography to be about, but they also provide
clues to the writer's analytic and substantive concerns.

One kind of ethnographic title communicates to the reader both the
general topic and exactly what people, setting, activity, or process was studied. For example:

> "Ritualized Drinking Behavior in the Fraternity System"
> "Interactional Dynamics of Ethnicity at an Urban High School"
> "Waiting to Die: An Ethnographic Study of a Convalescent Home"

Rather than simply stating the general topic, however, an author may attempt to convey the more abstract analytic theme of the ethnography in a
title. As Atkinson (1990:76) has noted, ethnographers often do so by placing a colon after a phrase containing the abstract, "generic" issue to link it
to another phrase specifying the general topic and concrete "local" setting
or activity:

> "Systems of Power: Authority and Discipline in a Boys Group Home"

Finally, the ethnographer may incorporate local members' terms or phrases as key elements of a title:

> "The Dynamics of Down: Being Cool with the Set"
> "'These Kids Live in Their Own Little Worlds': Interpretive Framework in a Halfway House"

In the first paragraph of the introduction to the ethnography, many authors begin with an attention-getting opening. They may use an incident from their fieldnotes that focuses on the topic or briefly describes common approaches to the topic. Next, the author very briefly introduces the topic and location of his own research as a bridge to presenting his thesis. In a thematic narrative, the author writes a "topical thesis" sentence that explains the general focus of the paper and lays out the themes to be examined. In that sense, the thesis sentence does not delineate every development in the ethnographic story, or foreshadow the conclusions to be made at the end. Rather, the thesis sentence gets the story going. Finally, the author generally provides an overview of the paper by presenting the thematic statement for each upcoming section.

For example, the author of "Interactional Dynamics of Ethnicity at an Urban High School" writing in the early 1990s began by orienting the reader to his topic.

> In everyday life, we commonly assume ethnicity as a given category. People belong to distinct groups with unique cultural practices. We say that the President of the United States is white, that the magic of a people in Africa is Azande witchcraft, that rap is black music, that Cinco de Mayo is a Mexican holiday, etc. We assume that we are describing what is objectively there. We are simply stating the "natural facts" of the world. When we do become more aware of ethnicity as a category, it is often because of conflict. The newspaper reports that a "black" girl was shot by a "Korean" storekeeper and that a "White Power" group is marching in a "Jewish" neighborhood. We ask, How did this happen? How can diverse peoples get along? But we still imply that definite aggregates of people exist and that they have distinct cultures.

In this introductory paragraph, the author points out that, in their talk about ethnicity, people commonly assume that terms that identify ethnicity refer unambiguously to naturally occurring and distinct "aggregates of people." In his next paragraph, he makes explicit the analytic stance that he takes toward ethnicity:

> What we ignore in this everyday discourse is that ethnicity is "social work": People identify a person, place, or thing as having a certain "character" through an implicitly interactional dynamic of inclusion or exclusion. This process creates what Barth calls "boundaries" in interaction (1969). These boundaries are not objective, but subjective borders, and they are constantly being recreated, reaffirmed, negotiated, and even discarded. Thus, in everyday life, ethnicity is a local phenomenon originating in specific situations.

He proposes to look at ethnicity not as an objectively given "fact" but rather as a product of "social work," namely, of local, interactional negotiations of inclusion and exclusion. By citing another researcher, he suggests that this issue also interests other scholars and implies that his "new angle" contributes to a scholarly discussion.

The author next substantiates his topic, first by identifying the subjects and setting of his research and, then, by specifying the sort of data he will rely on:

> In this paper, I examine ethnicity and ethnic groups at an urban high school in Southern California. The fieldnote excerpts describe the processes by which people use ethnicity in everyday life.

Next, he presents his general thesis about ethnicity in an interpretive statement about ethnicity as situationally "recreated and modified":

> I argue that through people's interactions, "ethnicity" is perpetuated by constantly being recreated and modified within a situation. This "social work" in situations and through interactions then generates the discrete units of specific groups, recognized as having particular cultures, symbols, styles, and objects. Thus, this paper is a study of how people "ascribe the ascribed" (Garfinkel 1967).

Finally, he closes this portion of the introduction with an overview of his argument, briefly describing the main idea for each upcoming section (see "Developing a Thematic Narrative," above).

In contrast to an introduction that begins by setting up an analytic idea and then subsequently identifies just what was studied, some ethnographers begin with an actual fieldnote-based description or observation. Following the presentation of the specific details, they then pinpoint a more general analytic issue or problem that this incident represents. The above ethnographer, for example, might have begun by describing an especially perspicuous instance of the "social work" that contributes to recreating and maintaining a particular ethnic identity, for example, an extreme or dramatic instance of a white student dressing, talking, or acting black. He could then have moved to identifying the general analytic problem or issue that he saw reflected in, or illustrated by, this incident.[16]

Linking the Study to Other Research

As part of the introduction (or in a section immediately following it), ethnographers generally link their interpretation to wider issues of scholarly interest in their disciplines. In that way, they invite their readers to consider seriously the topics to be discussed and how their research furthers or deepens an understanding of them. At this point, the writer thinks again of his intended readers and selects words and ideas familiar to them.

For example, the author of the paper on ethnicity writes for sociologists and thus discusses the concept of "ethnicity" as it is used by sociologists. In each paragraph, he addresses some feature of the problem of research on ethnic issues. Although he discusses other scholars' research, he only raises those ideas about ethnicity that he addresses later in the body of the paper. In his findings, he then offers analytic ideas and fieldnote excerpts that touch on the problems he raises:

> Marger (1991) notes that sociologists classify ethnic groups based on three indices: unique cultural traits, sense of community, and ascription. First, ethnic groups have some unique behavioral characteristics that set them off from other people. Second, ethnic groups display a sense of community among members. This "we" almost seems to necessitate a "they" and leads to the creation of ethnic group boundaries separating insiders and outsiders. Third, ethnic status is almost always ascribed which usually means given by birth. In presenting these traits, Marger emphasizes a supposed objective criteria for ethnicity. Ethnicities are seen as discrete collectives that can be studied in relation to each other. This approach is typical in many studies of race and ethnic relations in the United States. And the demographic data for this paper is analyzed thus.
>
> Unfortunately, while this approach offers information for macro studies of society, it leads to a neglect of the subjective perception and dynamic features of ethnicity in everyday life. It downplays how "ethnic identity is an acquired and used feature of human identity available for employment by either participant in an encounter and subject to presentation, inhibition, manipulation, and exploitation" (Lyman and Douglass 1973). In this approach, ethnicity is a resource to be used in strategic creation and maintenance of self. . . .
>
> For purposes of this study, an ethnic group is defined as "a reference group

invoked by people who identify themselves and are identified by others as sharing a common historical style" (Royce 1982). An ethnic group, thus, is a subculture with symbols, style, and forms. Unlike many other subcultures though, membership in the ethnic group is held to be ascriptive.

These few paragraphs briefly raise problematic issues in ethnic studies. In this introductory section on other research, the author does not attempt to provide an overview of all possible approaches to ethnicity. Rather, he only selects those researchers' works and ideas that provide a context for his own study. Thus, this writer implicitly demonstrates the relevance of his research to the other sociologists who are his intended readers.

In sum, the ethnographer does not review "the literature" on the topic nor does she simply cite several works of others. Rather, she carefully selects other research that provides a context for the upcoming findings and only discusses those ideas that highlight her own analysis.

Introducing Setting and Methods

Before launching into the ethnography proper, authors introduce their setting and their methods for learning about it. Setting and methods can be discussed either in separate sections or in a single section addressing both topics.

In describing the *setting*, the ethnographer orients readers to the place, people, and situations to be examined in detail in the subsequent ethnography. This description should help the reader picture the physical and social features of the setting. It should also provide overviews of the key individuals and of procedures or processes that are central to the substance of the ethnography. The overview of key individuals, for example, might trace differences between core and volunteer staff in a community mental health center or between managers and canvassers in a political action committee; the overview of procedures would address how clients enter and move through the program, what basic job responsibilities entail, and perhaps the overall organization of door-to-door canvassing.

This discussion of the setting, its personnel, and its routines should also anticipate and highlight specific features of the setting that are central for subsequent analyses. For example, an ethnographer writing about the nature and consequences of staff practices for categorizing or *labeling* resident clients of a homeless shelter provides a two-pronged introduction to the setting. First, he presents the types of clients sought by the shelter:

My fieldwork was carried out in an emergency shelter for the homeless in the downtown area of Los Angeles. The shelter has a capacity of 54 persons but had an average house total of 35 or so for the time I was there. The shelter's primary service is to provide food and housing for persons who are absolutely broke. While in the shelter, the "clients," as they are called by the staff, are also provided with some assistance in looking for housing and dealing with the welfare bureaucracy. That stated target group for the shelter is the "new homeless"; that is, persons who have only recently lost their homes and been thrust upon the streets. This is in contrast to those the staff refer to as the "chronic homeless" or "shelter hoppers" who have been living on the streets for some time and who are understood to move from shelter to shelter with no intention of finding a more stable residence. . . .

The shelter's other general criterion for admission is that they will take any sort of client except for single men. They are one of the few shelters that will handle homeless families with children, a fact that they pride themselves on. In practice, the predominant client group consists of a woman with several young children.

The author then introduces the frontline staff whose routine work practices are to be examined:

The staff most relevant to the typifying tasks in the shelter are six Program Aides [PAs]. The six PAs are four black women between the ages of approximately thirty and fifty, a younger white woman recently graduated from college, and a twenty-one-year-old white male seminary student. None are trained social workers, perhaps due, at least in part, to the extremely low pay PAs receive. The PAs spend most of their working time in the office which overlooks the lounge on the second floor of the shelter (the first floor contains the offices of the shelter while the third floor consists of the clients' rooms). The schedule is such that there is only one PA on duty at a time, apart from a one hour overlap period at the boundaries of the shifts.

He continues by describing PAs' routine duties: answering the phone, screening possible clients, maintaining logs, and so on.

The ethnographer may move directly from such a description of key features to an overview of her entry into the setting and of the nature of her participation in it. Here, the ethnographer summarizes what she actually did to get close to and learn about the events and issues considered throughout the ethnography. In so doing, it is important to explain how, and in what capacity, she obtained initial access to the setting, how those in the setting understood what she was doing and/or was interested in, and how different members of the setting reacted to or treated her.

It is generally useful to consider different stages or phases in the research, distinguishing, for example, between processes of initial entry, of getting used to the setting and its participants, and of established, longer-term participation. An ethnographer working in a community mental health center, for example, traces her socialization from initial encouragement to participate in a few routine activities under staff supervision through observation and testing of her competence in dealing with highly disturbed patients to eventually being charged with conducting community meetings with the clients.

In presenting their methods, ethnographers seek to depict the varied qualities of their participation and their awareness of both the advantages and constraints of their roles in a specific setting. The ethnographer of a community mental health center, for example, analyzed these qualities of her role in the following terms:

> My status is that of a "volunteer intern." When I first arrived here, I was not sure what this title/status entailed. As I became associated with the staff and socialized into a staff role, I have realized that my role is that of a lower staff member. I do not have the power, nor the privileges, of a core staff member. For example, although I am encouraged to participate in Case Review Meetings, my "insights" are not required to be considered for staff decisions.

Such an analysis demands that the ethnographer reflect on the specific kinds of interactions and events to which she had or was denied access. For example, one student ethnographer described how her participant role in a feminist political-action committee shaped and delimited her access to, and observations of, key interactions in political canvassing:

> I play more than a passive observer role. I am a canvasser and, as such, go out with the rest of the crew and canvass at least once a week. But I am also part of management in that they are grooming me for the position of field manager in the summer. This puts me in the ideal position to see what the canvassers are feeling and thinking and, at the same time, gives me access to information not otherwise available to canvassers. This does, however, work against me in that sometimes the canvassers will label me as management and therefore be less likely to confide in me. This becomes a particular problem when I have to act on behalf of management (such as doing retrainings) or when issues become polarized, and one has to take either management's or the canvassers' perspective. . . . [Furthermore] it is hard to go to the field to observe as a researcher because to observe means that I am there on behalf of management, and I am the authority rather than a peer.

Finally, in presenting and analyzing methods and their implications, it is helpful to include fieldnote excerpts to illustrate and support key points. The ethnographer in the study of the community mental health center, for example, presented the following fieldnotes—the first to show the character of the "testing" that she was subject to from one staff member during her first week at the center and the second to illustrate how her role differed from "regular staff":

> I was playing ping-pong with a client when I saw Cathy, a caseworker, point David in my direction. David walked over to me and said: "Hi. I'm the President, and I demand that you go to the Alaskan pipeline to save the world and my sister in Kansas. You must do this—it is your duty to your Country. You must save the world." Out of the corner of my eye, I saw Cathy and a couple of other staff members giggling. I responded: "Well, David, I'm sorry but that's just too big of a responsibility for me." David: "You must save the world." He then walked away. Cathy came over to me and said: "He's really crazy, isn't he?" She laughed. "Don't worry. He's just about the craziest one we've got."

> ---

> Today we were having client nominations for government. The clients were nominating other clients for President and Vice President. Norman (a client) nominated me for VP. Arlene (art therapist) stepped in and said to Norman: "Karina cannot be nominated. She is a staff member and cannot be nominated."

While discussions of the setting and of the complexities of doing field research highlight features and processes that are central to upcoming ethnographic analyses, they can also lend credibility to the final document.[17] These descriptions may allow readers to assess whether or not the enthnographer had access to the kinds and quality of observations needed to sustain subsequent analytic claims. With this background information to draw on, the reader may be more inclined to assume that the author is credible and informed. Indeed, ethnographers may select fieldnote excerpts about their involvement exactly in order to implicitly convince the reader "that I was there and experienced this firsthand."

Writing a Conclusion

Finished ethnographic texts usually end with a section that reflects on and elaborates the thesis addressed in the introduction to the paper. Hence, while naturally among the last pieces of writing the author does, conclusions are intricately tied to introductions.[18] Often, the conclusion explores the implications of the theoretical and/or substantive issues raised in the paper's introduction. In an ethnographic paper, the wording of the introductory thesis focuses the reader on the central idea, but often this idea may not be as sharply delineated as the concluding presentation of the thesis. Whereas the introduction prepares the reader to understand the upcoming analytic points and excerpts, the conclusion more precisely interconnects the ideas because, by the paper's end, the reader has read the whole ethnographic story and absorbed the details of its fieldnote excerpts. In other words, the ethnography tells a story that can be understood fully only by reading the progression of analytic ideas and fieldnote excerpts. Each section with its theme, points, and discussion of excerpts moved the reader further along toward the conclusion with its more finely tuned thesis.

To write a conclusion, the ethnographer should review the now completed tale, paying particular attention to the framing of that story in the introduction. In most cases, it is useful to write a *summary* of the major findings and themes of the paper. This summary should generally restate the thesis of the paper and then in short, concise sentences suggest how each section advances or contributes to this thesis. In some cases, the ethnographer may choose to use the summary to begin the conclusion. In others, he may move directly to other issues without a summary. Yet, even when one does not plan to make a summary part of the conclusion, writing one is beneficial to the ethnographer; it forces the author to turn from the minute problems of writing up specific ideas and segments to a review of the overall structure and flow of his paper. The result is a gestalt view of the ethnography's initial promises compared to where it has actually gone that gets the writer thinking about some of its wider implications.

Whether the author summarizes or not, conclusions take up the paper's thesis. The ethnographer may do so in at least three ways: (1) by extending or modifying the thesis in light of the materials examined; (2) by relating the thesis to some more general theory or current issue in the relevant literature; and/or (3) by offering a *meta-commentary* on the thesis, the methods, or assumptions associated with it. An author might employ only one of these options, or she might weave together two, or even all three, options in one longer, more elaborate conclusion.

As an example of the first option, consider some of the concluding portions of the ethnographic study on how family caregivers of persons with Alzheimer's disease manage the stigma associated with this condition. The introduction to this study had highlighted Goffman's (1971) concept of the "family information rule," namely, the preference for family members to keep knowledge of the stigma (discrediting information) within the family to prevent outsiders from learning about the problem. In the conclusion, the author returns to this issue, suggesting that, as the disease worsens, there is a radical change in the family's ability to honor this information rule:

> The Alzheimer's caregiver will try for as long as possible to collude with the family member, continuing to abide by the family information rule to the extent that she or he is able and limiting initial disclosures to intimates and medical personnel. However, there may well come a point where the caregiver realizes that she or he cannot count on the person with Alzheimer's to be cognizant of what is discrediting, let alone motivated or able to collude in trying to cover it up or minimize its embarrassment. Thus, the information control within the family tends to give way to more direct caregiver interpersonal and interactional control.
>
> The caregiver increasingly relies on a variety of management practices to control the individual, both within the private family domain as well as outside it. And, as the person with Alzheimer's can no longer play the collusive game, caregivers gradually come to align with outsiders, disclosing discrediting information.

Here, the author argues that while the family caregiver initially seeks to honor the family information rule, to do so requires cooperation from the person with Alzheimer's disease. When such cooperation can no longer be counted on, the caregiver increasingly violates the rule by disclosing discrediting information to outsiders in order to enlist their help in managing the patient. In this way, the author highlights how her findings would modify Goffman's notion, pointing out previously unnoted conditions underlying the operation of the family information rule and identifying the circumstances that lead family members to violate it.

Another way that authors might extend a thesis statement is to develop theoretical linkages between separate components of the thesis. For example, in the introduction to the study of residents in a home for ex–mental patients, the introductory thesis pointed to two conflicting tendencies within the home: residents' dependence on staff members and the residents' ability to actively influence staff views of them. In the conclusion, the author uses her more specific analyses of these relations to explicitly connect these contradictory tendencies as parts of an ongoing vicious circle. Residents feel vulnerable to the power of staff and may respond by trying to build credit and goodwill with them. In order to do this, they participate in therapy sessions and other staff-initiated activities. As a result, they gain the staff's support and protection, but, in so doing, they become more directly dependent upon the staff members who "sponsor" them. This analysis thus links two patterns that initially appear separate and even contradictory, pointing to an ironic outcome whereby residents' actions intended to lessen vulnerability and dependence on staff end up tightening that dependence. In this option, the writer tells an ethnographic story that progresses from an initial thesis that highlighted conflicting tendencies through an in-depth discussion of analytic points with appropriate excerpts to finally come to a conclusion that intertwines these conflicting strands.

A second tactic for writing a conclusion is to connect the ethnography's thesis to issues raised in a relevant disciplinary literature. In the study of Alzheimer's family caregiving, after the paragraphs quoted above, the author relates the contrast between colluding with the person with Alzheimer's and colluding with outsiders to a more general issue in the sociology of deviance: When do family members *accept*, tolerate, and continue to look out for another family member with some kind of stigmatizing condition or behavior, and when do they turn against, exclude, and implicitly *reject* this family member? This issue had been addressed in a journal article entitled "Toward a Sociology of Acceptance: The Other Side of the Study of Deviance" (Bogdan and Taylor 1987) that the author cites in developing her argument:

> Recognition of these two phases of caregiver stigma management, collusion with the person with Alzheimer's, and a realignment and collusion with outsiders, allows for an integration of a sociology of acceptance with a sociology of rejection (Bogdan and Taylor 1987).

Here, the author suggests the possibility of unifying sociological theories about why and how people tolerate deviants with theories about why and how people exclude and reject deviants. These reactions need not be opposed, alternative courses of action; some forms of exclusion develop exactly because of a deep and abiding commitment to caring for another under conditions where the afflicted family member can no longer be "counted on" by the caregiver. This unity of acceptance and rejection is frequently highlighted, the author argues, in caregivers' deeply ambivalent feelings about having to take overtly rejecting actions toward the person with Alzheimer's disease:

> Many caregivers were disturbed about having to take more and more control over their family members. In monitoring the person as well as using physical coercion, they made such comments as, "I hate my nagging voice." Or as one caregiver said with regard to taking control over his wife: "I have no right."

In this way, the concept of acceptance is also extended to encompass rejecting actions that are performed reluctantly and are combined with deep regret.

A third option in writing a conclusion is to pause, step back, and reflect on the ethnography in offering some *meta-commentary* on its methods, assumptions, tone, or conclusions. In the study of resident life in the home for ex–mental patients, the author not only addressed staff-resident relations but also considered how residents related to, and developed important social and supportive ties with, one another. One section of the ethnography explored the ways in which residents regularly exchanged certain items with one another—cigarettes, food, and small amounts of money. The author suggested that these exchanges and the continuing relations they created and sustained helped residents deal with the chronic deprivation that they faced. In one portion of her conclusion, however, she reflected on how this earlier consideration of resident exchange "strategies" presented an "overly rationalized," game-playing view of these exchanges. This view, she argued, needed to be complemented by appreciation of the caring and emotional qualities also characteristic of these exchanges as well as the role of these exchanges in fostering a sense of sharing and community among a number of residents. The prior strategies-and-tactics analysis, she argued, tended to obscure and distort these critical processes.

In all these approaches to writing a conclusion, the ethnographer takes up, once again, the problem of identifying and writing out, in explicit, elaborated form, the relevance of some of her experiences, observations, and insights into others' ways of life for an outside audience. But by proceeding in a way that keeps fieldnotes at the center of the analytic process, the ethnographer is often able to reach understandings and make connections that do not neatly fit existing explanations and theories in the discipline. The refined, more precise thesis to be presented in the conclusion will more likely privilege members' views and show what is interesting (and has theoretical import) about this local life in ways that convince one's scholarly readers. Thus, the more explicit thesis in the conclusion not only represents what the ethnographer saw and heard of members' experiences but also further clarifies known issues or proposes an entirely original perspective.

REFLECTIONS: BETWEEN MEMBERS AND READERS

In producing an ethnography for wider audiences, fieldworkers are constantly pulled by conflicts between representing some indigenous world and its meanings for members and making their own experiences with that world speak to the very different concerns of scholarly readers. In creating a finished ethnographic story, the ethnographer self-consciously orients toward the latter. In regularly returning to his fieldnote record and to the memories bound up with and evoked by this record, he is again and again reminded of the former.

While the give-and-take of relations in the field continues to shape the ethnographer's understanding, the finished ethnography is the ethnographer's version of those happenings and events. Most ethnographic conventions allow the writer to represent others (and her experience with them) as she sees best. In this sense, the ethnographer openly assumes and exercises authorial privilege.

Even in those instances when ethnographers ask members to read portions or to comment on certain analyses, the author has the final say about both the text itself and the extent of members' evaluations of it (see Bloor 2001; Duneier 1999; Emerson and Pollner 1988; Rochford 1992). Despite the efforts of intensive participation, the attempts to learn members' meanings, and the self-reflection in representing others' realities, the final document turns into a rather linear narrative, defined and controlled primarily by the author.[19] Only when the reader's interpretation differs from that of the fieldworker do the many ways to interpret a set of notes become explicit. But if this ethnographer keeps these various possibilities in mind while writing, he might feel paralyzed, preventing any story from being told. Hence, an ethnography remains one author's vision of field experiences and members' worlds. And, thus, because the author controls the text, she takes on an authoritative voice in writing.

Nonetheless, the ethnographer sometimes provides unintended glimpses into others' everyday lives as readers discern things that the ethnographer did not intend to reveal. In fact, reader participation in text-making can be a double-edged advantage in ethnographies built around fieldnote excerpts. On the one hand, readers more directly engage in the described social scenes and, thereby, closely follow the story line. On the other hand, they can also more readily assess the proposed analysis, at least the version presented by the author, and derive different insights from the fieldnotes.

Hence, by choosing fieldnotes for their rhetorical effects, as well as for their signifying and conceptual functions, an ethnographer tries to prefigure a reader's likely range of interpretations. But, readers ultimately make their own sense of these fieldnote excerpts, even though the note-taking ethnographer created, selected, and arranged them to tell a particular story in the text. The original fieldnotes stand there, embedded within the analysis, allowing any reader to listen closely to members' voices, to vicariously experience their actions, and to imagine other interpretations. In the end, it seems, the reader has her say.

8

Conclusion

In the preceding chapters, we initially examined the processes whereby field researchers transform direct experience and observation into fieldnotes. We then considered ways of using fieldnotes to develop and tell an ethnographic story, exploring a variety of procedures that can facilitate the construction of fieldnote-centered texts. In this final chapter, we want to offer some further reflections on learning to write and use fieldnotes and on some broader implications of these writing processes for ethnographic research.

As we have seen, in writing fieldnotes, the ethnographer makes a number of specific writing choices; through these choices, she transforms experience and observations into text and data. Obviously, many of these choices involve decisions about *what* to write—to note and describe the practical efforts of Alzheimer family caregivers, patterns of racial and ethnic distribution in a school playground, or audience participation in storytelling in a Zaire village. But these choices also involve intricate decisions about *how* to write about what has been observed and experienced. As we have emphasized, writing fieldnotes is not simply a matter of putting observed details on paper. Rather, the ethnographer draws on a variety of writing conventions in order to actively create characters and scenes on a page, to dramatically depict action and speech, and to effectively convey the meanings of events as perceived by those involved in them.

Ethnographers, of course, may not always make these choices consciously; because the immediate task is to get descriptions and accounts on the page, experienced writers may use skills and make choices without a conscious thought. But increased awareness of the options that make such choices possible will, we believe, improve the overall quality of ethnographic research. In the first place, heightened consciousness about writing should help ethnographers produce richer, more varied, and useful fieldnotes. In becoming aware of and adept at using effective writing conventions, the ethnographer is more likely to capture significant detail, create vivid imagery, and provide nuanced depictions of talk and events. The field researcher will have greater flexibility in making writing choices. He will know and employ to his advantage the different effects of writing in the third, as opposed to the first person, of describing a scene or event from particular or from varying points of view, and of writing up others' talk as direct or indirect speech.

But in addition, increased awareness of writing choices can also inspire the ethnographer to be more attentive to details while in the field. Envisioning scenes as written can make the researcher a better observer. With knowledge of writing options, he will be attuned to features of action and talk that might be captured on paper. Furthermore, a researcher who makes choices about different points of view in his writing is less likely, when observing, to confuse his own perspective with the views of others; hence, he will be able to recognize and represent those members' voices more fully.

Furthermore, sensitivity to writing options in constructing a final fieldnote-centered text also allows field researchers to produce more compelling and detailed ethnographic stories. The writer, for example, becomes explicitly attuned to responding both to voices from the field and to the voices of envisioned scholarly readers. She realizes that she must translate and interpret members' voices into the analytic language of intended readers in order to address issues, theories, and concerns that might interest them. Thus, in creating a fieldnote-centered final text, the ethnographer includes excerpts that report members' voices but with an awareness that she controls and orchestrates their presence; she reframes and reorders members' words and doings into her own ethnographic story. Sensitive to members' concerns and meanings, she can directly confront the task of re-presenting those meanings—for example, making them "interesting" or "relevant" to the concerns of anticipated readers. As a result, in a good ethnography, the reader can hear these two sets of voices speaking in harmony or at least not creating dissonance. The ethnography should provide a vehicle through which the voices from the field can, in their own distinctive ways, speak; and at the same time, the ethnography should also speak the language of the readers, addressing their issues, theories, and concerns.[1]

In all these ways, increased awareness of writing choices allows for a deepening appreciation of the power and implications of writing. The ethnographer cannot help but realize that he is not simply recording witnessed events; rather, through his writing, he is actively creating realities and meanings. In writing fieldnotes, he is not simply preserving those moments in textual form, but, rather, he is shaping observed moments as scenes, characters, dialogue, and recounted actions in the first place. Subsequently, in reworking fieldnotes and transposing them into a final ethnographic story, he does not simply recount the tale of something that happened; instead, he reconstructs "what happened" so as to illustrate a pattern or a make a point. Inevitably, in interpreting his fieldnotes for readers unfamiliar with that world, he constructs a version of events. Thus, while writing and analyzing fieldnotes, the ethnographer-as-author grows increasingly aware of his role and responsibility in telling the story of the people he studied; for in writing, he re-presents their everyday world.[2] In so doing, he is continually reminded about how the act of writing constructs meaning and knowledge.

In this sense, awareness of writing choices generates an appreciation of the *reflexivity* of ethnographic research. Reflexivity involves the recognition that an account of reality does not simply mirror reality but, rather, creates or constitutes as real in the first place whatever it describes. Thus, "the notion of reflexivity recognizes that texts do not simply and transparently report an independent order of reality. Rather, the texts themselves are implicated in the work of reality-construction" (Atkinson 1990:7).

Critical analyses of ethnographies that focus on reflexivity (e.g., Atkinson 1990; Clifford and Marcus 1986; Van Maanen 1988) have tended to address the rhetorical structure or unstated political and cultural presuppositions of completed ethnographies, examining how the ethnographer represents another culture, develops a particular line of analysis, or constructs a persuasive argument or engaging tale in a published account. However, these analyses reveal significant limitations in themselves, for they implicitly depict final ethnographies as original, unconstrained constructions produced wholly from the ethnographer's struggles to come to terms with experiences in the field. While polished ethnographies are, in part, culled from memories of and reflections on field experiences, they also draw heavily on the already created fieldnote record of that experienced reality. Final ethnographies, then, are rarely new edifices built up entirely by original writings but are more commonly jerry-built projects incorporating and constrained by prior fieldnote writings. The representational processes through which fieldnote segments are selected (or ignored), linked to one another, reworked into a consistent voice, and integrated to produce a clearly recognized rhetorical style have received little or no attention. In this way, most reflexive analyses neglect or marginalize fieldnotes in the construction of finished ethnographic accounts and, thereby, ignore the role of fieldnotes in the in-process work of actively constructing a polished ethnographic account.

Such critical analyses have overlooked not only the use of fieldnotes in writing final ethnographic accounts but also the prior processes whereby ethnographers actually created a fieldnote record in the first place. Yet, this initial transformation of field experiences and observations into written texts involves equally profound and consequential reconstructions of social reality as does the production of polished, full ethnographies. Growing consciousness of the reflexive qualities of ethnographic texts, however, has advanced by and large without attention to day-by-day writing practices for producing what comes to be treated as ethnographic data.

To fill this gap between reflexive analysis and practice, one must look closely at exactly how ethnographers go about writing fieldnotes: how they produce, process, and finally assemble fieldnotes into texts intended for wider audiences. For, in significant ways, describing people, events, and scenes in fieldnotes gives definite shape and substance to these matters for the writer. The writer, after all, does not simply sit down and put directly on paper something already worked out in his head. Rather, he constructs his descriptions: He must decide where to start, what to put first and what later, what to include, and what to ignore. While writing, he determines whose points of view to present, what is significant about a person or event, and what is incidental and can be left out. These decisions are even more salient for subsequent readers who have no independent access to the reality often presumed to lie behind and to have shaped the written account. From a reader's perspective, then, the text about a people's way of life creates that world as a phenomenon.

In the preceding chapters, we have emphasized several specific writing choices that can highlight awareness of the reflexive character of ethnographic research. First, we have advocated writing fieldnotes so that the ethnographer can be seen and heard in them, since the ethnographer's interactions in the field shape her writing. In this way, the processes whereby ethnographic texts come to be produced can be preserved and made available to readers: "Being reflexive is structuring communicative products so that the audience assumes the producer, process, and product are a coherent whole" (Myerhoff and Ruby 1982:6). But, in so writing, the ethnographer reminds herself that what she learned and writes about occurred on a specific occasion and was shaped by her own methods and mode of participation.

Second, we have urged writing fieldnotes in ways that effectively capture and represent members' meanings—the perspectives, understandings, concerns, and voices of those studied. In order to do this effectively, the writer must clearly understand that she is, in fact, re-presenting member's meanings, creating, to paraphrase Geertz (1973), "meanings of meanings" or "interpretations of interpretations."

But a seeming problem arises when we recognize that members' meanings are not things in themselves but representations of something: Why should members' meanings have priority over any other representation an ethnographer might make? Here again, we hold that fieldnotes and finished ethnographies are inevitably and unavoidably mediated by the ethnographer's person, experiences, point of view, and theoretical priorities. But the researcher's point of view and theoretical priorities are not simply pregiven; they are shaped and influenced by the relationships he forms with the people whose social worlds he is trying to understand. As a participant who has a place in the local setting and who has some degree of involvement with the people in it, the researcher is part of the world being studied and not a neutral, detached observer. The process of forming relationships with specific people subjects the ethnographer to their meaning systems, ones that must be learned and understood, if only in order to get by. The more the ethnographer involves himself in others' social worlds, the more he subjects his own presuppositions, his own ways of doing and giving meaning to events and behavior, to the challenges of members' everyday lives. The ethnographer's fieldnotes, then, consist of descriptions of, and reflections on, the meanings acquired and jointly constructed over the course of participation in relationships with those studied. Hence, fieldnotes reflect understandings gained through subjecting oneself to the logic of others' social worlds, a logic that comes to partially constitute the lens through which the ethnographer views and understands those worlds. In the end, what he inevitably writes is his version (informed by theoretical and other concerns and priorities) of their version. But the versions that an ethnographer constructs are negotiated and mediated by members' points of view, logics, and constructions of the world as well as by the researcher's. Hence, through relationships with others, the possibility exists for appreciation and understanding of the interactions that the researcher observes in their, not simply his own, terms.

Reflexivity is central both to how we understand the worlds of others as well as to how we understand the research enterprise. Reflexivity, when applied to the understanding of members' worlds, helps us to see those worlds as shaped, not by variables or structures that stand above or apart from people, but, rather, as meaning systems negotiated and constructed in and through relationships. Hence, when self-consciously applied to ourselves as researchers, the reflexive lens helps us see and appreciate how our own renderings of others' worlds are not, and can never be, descriptions from outside those worlds. Rather, they are informed by, and constructed in and through, relationships with those under study. Hence, in training the reflexive lens on ourselves, we understand our own enterprise in much the same terms that we understand those we study.

Notes

Preface to the First Edition

1. Consider the treatment by Schatzman and Strauss of "Strategy for Recording" in their *Field Research: Strategies for a Natural Sociology* (1973:94–101). Good advice abounds on such matters as when and when not to jot notes in the field, the relative advantages of typing as opposed to taping full notes, and the utility of distinguishing between observational, methodological, and theoretical notes. Yet, nothing is said about what and how one actually writes, about learning writing skills, or about the consequences of different writing styles.

2. This research was supported by the National Science Foundation grant SES-8713255, "The Pro Se Litigant: Self-Representation in Consequential Civil Cases," co-principal investigators Robert M. Emerson and Susan McCoin, 1988–89.

3. Rachel Fretz's research on storytelling among the Chokwe in Zaire in 1982 was supported by a Fulbright-Hayes award and the subsequent Zambian research in 1992 by a Fulbright grant for advanced research.

4. See, for example, Burgess 1982, 1984; Denzin and Lincoln 1994; Ellen 1984; Emerson 1988; Hammersley 1992; Hammersley and Atkinson 1983; Lofland and Lofland 1995; Schatzman and Strauss 1973; Schwartz and Jacobs 1979; Spradley 1980; Taylor and Bogdan 1984.

Chapter One: Fieldnotes in Ethnographic Research

1. For more extended discussions of social constructionism and of interactionist and interpretive paradigms in sociology, see Corbin and Strauss (2008:1–17); Emerson (2001:1–53); and Gubrium and Holstein (1997).

2. The term "member" is drawn from ethnomethodology and its concern with or-

dinary persons' "mastery of natural language" and, ultimately, with the "common-sense knowledge of everyday activities" or "competences" reflected in the use of such language (Garfinkel and Sacks 1970:339). See also ten Have (2004).

3. Here we are assuming that the fieldworker is a "known researcher" in the setting or scene of interest. Many ethnographers now avoid the classic distinction between "overt" and "covert" field research, considering, instead, the more subtle and complex variations within and between "known" and "unknown" research roles (Emerson 2001; Fine 1993; Lofland et al. 2006:40–47; Schwartz and Jacobs 1979; Warren and Karner 2010:50–53).

4. As Mishler (1979:10) has suggested: "[any phenomenon] contains multiple truths, each of which will be revealed by a shift in perspective, method, or purpose. . . . The task is not to exhaust the singular meaning of an event but to reveal the multiplicity of meanings, and . . . it is through the observer's encounter with the event that these meanings emerge."

5. On occasion, the ethnographer may feel as if he has "nonconsequential presence," i.e., is naturally and unproblematically "just an observer." But this sense is, in fact, a contingent and effortful achievement dependent upon the collusive cooperation of the observed (Emerson and Pollner 2001). Field researchers rely upon a variety of interactional practices to achieve and sustain the role of "observer" in the face of various pulls and seductions to participate more fully in unfolding events and, hence, in some sense, to dissolve the very distinction between "observer" and "observed."

6. Georges and Jones (1980) describe many examples of fieldworkers whose research developed directly from the kind of relationships they formed with those encountered in the field.

7. Geertz (1983:55–70) and Bittner (1988) explore several of the implications that flow from recognizing that an ethnographer must remain at least a partial outsider. First, having "been there" and "seen for myself" does not provide compelling authority for written accounts of another world, given that the ethnographer's experience of another world approximates, rather than absolutely replicates, members' experiences. See also the discussion of "ethnographic realism" in Marcus and Cushman (1982). Second, the ethnographer's limited commitment and appreciation of constraint promotes an understanding of other worlds as subjectively perceived and constructed, hence, without the "traits of depth, stability and necessity that people recognize as actually inherent in the circumstances of their existence" (Bittner 1988:155).

8. We would like to acknowledge Caitlin Bedsworth and Nicole Lozano for making these materials available.

9. All of these matters must be handled through the development of a series of writing conventions. See Psathas and Anderson (1990) for a review of the key "transcription symbols" used in making transcripts for conversation analysis

10. In comparing fieldnotes with transcripts made from audio and visual recordings as different methods for reducing ongoing social life to texts, we do not mean to suggest a model of ethnographic research that employs only the former. Rather, most contemporary field researchers rely heavily upon *both* fieldnotes and record-

ings. Fieldwork guides now regularly discuss varied methods for documenting research, emphasizing both audio recording (e.g. Ellen 1984; Goldstein 1964; Jackson 1987; Stone and Stone 1981; Wilson 1986) and the use of video and photography (Ball and Smith 2001; Harper 2005; Warren and Karner 2010).

11. The relative emphasis placed on writing fieldnotes as opposed to recordings, however, varies with the nature of the field researcher's discipline and project. Many ethnographers, for example, often make audio recordings of informal interviews as well as write extensive notes—an essential practice when working in a foreign language and often valuable when working in one's own language and culture. Similarly, other fieldworkers complement their fieldnote research by systematically using audio recordings to capture significant occasions or recurrent events that are central to their theoretical concerns. In contrast, field researchers studying face-to-face interaction, forms of expression, and oral traditions often give primacy to audio recording but, nevertheless, write detailed fieldnotes to supplement verbal accounts with contextual details.

12. Some field researchers urge writing "natural histories" of the research process to link methods and findings (Altheide and Johnson 1994; Athens 1984; Becker 1970). A number of ethnographers have examined specifically how human relationships in field research have influenced final research findings: see the case studies by Duneier (1999:333–57), Ellis (1991), Fine (1996:233–53), and Kleinman (1991), and reviews by Emerson (2001:113–31), Georges and Jones (1980), and Lareau and Shultz (1996).

13. As several researchers (Clifford 1983; Stoddard 1986) have shown, the seeming objectivity and "authority" of ethnographic data (and "scientific data" more widely; Gusfield 1976) is achieved, in part, exactly by suppressing or ignoring their dependence upon the person of the researcher and her methods of inquiry and writing.

14. Seeking to capture indigenous meanings in fieldnotes, however, leaves open issues of whether or not and how to incorporate indigenous meanings into finished ethnographic analyses. Some ethnographers insist that indigenous meanings should not direct and undergird sociological analysis (e.g., Burawoy 1991, 1998; Wacquant 2002). Others—symbolic interactionists and ethnomethodologists within sociology (Pollner and Emerson 2001) and anthropologists concerned with providing "accounts of other worlds from the inside" (Marcus and Fischer 1986:26)—seek to analytically incorporate and represent members' understandings in their finished analyses.

Chapter Two: In the Field: Participating, Observing, and Jotting Notes

1. Jackson (1990b:23), for example, quotes several anthropologists who emphasized the pure "doing" of ethnography as follows: "Fieldnotes get in the way. They interfere with what fieldwork is all about—the doing." And: "*This* is what I would call fieldwork. It is not taking notes in the field but is the interaction between the researcher and the so-called research subjects."

2. Jackson (1990b:25) provides an example of the former, quoting an anthropologist who gained "insight into Australian Aboriginal symbolism about the ground

while on the ground": "You notice in any kind of prolonged conversation, people are squatting, or lie on the ground. I came to be quite intrigued by that, partly because I'd have to, too . . . endless dust." Emerson and Pollner (2001:250) present an instance of the latter when a previously marginalized and detached observer is suddenly brought stage center into an in-the-home psychiatric evaluation.

3. Some ethnographers committed to ez xperiencing immersion may put off systematic writing almost indefinitely, often until leaving the field permanently. Given our commitment to more or less contemporaneously written notes, we do not address procedures for writing fieldnotes long after the occurrence of the events of interest.

4. This term is taken from Jackson (1990b:5), who credits it to Simon Ottenberg.

5. Gottlieb and Graham (1993) depict these processes of note-taking in their narrative of the course of their ethnographic research in Africa.

6. However, Catherine's placement of this remark immediately following introductions indicates that she considers it important "news" that should be delivered to Ellen in a timely fashion, And the remark takes on further import since it involves an explicit change in topic that excludes the newcomer by referring to someone she clearly does not know.

7. These jottings were originally written in a version of speed writing that is incomprehensible to most readers. We have translated them into readable form.

8. Wolfinger (2002) notes that fieldworkers rely heavily on tacit social knowledge and taken-for-granted assumptions when they determine what to observe and what to recall in writing jottings and fieldnotes. These emergent and situational decisions vary with the concerns and personal dispositions of the fieldworker.

9. This excerpt, as well as others in this and subsequent chapters, draws on interviews conducted by Linda Shaw in which student fieldworkers were encouraged to "talk out loud" while seated at their computers writing fieldnotes from jottings and headnotes.

10. It is possible, of course, to *interview* those involved in the social world under study and to ask directly about their own inner states and motives as well as about their assessments of those of others. Such interviews, however, do not provide definitive answers to these matters but only another set of observations that the ethnographer must still assess and evaluate. See Emerson and Pollner's (1988) consideration of the contingent, deeply problematic interpretations required to evaluate the interview statements of a mental health clinic worker asked to assess ethnographic writings describing his own work circumstances and decision making

11. This student ethnographer offered these reflections on this process: "Before, I never could write about it. I just never could remember them [concrete events]. It seemed very small and insignificant because everything with these children is in very small steps, and nothing really outstanding ever happens, but this really stood out in my mind, and I wanted to remember it. At the time, I told myself, 'Remember that.'"

These notes also reflect this student intern/fieldworker's distinctive *commitments* in this setting as is evident in the point of view implicit in her writing. She not only identifies the incident that has just taken place as "listening to the teacher" and as a change from Nicole's prior pattern of behavior. But reflecting her real teaching responsibilities in the setting, she also *evaluates this change positively as an "accomplishment,"* as something that Nicole *should* learn. An ethnographer without job responsibilities in the setting might well characterize the incident differently (e.g., as an adult staff member's exercise of authority) and withhold immediate evaluation as to whether what Nicole did was "good" or "bad."

12. Indeed, Everett Hughes (1971:505) emphasized that it is less the published report than taking a detached outlook toward the personal and intimate that brings people's wrath down upon the field researcher: "The hatred occasionally visited upon the debunking historian is visited almost daily upon the person who reports on the behavior of people he has lived among; and it is not so much the writing of the report, as the very act of thinking in such objective terms that disturbs the people observed."

13. In part, this lack of knowledge about what the field researcher is doing may result from the latter's evolving analytic purposes and concerns, which are not pre-established but which change with immersion in the setting (see Emerson 2001:282–95). As Thorne (1980:287) emphasizes, "fieldworkers usually enter the field with an open-ended sense of purpose; they tend to work inductively and may shift interests and outlooks as the research proceeds; practical exigencies may force extensive change of plans."

14. Similarly, those observed often use humor to comment on the role of the note-taking ethnographer. Again, from the HUD office: "The workers are talking and laughing as Sam decides where to put his desk in his new office. I hear one of the workers say, 'I hope Bob didn't write that down.' I walked up. 'What?' 'Oh, I just told Sam it's good he's got space for his machete behind his desk.' They laugh."

15. Here, further complications arise about whether the ethnographer will write fieldnotes about matters that she avoided making jottings on or was asked not to make jottings on. On the one hand, a fieldworker might feel that her fieldnotes are her personal (as well as scientific) record and that she can write anything and everything in those notes that she desires. Such a practice puts off any decision about whether or not to use these particular fieldnote writings in a paper to be seen by any outside audience. On the other hand, the ethnographer might well feel constrained by an implicit agreement not to take jottings about a particular event and to also avoid writing full fieldnotes about the event, independently of whether anyone would ever read that material. Here, the fieldworker honors the personal, ethical bond with the person observed over any commitment to her fieldnotes as research record.

16. Thus, making jottings "off-phase," recommended by Goffman (1989:130) as a means of minimizing reactive effects (i.e., "don't write your notes on the act you're observing because then people will know what it is you're recording"), may risk offending others when the focus of the jottings appears to be the *current* activity or topic.

17. For example, to have made jottings during a Chokwe initiation ceremony (*mwadi*) when the older women were teaching a young woman how "to dance with a

husband" by simulating the sexual act might have appeared inappropriate and might have drawn immediate criticism from participants.

18. The seductions of the field, seductions that impart "liminal" or "betwixt-and-between" qualities to fieldnotes and the experience of writing them, are strikingly revealed in Jackson's (1990a) interviews with anthropologists. Many reported feeling inclined to let fieldnotes go as they began to fit into the rhythms of local life. For example: "I slowed down. More concerned with the hour by hour. You forget to take notes because you feel this is your life" (Jackson 1990a:18).

19. Field researchers routinely use a number of tactics to maintain research distance in the face of pressures for heightened involvement from those under study (Emerson and Pollner 2001). These practices involve "a variety of distancing practices to manage overtures to deeper involvement," including "interactional efforts to preclude, to finesse, and to decline" such overtures, and "cognitive reminders to retain the 'research' framing of one's experiences in the field" (Emerson and Pollner 2001: 248).

20. Many ethnographers also create that same separate stance through photographing or filming events. See Jackson (1987).

Chapter Three: Writing Fieldnotes I: At the Desk, Creating Scenes on a Page

1. Sanjek (1990b), for example, reports a full year passed before he went from notebook to full fieldnotes; obviously, he spent a great deal of time and care in writing up descriptions and events in these handwritten notebooks.

2. Along these lines, Goffman (1989:127) advises against bringing spouses into the field because "it does give you a way out. You can talk to that person, and all that, and that's no way to make a world."

3. As a general rule, it is important to preserve discrepant reports about the same event to avoid deciding what "really happened" in accepting one account over the other. Here, for example, we can now understand the difference as a likely product of Laura's self-expressed uneasiness with explicit, earthy sexual references.

4. Description is often referred to as one of the four chief types of composition—along with argumentation, exposition, and narration. But here we consider describing as a key strategy for picturing settings, people, objects, and actions as a part of the larger ethnographic narrative that the ethnographer tells throughout her fieldnotes, beginning with the first day that she enters the site and closing when she leaves and writes her last notes.

5. Lofland (1985:15) terms this "categoric knowing" in which "one knows who the other is only in the sense that one knows he can be placed into some category," particularly gender, age, and race, since these categories are readily gleaned from appearance only. In contrast, "personal knowing" involves knowledge of at least some aspects of the other's actual biography.

6. In this sense, this description might be a product of, as well as advance, the ethnographer's theoretical interest in ethnic identity. That is, the observer might have come upon this scene with a preexisting interest in how white students affiliate with

African Americans, this sensitivity leading him to appreciate the ironic symbolism and to write so vividly about the jacket. Alternatively, writing a description of something that made an immediate impression on him might have made him begin to think about issues of cross-cultural affiliation. In either case, in subsequent field-notes, this ethnographer continued to focus on this woman and other white students who hung out with blacks, describing other instances of ethnically distinct clothes, whites' use of black conversational styles, etc.

7. A combination of field observations and tape recordings of specific interactions marks many ethnographic studies of institutional settings, including medical clinics (Maynard 2003), lawyers' offices (Sarat and Felstiner 1995), and public schools (Garot 2010). However, a number of ethnographers found that tape recorders inhibited and distorted talk in informal settings and exchanges; e.g., see Desmond (2007:291–93) on the problems of attempting to tape-record daily activities among wildland fire-fighters.

8. Often her fieldnotes were written in English, though she listened in another language; she therefore included many non-English terms to preserve local meanings.

9. For a discussion of how researchers working in second languages or explicitly focusing on verbal expression combine and integrate these methods, see Stone and Stone (1981). Some sociological field researchers advocate the use of similar sorts of "triangulation" procedures—for example, conducting later interviews with participants about what they were thinking and doing during a recorded exchange; see Cicourel (1974:124ff).

10. Shaw (1991) explores a number of other expressions of this feeling of falling short of achieving a "normal" life, and the resulting pervasive sense of stigma, that afflicts ex–mental patients in their dealings with more conventional people.

11. Grouping details not only makes writing up easier, but the habit of marking paragraph breaks also speeds up reading and making sense of fieldnotes later on.

12. Stoller (1989) suggests that many ethnographers, reflecting their Western culture, have a bias for visual detail even though members might be attending more to other sensory impressions, such as smell, sound, or movement. In this respect, the kinds of sensory details that are dominant vary from one culture to another.

13. Lederman (1990:84) emphasizes that units such as *"events"* have "an apparent 'wholeness'" that makes them "good modes of entry into fieldnotes" and useful analytic units in her ethnography. One can write up an event as a brief episode or more fully describe it in a tale.

14. Schatzman and Strauss (1973:99–101) recommend tagging each fieldnote segment with an initial label, either "Observational Notes" (ON), "Theoretical Notes" (TN), or "Methodological Notes" (MN). Many field researchers find this procedure helpful in marking transitions in writing focus and intent. We generally avoid using these tags because we think that the distinctions are not only theoretically problematic but also practically difficult to apply in many instances.

15. Although not focused specifically on fieldnote descriptions, Wolf (1992) pro-

vides a provocative illustration of the potential variation in how ethnography can portray different slices of life; she presents the "same" series of events in three different story formats—original fieldnotes, a more formal analytic account, and a fictional short story.

Chapter Four: Writing Fieldnotes II: Multiple Purposes and Stylistic Options

1. As Flower (1988) emphasizes, a writer's purpose is not unitary, conscious intention but, rather, a set of interconnected goals; during the writing process, writers regularly revise and prioritize these goals.

2. In addition, the field researcher with actual readers may not want to disclose what they regard as revealing or overly personal incidents to these others, whether instructor, classmates, or coworkers (Warren 2000). We would advise writing up these notes in a separate document. This procedure produces a written account but one seen only by the fieldworker. At a later point, the latter may feel that the account is important and should be included in a final analysis; or, he may decide that it is too personal and keep it private.

3. As Ong (1975) points out, writers envision audiences by imagining the kinds of readers who have read similar pieces of writing. Thus, the writer's stylistic choices are a means of addressing those imagined audiences.

4. As one ethnographer commented, "That might be closer to a definition of a fieldnote: something that can't be readily comprehended by another person" (Jackson 1990b:20).

5. Strictly speaking, point of view is the angle from which one sees activities and events and how that angle is presented in writing. However, Beiderwell and Wheeler (2009:389) point out; "More broadly, point of view signals narrative perspective—the way a story is related. Thinking in terms of point of view involves considering who tells the story as well as how the teller's interests, personality, motives, and background influence what is observed and reported."

6. Here, we refer to "voice" as representing the unique speaking style and the distinctive perspective or "ethos" of an individual (Abrams and Harpham 2009; Beiderwell and Wheeler 2009). Thus, if the ethnographer-as-writer wants to present multiple voices and points of view in her fieldnotes, she must also be sensitive to varied people's perspectives and voices while in the field. In this sense, writing fieldnotes is reflexive, illustrating how writing can play back on and affect what the ethnographer does in the field!

7. Thus, one researcher noted, "I kept track of a student who got in an argument with his teacher. I was not able to read his mind, but based on visual cues from the way he walked, the way he talked, and through his [other] body language, I could get a better insight into how he may have been feeling and what thoughts might be running through his head."

8. Similarly, in writing notes on a checkout line in a grocery store, the fieldworker might describe activities, at different times, from the position and perspective of the checker, the bagger, a customer being served, and customers waiting in line.

9. Many of these objections to an omniscient point of view weaken or even dissolve entirely when we turn from writing fieldnotes to writing final ethnographies. Indeed, existing discussions of omniscience in ethnographic writing all treat final ethnographies, not fieldnotes. Van Maanen's (1988:45–72) "realist tales," for example, are complete ethnographies that involve many omniscient qualities—the absence of the author from the text, minutely detailed descriptions and overviews, and "interpretive omnipotence." Similarly, Brown (1977) sees the omniscient point of view as characteristic of many classic ethnographies; the ethnographer adopts an omniscient point of view, for example, when he chooses which members' voices to present and shifts from one person's view to another's.

10. Writing different points of view involves a shift in the writer's attention. One student points out that when she consciously shifted between points of view, she actually noticed the shifting emphasis within herself: "When I look over my jottings and begin to write up the fieldnotes, my brain thinks differently for first person than it does for third person. When I wrote the fieldnotes in first-person, I found that as much as I wrote about the people around me, I actually thought about the events unfolding from my perspective. When I wrote the fieldnotes in the third-person point of view, I thought more about the other members, what they were doing, and it made me focus a little more on them, rather than on what I was doing." As this student points out, the shifts in point of view are consequential—shaping what and how one sees and reports—and not just matters of taste or technique.

11. Beiderwell and Wheeler explain that although a first-person narrator speaks from the "perspective of one inside the story; that is to say, the narrator speaks as 'I,'" this writing technique is not limited to the narrator's vision. The first-person narrator may have the function of reporting about others (2009:383). This additional use of the first-person technique would appear to be common in writing fieldnotes, where the ethnographer speaks in her own voice to narrate activities with someone else as the central character in the event. This use of first person blurs the boundaries between the writing techniques of first-person and third-person points of view.

12. In this project, Rachel Fretz carried out many of her observations in conjunction with two other researchers working in the same village, art historians Elisabeth Cameron and Manuel Jordan. Researchers who work together in the same site can document and represent the different voices and points of view of various members.

13. Johnstone (1990:18) defines a story as a "*narrative* (that is, it presents a sequence of events) with a *point* (a reason for being told that goes beyond, or is independent of, any need for the reporting of events)." However, the way storytellers structure their narratives to convey ideas varies from one storytelling tradition to another (Johnstone 1990; Riessman 1987; Stahl 1989). In Western hero tales, for example, the protagonist sets forth on a quest, moves through difficulties, and conquers the monster or finds the holy grail. The story is one of personal success and conquest. In contrast, in many cultures the focus is less on an individual's success and personal development and more on the way relationships between people unfold and have consequences for their community or extended family. In such narrative traditions, the

listeners pay attention to how the characters negotiate their relationships and to whether or not they act appropriately toward their relatives and friends. Thus, the teller of a story about an authority figure and a young person in an educational situation might be concerned with the effects of the student's actions on his family, about the student's respect for authority, and about the disciplinarian's opinion of the students' relatives.

14. The current ending of the police tale results from our editing decisions and reflects our search for a loosely structured tale that was relatively short. Had we begun the cut at an earlier point or ended at a later one, the reader's sense of the story line might differ. Or, if we had shortened it further, to begin with the stop at the 7-11 store and to end with the second car stopping, the tale might have seemed more cohesive and more clearly the story of mundane police work broken by moments of excitement.

15. Grounded theorists (Charmaz 2001; Strauss 1987), in particular, emphasize beginning analyses early on in data collection: The researcher is urged to make analytically explicit observed phenomena as theoretical categories, to systematically identify the properties and dimensions of these categories, to formulate provisional questions or hypotheses about the occurrence or relations between these categories, and to then seek out new data in the field specifically relevant to these refined or focused issues.

16. See chapter 6 for discussion of memos connected with coding and analysis when attention has turned from fieldwork to writing a finished ethnographic text.

17. Some ethnographers come to view their own fieldnotes as poor substitutes for their actual experiences and observations in the field. Jackson (1990a: 19), for example, quotes one person's comment: "I was disappointed that they weren't as magical as my memory . . . there are a lot of visual features to my memory, whereas fieldnotes were much more sort of mere rendering." While fieldnotes may never completely capture the lived experience in the field, improving writing skills will suffuse notes with at least some of this "magic." We see wide gaps between memory and fieldnote as evidence of insufficient attention to writing.

Chapter Five: Pursuing Members' Meanings

1. Many studies do not directly claim that a group's beliefs and practices are fallacious or ineffective but indirectly diminish these beliefs and practices by depicting them as self-serving. Berger (1981) proposes the concept of "ideological work" as an alternative way of handling these issues. Many sociological analyses, he argues, "take as their task 'exposing' the 'real' interests served by ideas or 'unmasking' or debunking ideas by revealing the contradictions between what ideas apparently profess and the day-to-day behavior of those who profess them" (1981:19–20). The ethnographer has a different task—"not to expose discrepancies or contradictions between practice and preachment" (1981:114) but, rather, to look closely at and document the ways in which people resolve and reconcile any such discrepancies. For example, rather than "unmasking" rural hippies' use of chain saws as a contradiction of their pro-

fessed distrust of modern "technology," Berger carefully and noncynically examines how these hippies come to view the chain saw as a "tool" distinct from "technology" (1981:116). These sorts of interpretive acts, "aimed at bridging gaps, sweetening dissonances, and restoring (perhaps only temporarily) a measure of harmony and consistency" between practice and belief, represent "remedial ideological work" (1981:114).

2. Jordan's (1993:41–61) discussion of masking traditions in the circumcision (*mukanda*) rituals of Northwest Province, Zambia, explains variation as characteristic of these rituals; he found that innovation in mask decorations can be a means through which people cope with political realities in the region. See also the discussion by Cameron and Jordan (2006) on ritual play in this same area.

3. Hunt's (1985) analysis of the use of force by police illustrates an alternative, more naturalistic approach that seeks to identify what sorts of force the police themselves recognize as excessive or "brutal" and what sorts as legitimate or "normal." Hunt refrains from passing her own judgments in order to learn how and where particular officers apply these distinctions to specific instances of the use of force.

4. Ben-Amos (1982), in particular, has argued that the examination of indigenous classifications has been hindered by the "discrepancy" between ethnic and analytic systems and advocates that researchers document and explain the terms and categories that the people studied use. However, scholars studying oral traditions continue to insist on the comparative value of analytic categories. Okpewho (1992), for example, urges continued use of analytic categories to further comparative discussion even while he commends the practice of using indigenous terms for narrative categories. In an introduction to "folk narratives," Oring (1986) identifies analytic features generally associated with "myth," "legend," and "folktale." Current focus on autoethnography further complicates the distinctions between analytic and indigenous categories; Butz and Besio (2009) provide a review of some autoethnographic practices that include personal experience narrating.

5. Ethnographers may also receive "nonanswers" when they appear to be woefully ignorant of the matters they ask about. Diamond (1989) recounts the story told by an eminent ethnobiologist who has spent years with the Kalam people of the New Guinea Highlands working with native informants to identify folk terms for 1,400 species of animals and plants. Yet, when at one point he asked about rocks, his Kalam informants insisted they had just one word covering all rocks. A year later he returned with a geologist friend who within an hour came back with a long list of Kalam terms for rocks. The ethnobiologist angrily confronted his Kalam informants, demanding to know why they had lied to him about not classifying rocks. They answered: "When you asked us about birds and plants, we saw that you knew a lot about them, and that you could understand what we told you. When you began asking us about rocks, it was obvious you didn't know anything about them. Why should we waste our time telling you something you couldn't possibly understand? But your friend's questions showed that he does know about rocks" (Diamond 1989:30). Diamond concludes that the ethnoscientist has "to know almost as much" as those questioned in order to elicit their native terms and classificatory principles.

6. Cognitive anthropologists, in particular (e.g., Agar 1982; Frake 1964; Spradley 1979), have sought to provide techniques to avoid imposing outside categories by "discovering" appropriate and meaningful questions from within another culture.

7. Frake's classic ethnography, "How to Enter a Yakan House" (1975), includes a detailed analysis of local ways of passing by and greeting others in Yakan society.

8. Of course, paying close attention to ordinary questions and appropriate answers also helps the field researcher learn how to participate in conversations in a natural way, and, hence, is a key part of the resocialization process involved in fieldwork.

9. In a similar vein, see Sudnow's (1967:36–42) subtle observations of the patterned differences in how new medical personnel talk about deaths as "countable" occurrences.

10. Many other fieldworkers also recount socialization through teasing and laughter (cf. Yocom 1990).

11. In general, formulations of "what happened" will not only involve summaries or "glosses" but will be framed to anticipate or influence the specific persons to whom they are recounted.

12. In his classic field study, Cicourel (1968) examines how police and probation officers dealing with youth read and interpret the various written records generated in delinquency cases, including arrest reports, probation investigations, and school reports. He also emphasizes the distinctive practical and strategic considerations that shape how police and probation officers turn their conversations with youth into written reports in the first place (see particularly the case of Audrey; Cicourel 1968:130–66).

13. Johnstone (1990) discusses the way people structure and give meaning to experience through storytelling, both drawing on the group's conventions for storytelling and expressing themselves in their own unique style. Stahl (1989) points out that storytellers often pattern their experiences to fit community values and notions of a story. In interpreting stories, the researcher must infer the implicit values of the teller. Cashman (2008) notes that, although the storytellers of the northern Irish border express their political differences in their stories, they also actively emphasize community values through anecdotes about characters they all know.

14. Of course, this story is also told to the researcher, and, presumably, has been adapted to his concerns and interests and to his relationship with the teller. Consequently, the ethnographer should not only tell "the story" in his fieldnotes but also describe the context of the storytelling: what conversational questions or comments triggered the story, where the storytelling happened (in private or as a part of other activities), and who else was listening.

15. Mills (1990) notes that folklorists, with their emphasis on face-to-face interactions in oral expression, have documented in detailed transcriptions the multiple voices and differing perspectives expressed during performances. Viewing oral performances as emergent and unique, many scholars of oral narrative (for example, Bauman 1992a, 1992b; Briggs 1988; Georges 1981) analyze in detail the dynamics of each performance. Particularly in examining several versions of the "same" oral story,

they show how narrators shape their style and themes to accommodate the audience, situation, and specific circumstances. For example, Cosentino (1982) in his study of Mende storytelling in Sierra Leone, documents three women who argue with each other through their contrasting versions of a folktale: Each story has distinctly different details and clearly differing outcomes. Yitah (2009) notes that Kasena women of northern Ghana argue through proverbial jesting to establish their sense of female personhood as well as to subvert sexist ideology inherent in the proverbs.

16. This discussion is based on Rachel Fretz's research among the Chokwe of Northwest Province, Zambia, in 1992–93. It elaborates and extends the earlier discussion in Fretz (1987) based on research in Bandundu Province, Zaire/Congo.

17. Ben-Amos (1982) suggests that in studying indigenous categories of expression, the researcher should describe the cognitive, expressive, and behavioral levels. He points out that sometimes a people's system of expression includes distinctions made behaviorally but which are not marked by distinct terms and therefore must be discerned through observation of actions in differing social situations.

18. The Chokwe distinguish between two different kinds of *yishima*—longer stories and short sayings or proverbs. Although they do not use distinct terms for each, if pressed, people might say "the long ones" (*yishima yisuku*) for stories or "the short ones" (*yishima yipinji*) for proverbs. People employ the latter in informal and formal conversation (e.g., court sessions) to make a point. In contrast, people tell the longer *yishima* only at night as they sit around their fires visiting and entertaining themselves. In these latter situations, narrators are inventive composers playing to the enthusiastic responses of listeners; thus, different narrators will tell different versions of the same story, and the same narrator's version of a story will vary from telling to telling. A good storytelling performance is described as *chibema*. See also Van Damme (2003) for a review of the study of aesthetics in African cultures.

19. Holstein and Gubrium suggest that members' invoking of context should be examined both from the "bottom up"—looking at how context is built up moment by moment in the sequencing of ordinary talk and interaction—and from the "top down"—looking at how local discourse and culture incorporates broader social structures and cultural understandings. The bottom-up approach focuses on "why that now," that is, on how something said or done previously is invoked as grounds for saying or doing something now. A top-down approach looks at the ways in which broader cultural and social understandings are used in the local setting. For example, the local import of Julie's act of cutting her hair derives from prior staff experience with this resident and from recognition in the local institutional culture that its treatment regime involves sufficient deprivation and isolation that residents often feel drawn back to the fast life of hooking and drugs.

20. Here we draw directly from Moerman's (1969:464) idea of "intracultural contrast." Moerman notes that the seemingly innocuous descriptive claim, "the Thai are noisy in temple," implicitly involves an *inter*cultural comparison on the order of, "The Thai I saw in temple were noisier than Methodists are supposed to be in church." Intracultural contrast of Thai religious behavior would require the eth-

nographer to compare behaviors in different settings within the society, contrasting organizational and interactional patterns found within them. Thus, one might compare the noise (and other aspects of social behavior) in temples with the noise in other locally comparable situations (among the Thai, for example, dispute hearings, village meetings, and casual conversations).

21. As a general practice, Becker advises that when people make distinctions between "us" and "them," "treat these distinctions as diagnostic of that organization, those people, their situation, their careers" (1998:150). Or as he notes concerning medical students' designations of some patients as "crocks": "To put it most pretentiously, when members of one status category make invidious distinctions among the members of another status category with whom they regularly deal, the distinction will reflect the interests of the members of the first category in the relationship" (1993:31).

22. In this instance, what counts as a satisfactory, "official" explanation shifts as speakers change language, but neither explanation fully describes what people do about AIDS/sorcery illnesses. The ethnographer needs to recognize that explanations often are no more than pointers to how the people momentarily see events or how they wish them to be. Explanations do not constitute experience/reality. Jackson (1982:30–31) in his study of the Kuranko people in West Africa, suggests that people invoke verbal, official explanations in times of crisis to validate some claim but that people's everyday experience rarely conforms to such explanations. Verbal explanations and actions are two different types of experience.

23. Classifications, then, should be seen not as determined by particular attributes of the objects being categorized (that is, as "trait driven") but, rather, as driven by actors' "practical purposes at hand" (Schutz 1964). This stance directs attention away from cognitive categories residing inside of actors' heads toward actual interactions and the practical "purposes at hand" that actors pursue in social settings; attributes take on actual salience or relevance vis-à-vis these shifting, emergent purposes. Such purposes at hand will vary widely from moment to moment and situation to situation as actors' purposes emerge, develop, and change.

24. Researchers working within the interdisciplinary field of "the ethnography of speaking" have as their aim a detailed record and description of the differing kinds of expression within a community. Sherzer (1983, 1992) notes that such studies examine not only the range of expression but also their functions within the community.

25. The fieldnote account leaves opaque Ellen's perspective on these events, indicating only, "I heard her out," but without reporting what she said specifically in her own defense. Her reported claim that she did not realize that the author was helping the wife would suggest that she recognized that she had "mistakenly" made the sale to the husband, a stance that might suggest it was not "snaking" because she had not taken the sale "deliberately." It is also possible that she maintained that she had made the sale legitimately, that the customer in fact "belonged" to her because he was making a purchase independently of his wife, or because of the practical contingencies of managing the purchase of a surprise present.

26. In this instance, it is likely that a female ethnographer's presence at the chief's pavilion initially encouraged a woman to narrate; she may well have been reprimanded later for having done so; in any case, no women narrated in that location again. The researcher's gendered presence is frequently consequential in field settings, although often in subtle ways that can only be identified with close, long-term observation. For examinations of the influence of gender in field research, see Camitta (1990); DeVault (1990); Hunt (1984); Lawless (1993); Mills (1990); Thorne (1993); Warren (2001); and Warren and Hackney (2000).

27. Whyte (1955/1993) and Liebow (1967) provided early discussions of these issues. For a comprehensive review of the advantages and drawbacks of "insider" and "outsider" roles based on race/ethnicity, gender, or age, see Emerson (2001:116–23).

28. Dorothy Smith's institutional ethnography (2002, 2005) has played a major role in focusing ethnographers' attention on the relationship between outside influences and everyday life. While we emphasize how members engage, negotiate, and make meaning of interactions carried out within particular social conditions, Smith's focus is on social structures and organization and how they both shape and are reflected in daily activity.

29. Wiseman's (1970) study of how alcoholics "make the rehab route" on skid row in the 1960s uses just such a procedure to examine how a category of people similar to the homeless made contact with and moved through various "supporting institutions." Similarly, Dingwall et al. (1983) studied the identification and processing of neglected and abused children across a variety of institutional points, ranging from hospital emergency rooms and pediatric medical offices through health visitors, child protection, and social service agencies to courts and probation offices.

30. However, field researchers would be well advised to interview people specifically about interactions and occasions, both those they have observed directly and those that occurred out of their presence; such interviews can provide truncated, but often invaluable, accounts of relations and interactions (see Emerson 2009), as well as insight into others' perspectives on these events.

Chapter Six: Processing Fieldnotes: Coding and Memoing

1. Qualitative social scientists have given substantial attention to how to come up with, develop, and elaborate qualitative analyses of social life. The following provide useful orientations to analysis and specific procedures for developing concepts from fieldnote data. Becker (1998, 2001) lays out a series of "generalizing tricks" that provide "ways of expanding the reach of our thinking, of seeing what else we could be thinking and asking, or increasing the ability of our ideas to deal with the diversity of what goes on in the world" (1998:7). Lofland et al. (2006: chapters 6–8) delineate a variety of possible conceptual "topics" for analyzing fieldnote and other qualitative data and suggest how relevant topics can be elaborated and developed into more finished analyses of "generic" social processes (see also Prus 1996). Corbin and Strauss (2008) provide an updated approach to grounded theory that focuses on identifying the properties and dimensions of key components of social life. Finally, Katz (2001b)

suggests a number of general conceptual "warrants" that ethnographers have frequently relied on and that can provide relevance for, and interest in, analyses of field data.

2. Several practitioners of grounded theory now avoid making sharp distinctions between different types of coding and memos. Corbin notes, for example, that while the 1990 edition of *Basics of Qualitative Research* (Strauss and Corbin 1990) discussed code notes, theoretical notes, and operational notes as three different types of memos, "we now want to get away from thinking about memos in a structured manner." She explains: "The reason is that novice researchers often become so concerned with 'getting it right' that they lose the generative fluid aspect of memoing. It is not the form of memos that is important, but the actual doing of them" (Corbin and Strauss 2008:118). We continue to distinguish between in-process memos, code memos, and integrative memos, not on the basis of form, but in terms of their uses and timing in analyzing fieldnotes.

3. Early statements of the grounded theory approach include: Glaser and Strauss (1967); Schatzman and Strauss (1973) and Glaser (1978). Contemporary treatments include Charmaz (2001, 2006); Corbin and Strauss (2008); and Strauss (1987). Substantively, much of the field research using grounded theory methods has examined the treatment and experience of illness; see particularly Biernacki (1986); Charmaz (1991); Corbin and Strauss (1988); and Glaser and Strauss (1965).

4. Of course, quantitative research involves similar sorts of category creation and refinement, typically at the pretest stage, but it does not term this "coding."

5. Corbin illustrates the use of one such program, MAXQDA 2007, to develop and expand her grounded theory analyses of the experiences of Vietnam War veterans; see Corbin and Strauss 2008.

6. Qualitative data analysis reverses the sequence of procedures employed in quantitative analysis: rather than using preestablished categories to sort and then analyze the data, the researcher first analyses the data by means of initial coding and only subsequently sorts it. Thus, in qualitative data analysis, sorting is subordinated to developing and refining analyses; it is more a by-product of the coding process than the end of that process.

7. See Blum (1991) for the completed analysis of these and other issues.

8. That is, that you have only one instance or case in your data does not affect many of the analytic claims that you can develop from it. What is important is the theoretical relevance or import of the instance. A single unusual incident may reveal critical, but rarely observed, processes within a particular setting (Harper 1992) or reflect issues that rarely surface in everyday life but that are of deep concern to members. Similarly, advocates of the sociological procedure of "analytic induction" insist that finding a *single* negative case that contradicts the theoretical explanation that the researcher has developed requires modifying either that explanation or the phenomenon to be explained (Katz 2001a). In this way, theory grows more dense and sophisticated when the researcher looks for and incorporates such negative cases into her analysis.

9. In writing integrative memos, it may be useful, as in this case, to note parallels, connections, or differences from the concepts and findings of published books and articles. However, it is advisable to stay focused on connecting and elaborating the ideas and empirical materials in your memo and to avoid spending time, at this point, explaining the reference and the details of its relevance to your theme.

Chapter Seven: Writing an Ethnography

1. Richardson (1990), however, does discuss ethnographic writing for general audiences in high-circulation trade books and for mass-circulation magazines.

2. Our concept of thematic narrative in ethnography draws heavily upon Atkinson's (1990:126–28) discussion of "fragmented narratives" as the most common form of "conventional ethnography." Fragmented narratives are nonlinear, rearranging and presenting everyday events in "atemporal, paradigmatic relationships" (1990:126). Atkinson contrasts such fragmented narratives with the more classic "chronological narratives" that provide a linear "extended chronicle of events" (1990:126).

3. Many of our recommendations for writing final ethnographies resonate with, and often draw upon, the ideas and advice that Becker (2007) has developed for social science writing in general. Indeed, we strongly recommend that all field researchers who are turning to the process of writing final ethnographies consult Becker's book directly early on in their project.

4. Thus, in a logical argument, the thesis is explicitly stated at the outset, the subsequent points develop that thesis, and the evidence illustrates and confirms the points. Richardson (1990:13) notes how such arguments draw on "logicoscientific codes" of reasoning and representation that stand in sharp contrast to the narrative forms employed in most ethnographies. In practice, the local, concrete commitments of ethnography preclude the highly formal forms of analytic argumentation that may be found in other areas of social science. See also Richardson and St. Pierre's (2005:960ff) discussion of the historically changing styles of social science and ethnographic writing.

5. Each of these topics suggests a theoretical concern related to a specific scholarly literature; indeed, each might well have been formulated because of familiarity with such a literature. "Ethnicity as social construction in high school," for example, expresses an interest in examining ethnic differences as recognized and acted upon by high school students. Similarly, "parental involvement in juvenile court hearings" implicitly raises issues concerning the factors that influence outcomes in juvenile court proceedings. But neither theory nor literature need be explicitly addressed at this point.

6. This is exactly what is involved in the process of analytic induction, where one can modify either the conceptual category or what is being explained, or both, in order to "form a perfect relation between data and explanation" (Katz 2001a:331). Note, however, that modifying themes or conceptual categories to fit fieldnote data may make prior coding irrelevant; indeed, initial code categories often do not hold up throughout the writing.

7. For examples of ethnographies relying on integrative strategies, see Berger (1981), Desmond (2007), Diamond (1992), and Thorne (1993). DeVault (1991), Emerson (1989), Irvine (1999), and Lareau (2003) make heavy use of excerpt strategies.

8. Long incidents or episodes are difficult to handle in the excerpt style, requiring either intimidatingly long excerpts or arbitrary separation into a choppy series of shorter units.

9. Some critics argue that writing analytic ideas in the "ethnographic present" creates a false sense of continuous actions that are ahistorical. Fabian (1983) explores these issues in examining the conceptions of time and history underlying anthropological research. We contend that the included fieldnote excerpts and commentary clearly ground any discussion in specific times, places, and social conditions.

10. However, this excerpt might be used effectively to depict the probation officer's routine practices and concerns, a more appropriate focus given this ethnographer's strong identification with staff.

11. This issue was suggested by Okpewho's (1992:183–203) analysis of "historic legends." Okpewho argues that when telling about events that occurred within the recent past, the narrator produces an account that listeners, some of whom may have been witnesses, can accept as factual. Nevertheless, the teller uses well-known stylistic devices and narrating conventions to recount the event; as a result, "historic legends" sound very similar to "mythic legends" whose events no one witnessed.

12. This idea was, in part, triggered by Young's (1988:121–58) discussion of the links between landscape and narration. She points out that certain rock paintings among the Zuni people have narratives associated with them that people tell when they pass by them. In a similar vein, Kusenbach (2003) describes a "go along" procedure used to stimulate community residents to recount their memories and associations connected with local scenes and landmarks.

13. Under some circumstances, however, a researcher can effectively incorporate analytic or other commentary made in the original fieldnotes into a final text. One might well include such a commentary as a self-contained excerpt in order to dramatize how an initial theoretical insight gave way to a later, more comprehensive understanding. Or a field researcher might use an initial fieldnote commentary to set up or introduce the theme of a section of the final ethnography. For example, a student researcher studying how street people use a public library began a section entitled "Library Materials as Masks" in this fashion: "This is an observation I made early on in my setting: 'There is something that I have always wondered about the "street people" who sit all day at our library. I wonder, as they stare at the pages with that typically blank expression, whether they are actually reading or simply looking down with their thoughts focused on a completely different place in an entirely different time.'"

14. Consider the original brief transcribed quotation characterized by the journal editor as "incomprehensible" and the edited version that ultimately appeared in print (Emerson and Pollner 1988:193) (parentheses indicate passages that were either completely or partially inaudible).

Original: "How does that jibe with your feelings here about what ( ) other formulations seem to. Were there any parts that you thought were um, um ( ) say just way, way, way y' know (we were) stretching it, off the—off the mark? ohh"

Edited: "How does that jibe with your feelings? . . . Were there any parts that you thought were, say just way, way, way y' know, we were stretching it, off the mark?"

15. However, in his ethnography of New York street book vendors, Duneier (1999: 347–48) follows the journalist practice in providing the real names of those studied (with their consent), suggesting that this procedure holds descriptions to "a higher standard of evidence." Folklorists often offer the original names of storytellers, wishing to credit their creativity. In collaborative research, fieldworkers also list their assistants' and coauthors' names. However, when people describe sensitive issues—such as in telling some religious, political, or historical accounts—most ethnographers change the names as Rachel Fretz did in the Mushala fieldnote.

16. This strategy can also be used to introduce the theme of one section in the ethnography.

17. Indeed, Altheide and Johnson (1994:485) insist that "assessing and communicating the interactive process through which the investigator acquired the research experience and information" provide core components of the underlying "logic" or "ethic" of ethnographic research.

18. Indeed, Becker (2007:50) quotes the following advice from Everett Hughes to write introductions last: "Introductions are supposed to introduce. How can you introduce something you haven't written yet? You don't know what it is. Get it written and then you can introduce it." Becker (2007:55) himself recommends the following specific practice in this regard: "You usually find out, by the time you get to the end of your draft, what you have in mind. Your last paragraph reveals to you what the introduction ought to contain, and you can go back and put it in and then make the minor changes in other paragraphs your new-found focus requires."

19. Some ethnographers have struggled against these features of conventional narrative forms. Atkinson (1992:40), for example, considers ethnographic writings that attempt to avoid "monologic ethnography . . . dominated by the voice of the privileged narrator," either by creating *discursive* texts (transcribed conversations between the ethnographer and informant, as in Dwyer 1982) or *polyphonic* texts intended to represent the actual words and ways of thinking of those studied through extended quotations (e.g., Crapanzano 1985; Stacey 1998). Other ethnographers have tried to move beyond conventionally narrative-based texts by writing in a variety of literary forms, including poetry (Richardson 1992), plays (McCall and Becker 1990; Mulkay 1985), and fictional stories (Wolf 1992). For general overviews of these efforts, see Atkinson (1992) and Emerson (2001:306–11, "Ethnographic Conventions and Experimental Texts").

Chapter Eight: Conclusion

1. One problem with conventional ethnography is the one-sidedness of this arrangement: Since ethnographies are written for and circulated almost exclusively among scholarly audiences, those whose lives and voices are depicted rarely get an

opportunity to read and respond publicly to how they have been represented. A number of field researchers (e.g., Bloor 2001; Emerson and Pollner 1988, 1992; Handler 1985; Tedlock 1979) urge taking ethnographic accounts back to those whose lives they represent, not primarily to "validate" those accounts but, rather, to open up active dialogue between members and researchers about the meaning and import of such accounts. Such "dialogue" aims not to produce agreement or consensus but rather to highlight the inevitable differences that will mark the concerns of ethnographers and those whom they have represented (cf. Emerson and Pollner 1992:95–96).

2. Johnson and Altheide (1993:105) summarize these many conflicting demands by insisting that the ethnographer/writer must seek "to locate oneself vis-à-vis the subjects, to accept authority with its responsibility, fallibility, and limitations, and to tell 'your' story about the subject matter, making it clear that you have 'biased' the account with specific focus, selection, description, and interpretation of the materials."

References

Abrams, M. H., and Geoffrey Galt Harpham. 2009. *A Glossary of Literary Terms*. 9th ed. Boston: Wadsworth.

Adler, Patricia A., and Peter Adler. 1987. *Membership Roles in Field Research*. Newbury Park, CA: Sage.

Agar, Michael H. 1982. "Whatever Happened to Cognitive Anthropology: A Partial Review." *Human Organization* 41:82–86.

Ahmad, Sara. 2000. *Strange Encounters, Embodied Others in Post-Coloniality (Transformations)*. London: Routledge.

Aitken, Gill, and Erica Burman. 1999. "Keeping and Crossing Professional and Racialized Boundaries: Implications for Feminist Practice." *Psychology of Women Quarterly* 23:277–97.

Altheide, David L., and John M. Johnson. 1994. "Criteria for Assessing Interpretive Validity in Qualitative Research." In Denzin and Lincoln, *Handbook of Qualitative Research*, 485–99.

Athens, Lonnie H. 1984. "Scientific Criteria for Evaluating Qualitative Studies." In *Studies in Symbolic Interaction*, vol. 5, ed. Norman K. Denzin. Greenwich, CT: JAI Press.

Andersen, Margaret L. 1993. "Studying across Difference: Race, Class, and Gender in Qualitative Research." In *Race and Ethnicity in Research Method*, ed. John H. Stanfield II and Rutledge M. Dennis, 39–52. Newbury Park, CA: Sage.

Anderson, Elijah. 1990. *Streetwise: Race, Class, and Change in an Urban Community*. Chicago: University of Chicago Press.

Atkinson, Paul. 1990. *The Ethnographic Imagination: Textual Constructions of Reality.* New York: Routledge.

———. 1992. *Understanding Ethnographic Texts.* Newbury Park, CA: Sage.

Atkinson, Paul, Amanda Coffey, Sara Delamont, John Lofland, and Lyn Lofland, eds. 2001. *Handbook of Ethnography.* London: Sage.

Baca Zinn, Maxine. 2001. "Insider Field Research in Minority Communities." In Emerson, *Contemporary Field Research: Perspectives and Formulations,* 159–66.

Baldamus, W. 1972. "The Role of Discoveries in Social Science." In *The Rules of the Game: Cross-Disciplinary Essays on Models in Scholarly Thought,* ed. T. Shanin, 276–302. London: Tavistock.

Ball, Mike, and Greg Smith. 2001. "Technologies of Realism? Ethnographic Uses of Photography and Film." Chapter 21 in Atkinson et al., *Handbook of Ethnography.*

Barth, Fredrik, ed. 1969. *Ethnic Groups and Boundaries.* Boston: Little, Brown.

Batchelder, D., and E. Warner. 1977. *Beyond Experience.* Brattleboro, VT: The Experiment Press.

Bauman, Richard. 1992a. *Story, Performance, and Event: Contextual Studies of Oral Narrative.* Cambridge: Cambridge University Press.

———, ed. 1992b. *Folklore, Cultural Performances, and Popular Entertainments: A Communications Centered Handbook.* Oxford: Oxford University Press.

Becker, Howard S. 1970. *Sociological Work: Method and Substance.* Chicago: Aldine.

———. 1993. "How I Learned What a Crock Was." *Journal of Contemporary Ethnography* 22:28–35.

———. 1998. *Tricks of the Trade: How to Think about Your Research While You're Doing It.* Chicago: University of Chicago Press.

———. 2001. "Tricks of the Trade." In Emerson, *Contemporary Field Research: Perspectives and Formulations,* 353–60.

———. 2007. *Writing for Social Scientists: How to Start and Finish Your Thesis, Book, or Article.* 2nd ed. Chicago: University of Chicago Press.

Beiderwell, Bruce, and Jeffrey M. Wheeler. 2009. *The Literary Experience: Essential Edition.* Boston: Thomson Wadsworth.

Ben-Amos, Dan. 1982. "Analytical Categories and Ethnic Genres." In *Folklore in Context: Essays,* 38–64. New Delhi: South Asian Publishers.

Berger, Bennett M. 1981. *The Survival of a Counterculture: Ideological Work and Everyday Life among Rural Communards.* Berkeley: University of California Press.

Bhopal, Kalwant. 2001. "Researching South Asian Women: Issues of Sameness and Difference in the Research Process." *Journal of Gender Studies* 10:279–86.

Biernacki, Patrick. 1986. *Pathways from Heroin Addiction: Recovery with Treatment.* Philadelphia: Temple University Press.

Bittner, Egon. 1988. "Realism in Field Research." In Emerson, *Contemporary Field Research: A Collection of Readings,* 149–55.

Bleich, David. 1993. "Ethnography and the Study of Literacy: Prospects for Socially

Generous Research." In *Into the Field: Sites of Composition Studies*, ed. Anne Ruggles Gere, 176–92. New York: Modern Language Association of America.

Bloor, Michael. 2001. "Techniques of Validation in Qualitative Research: A Critical Commentary." In Emerson, *Contemporary Field Research: Perspectives and Formulations*, 383–95.

Blum, Nancy S. 1991. "The Management of Stigma by Alzheimer Family Caregivers." *Journal of Contemporary Ethnography* 20:263–84.

Blumer, Herbert. 1969. *Symbolic Interactionism: Perspective and Method*. Englewood Cliffs, NJ: Prentice Hall.

———. 1997. "Foreword" to Lonnie Athens, *Violent Criminal Acts and Actors Revisited*. Urbana: University of Illinois Press.

Bogdan, Robert, and Steven J. Taylor. 1987. "Toward a Sociology of Acceptance: The Other Side of the Study of Deviance." *Social Policy* 18:34–39.

Booth, Wayne C., Gregory G. Colomb, and Joseph M. Williams. 2008. *The Craft of Research*. 3rd ed. Chicago: University of Chicago Press.

Briggs, Charles L. 1988. *Competence in Performance: The Creativity of Tradition in Mexicano Verbal Art*. Philadelphia: University of Pennsylvania Press.

Brown, Richard H. 1977. *A Poetic for Sociology: Toward a Logic of Discovery in the Human Sciences*. Cambridge: Cambridge University Press.

Bulmer, Martin. 1979. "Concepts in the Analysis of Qualitative Data: A Symposium." *Sociological Review* 27:651–77.

Burawoy, Michael. 1991. *Ethnography Unbound: Power and Resistance in the Modern Metropolis*. Berkeley and Los Angeles: University of California Press.

———. 1998. "The Extended Case Method." *Sociological Theory* 16:4–33.

Burgess, Robert G. 1982. *Field Research: A Sourcebook and Field Manual*. London: George Allen & Unwin.

———. 1984. *In the Field: An Introduction to Field Research*. London: George Allen & Unwin.

Burns, Stacy Lee. 2000. *Making Settlement Work: An Examination of the Work of Judicial Mediators*. Burlington VT: Ashgate.

Butz, David, and Kathryn Besio. 2009. "Autoethnography." *Geography Compass* 5(3): 1660–74.

Cahill, Spencer E. 1985. "Meanwhile Backstage: Public Bathrooms and the Interaction Order." *Urban Life* 14:33–58.

Cameron, Elisabeth L., and Manuel A. Jordan. 2006. "Playing with the Future: Children and Rituals in North-Western Province, Zambia." In *Playful Performers: African Children's Masquerades*, ed. Simon Ottenberg and David A. Brinkley, 237–46. New Brunswick, NJ: Transaction.

Camitta, Miriam. 1990. "Gender and Method in Folklore Fieldwork." *Southern Folklore* 47:21–31.

Cashman, Ray. 2008. *Storytelling on the Northern Irish Border: Characters and Community*. Bloomington: Indiana University Press.

Charmaz, Kathy. 1991. *Good Days, Bad Days: The Self in Chronic Illness and Time*. New Brunswick, NJ: Rutgers University Press.

———. 2001. "Grounded Theory." In Emerson, *Contemporary Field Research: Perspectives and Formulations*, 335–52.

———. 2006. *Constructing Grounded Theory*. Thousand Oaks, CA: Sage.

Cicourel, Aaron V. 1968. *The Social Organization of Juvenile Justice*. New York: John Wiley.

———. 1974. *Cognitive Sociology: Language and Meaning in Social Interaction*. New York: Free Press.

Clarke, Michael. 1975. "Survival in the Field: Implications of Personal Experience in Field Work." *Theory and Society* 2:95–123.

Clifford, James. 1983. "On Ethnographic Authority." *Representations* 1:118–46.

———. 1986. "On Ethnographic Allegory." In Clifford and Marcus, *Writing Culture*, 98–121.

———. 1990. "Notes on (Field)notes." In Sanjek, *Fieldnotes*, 47–70.

Clifford, James, and George E. Marcus, eds. 1986. *Writing Culture: The Poetics and Politics of Ethnography*. Berkeley: University of California Press.

Corbin, Juliet M., and Anselm Strauss. 1988. *Unending Work and Care: Managing Chronic Illness at Home*. San Francisco: Jossey-Bass.

———. 2008. *Basics of Qualitative Research*. 3rd ed. Los Angeles: Sage.

Cosentino, Donald. 1982. *Defiant Maids and Stubborn Farmers: Tradition and Invention in Mende Story Performances*. Cambridge: Cambridge University Press.

Crapanzano, Vincent. 1985. *Waiting: The Whites of South Africa*. New York: Random House.

Denzin, Norman K., and Yvonna C. Lincoln, eds. 1994. *Handbook of Qualitative Research*. Thousand Oaks, CA: Sage Publications.

Desmond, Matthew. 2007. *On the Fireline: Living and Dying with Wildland Firefighers*. Chicago: University of Chicago Press.

DeVault, Marjorie L. 1990. "Talking and Listening from Women's Standpoint: Feminist Strategies for Interviewing and Analysis." *Social Problems* 37:96–116.

———. 1991. *Feeding the Family: The Social Organization of Caring as Gendered Work*. Chicago: University of Chicago Press.

———. 1995. "Ethnicity and Expertise: Racial-Ethnic Knowledge in Sociological Research." *Gender and Society* 1995:612–31.

Diamond, Jared. 1989. "The Ethnobiologist's Dilemma." *Natural History*, no. 6 (June): 26–30.

Diamond, Timothy. 1992. *Making Gray Gold: Narratives of Nursing Home Care*. Chicago: University of Chicago Press.

Dingwall, Robert, J. Eekelaar, and T. Murray. 1983. *The Protection of Children: State Intervention and Family Life*. Oxford: Basil Blackwell.

Douglas, Jack D. 1976. *Investigative Social Research: Individual and Team Field Research*. Beverly Hills, CA: Sage Publications.

Duneier, Mitchell. 1999. *Sidewalk*. New York: Farrar, Strauss and Giroux.

————. 2004. "Three Rules I Go By in My Ethnographic Research on Race and Racism." In *Researching Race and Racism*, ed. Martin Bulmer and John Solomos, 92–103. London: Routledge.

Dwyer, Kevin. 1982. *Moroccan Dialogues: Anthropology in Question*. Baltimore: John Hopkins University Press.

Ellen, R. F., ed. 1984. *Ethnographic Research: A Guide to General Conduct*. London: Academic Press.

Ellis, Carolyn. 1991. "Sociological Introspection and Emotional Experience." *Symbolic Interaction* 14:23–50.

Emerson, Robert M. 1987. "Four Ways to Improve the Craft of Fieldwork." *Journal of Contemporary Ethnography* 16:69–89.

————, ed. 1988. *Contemporary Field Research: A Collection of Readings*. Prospect Heights, IL: Waveland.

————. 1989. "Tenability and Troubles: The Construction of Accommodative Relations by Psychiatric Emergency Teams." In *Perspectives on Social Problems: A Research Annual*, ed. Gale Miller and James A. Holstein, 1:215–37. Greenwich, CT: JAI Press.

————, ed. 2001. *Contemporary Field Research: Perspectives and Formulations*. 2nd ed. Prospect Heights, IL: Waveland.

————. 2008. "Responding to Roommate Troubles: Reconsidering Informal Dyadic Control." *Law & Society Review* 42:483–512.

————. 2009. "Ethnography, Interaction and Ordinary Trouble." *Ethnography* 10: 535–48.

Emerson, Robert M., and Sheldon L. Messinger. 1977. "The Micro-Politics of Trouble." *Social Problems* 25:121–34.

Emerson, Robert M., and Melvin Pollner. 1976. "Dirty Work Designations: Their Features and Consequences in a Psychiatric Setting." *Social Problems* 23:243–55.

————. 1988. "On the Uses of Members' Responses to Researchers' Accounts." *Human Organization* 47:189–98.

————. 1992. "Difference and Dialogue: Members' Readings of Ethnographic Texts." In *Perspectives on Social Problems: A Research Annual*, ed. Gale Miller and James A. Holstein, 3:79–98. Greenwich, CT: JAI Press.

————. 2001. "Constructing Participant/Observer Relations." In Emerson, *Contemporary Field Research: Perspectives and Formulations*, 239–59.

Fabian, Johannes. 1983. *Time and the Other: How Anthropology Makes Its Object*. New York: Columbia University Press.

Fetterman, David M. 1989. *Ethnography: Step by Step*. Newbury Park, CA: Sage Publications.

Fielding, Nigel. 2001. "Computer Applications in Qualitative Research." In Atkinson et al., *Handbook of Ethnography*, 453–67.

Fine, Elizabeth C. 1984. *The Folklore Text: From Performance to Print*. Bloomington: University of Indiana Press.

Fine, Gary A. 1993. "Ten Lies of Ethnography: Moral Dilemmas in Field Research." *Journal of Contemporary Ethnography* 22:267–94.

———. 1996. *Kitchens: The Culture of Restaurant Work*. Berkeley and Los Angeles: University of California Press.

Flower, Linda S. 1988. "The Construction of Purpose in Writing and Reading." *College English* 50:528–50.

Forester, John. N.d. "Notes on Writing in and after Graduate School." Unpublished paper.

Frake, Charles O. 1964. "Notes on Queries in Ethnography." *American Anthropologist* 66, no. 3, pt. 2:132–45.

———. 1975. "How to Enter a Yakan House." In *Sociocultural Dimensions of Language Use*, ed. Mary Sanchez and Ben Blount, 25–40. New York: Academic Press.

Fretz, Rachel I. 1987. "Storytelling among the Chokwe of Zaire: Narrating Skill and Listener Responses." Ph.D. diss., Folklore and Mythology Program, University of California, Los Angeles.

———. 1994. "Through Ambiguous Tales: Women's Voices in Chokwe Storytelling." *Oral Tradition* 9:230–50.

———. 1995a. "Answering-in-Song: Listener Responses in *Yishima* Performances." *Western Folklore* 9:95–112.

———. 1995b. "Revising and Retelling: Ritual Images in Chokwe Narratives in Zaire and Zambia." Unpublished paper, Writing Programs, University of California, Los Angeles.

Frohmann, Lisa. 1991. "Discrediting Victims' Allegations of Sexual Assault: Prosecutorial Accounts of Case Rejections." *Social Problems* 38:213–26.

———. 1997. "Convictability and Discordant Locales: Reproducing Race, Class and Gender Ideologies in Prosecutorial Decisionmaking." *Law & Society Review* 31: 531–55.

Garfinkel, Harold. 1967. *Studies in Ethnomethodology*. Englewood Cliffs, NJ: Prentice Hall.

Garfinkel, Harold, and Harvey Sacks. 1970. "On Formal Structures of Practical Actions." In *Theoretical Sociology*, ed. J. C. McKinney and E. A. Tiryakian, 338–66. New York: Appleton Century Crofts.

Garot, Robert. 2010. *Who You Claim: Performing Gang Identity in School and on the Streets*. New York: New York University Press.

Gearing, Frederick O. 1970. *The Face of the Fox*. Chicago: Aldine.

Geertz, Clifford. 1973. "Thick Description: Toward an Interpretive Theory of Culture." In *The Interpretation of Culture*, 3–30. New York: Basic Books.

———. 1983. *Local Knowledge: Further Essays in Interpretive Anthropology*. New York: Basic Books.

Georges, Robert A. 1981. "Do Narrators Really Digress? A Reconsideration of 'Audience Asides' in Narrating." *Western Folklore* 40:245–52.

Georges, Robert A., and Michael O. Jones. 1980. *People Studying People: The Human Element in Fieldwork*. Berkeley: University of California Press.

Glaser, Barney G. 1978. *Theoretical Sensitivity*. Mill Valley, CA: Sociology Press.

Glaser, Barney G., and Anselm L. Strauss. 1965. *Awareness of Dying*. Chicago: Aldine.

———. 1967. *The Discovery of Grounded Theory: Strategies for Qualitative Research*. Chicago: Aldine.

Goffman, Erving. 1961. *Asylums*. Garden City, NJ: Doubleday.

———. 1971. *Stigma: Notes on the Management of Spoiled Identity*. Englewood Cliffs, NJ: Prentice Hall.

———. 1989. "On Fieldwork." *Journal of Contemporary Ethnography* 18:123–32.

Goldstein, Kenneth S. 1964. *A Guide for Field Workers in Folklore*. Hatboro, PA: Folklore Associates.

Gottlieb, Alma, and Philip Graham. 1993. *Parallel Worlds: An Anthropologist and a Writer Encounter Africa*. New York: Crown Publishers.

Gubrium, Jaber F., and James A. Holstein. 1997. *The New Language of Qualitative Method*. New York: Oxford University Press.

Gunaratnam, Yasmin. 2003. *Researching "Race" and Ethnicity: Methods, Knowledge, and Power*. Thousand Oaks, CA: Sage.

Gusfield, Joseph. 1976. "The Literary Rhetoric of Science: Comedy and Pathos in Drinking Driver Research." *American Sociological Review* 41:16–34.

Hammersley, Martyn. 1992. *What's Wrong with Ethnography?* London: Routledge.

Hammersley, Martyn, and Paul Atkinson. 1983. *Ethnography: Principles in Practice*. London: Tavistock.

Handler, Richard. 1985. "On Dialogue and Destructive Analysis: Problems in Narrating Nationalism and Ethnicity." *Journal of Anthropological Research* 41:171–82.

Harper, Douglas. 1992. "Small N's and Community Case Studies." In *What Is a Case? Exploring the Foundations of Social Inquiry*, ed. Charles C. Ragain and Howard S. Becker, 139–58. Cambridge: Cambridge University Press.

———. 2005. "What's New Visually?" In *Handbook of Qualitative Research*, 3rd ed., ed. Norman K. Denzin and Yvonna S. Lincoln, 747–62. Thousand Oaks, CA: Sage.

Heritage, John. 1984. *Garfinkel and Ethnomethodology*. Cambridge: Polity Press.

Hilbert, Richard A. 1980. "Covert Participant Observation: On Its Nature and Practice." *Urban Life* 9:51–78.

Holstein, James A., and Jaber F. Gubrium. 2004. "Context: Working It Up, Down and Across." Chapter 17 in Seale et al., *Qualitative Research Practice*.

Hughes, Everett C. 1960. "The Place of Field Work in Social Science." In Junker, *Field Work*, v–xv. Chicago: University of Chicago Press.

———. 1971. *The Sociological Eye: Selected Papers*. Chicago: Aldine.

Hunt, Jennifer. 1984. "The Development of Rapport through the Negotiation of Gender in Field Work among Police." *Human Organization* 45:283–96.

———. 1985. "Police Accounts of Normal Force." *Urban Life* 13:315–41.

Hymes, Dell. 1991. *"In Vain I Tried to Tell You": Essays in Native American Ethnopoetics*. Philadelphia: University of Pennsylvania Press.

Irvine, Leslie. 1999. *Codependent Forevermore: The Invention of Self in a Twelve Step Group*. Chicago: University of Chicago Press.

Jackson, Bruce. 1987. *Fieldwork*. Chicago: University of Illinois Press.

Jackson, Jean E. 1990a. "'Deja Entendu': The Liminal Qualities of Anthropological Fieldnotes." *Journal of Contemporary Ethnography* 19:8–43.

———. 1990b. "'I Am a Fieldnote': Fieldnotes as a Symbol of Professional Identity." In Sanjek, *Fieldnotes,* 3–33.

Jackson, Michael. 1982. *Allegories of the Wilderness: Ethics and Ambiguity in Kuranko Narratives.* Bloomington: Indiana University Press.

Johnson, John M., and David L. Altheide. 1993. "The Ethnographic Ethic." In *Studies in Symbolic Interaction,* ed. Norman K. Denzin, 14:95–107. Greenwich, CT: JAI Press.

Johnstone, Barbara. 1990. *Stories, Community, and Place: Narratives from Middle America.* Bloomington: Indiana University Press.

Jordan, Manuel. 1993. "Le Masque comme processus ironiques: Les *Makishi* du Nord-Ouest de la Zambie." *Anthropologie et Société* 17:41–61.

Jules-Rosette, Bennetta. 1975. *Vision and Realities: Aspects of Ritual and Conversion in an African Church.* Ithaca, NY: Cornell University Press.

Junker, Buford H. 1960. *Field Work: An Introduction to the Social Sciences.* Chicago: University of Chicago Press.

Karp, Ivan, and Martha B. Kendall. 1982. "Reflexivity in Field Work." In *Explaining Human Behavior: Consciousness, Human Action, and Social Structure,* ed. Paul F. Secord, 249–73. Beverly Hills, CA: Sage.

Katz, Jack. 1988a. "A Theory of Qualitative Methodology: The System of Analytic Fieldwork." In Emerson, *Contemporary Field Research: A Collection of Readings,* 127–48.

———. 1988b. *Seductions of Crime: Moral and Sensual Attractions in Doing Evil.* New York: Basic Books.

———. 2001a. "Analytic Induction Revisited." In Emerson, *Contemporary Field Research: Perspectives and Formulations,* 331–34.

———. 2001b. "Ethnography's Warrants." In Emerson, *Contemporary Field Research: Perspectives and Formulations,* 361–82.

———. 2001c. "From How to Why: On Luminous Description and Causal Inference in Ethnography (Part 1)." *Ethnography* 2(4):443–73.

———. 2002. "From How to Why: On Luminous Description and Causal Inference in Ethnography (Part 2)." *Ethnography* 3(1):63–90.

Kelle, Udo. 2004. "Computer-Assisted Qualitative Data Analysis." In Seale et al., *Qualitative Research Practice,* 443–59.

Kleinman, Sherryl. 1991. "Fieldworkers' Feelings: What We Feel, Who We Are, How We Analyze." In *Experiencing Fieldwork: An Inside View of Qualitative Research,* ed. William B. Shaffir and Robert A. Stebbins, 184–95. Newbury Park, CA: Sage Publications.

Kusenbach, Margarethe. 2003. "Street Phenomenology: The Go-Along as Ethnographic Research Tool." *Ethnography* 4:455–85.

Lareau, Annette. 2003. *Unequal Childhoods: Class, Race, and Family Life.* Berkeley: University of California Press.

Lareau, Annette, and Jeffrey Shultz, eds. 1996. *Journeys through Ethnography: Realistic Accounts of Fieldwork*. Boulder CO: Westview Press.

Lawless, Elaine. 1993. *Holy Women, Wholly Women: Sharing Ministries through Life Stories and Reciprocal Ethnography*. Philadelphia: University of Pennsylvania Press.

Lederman, Rena. 1990. "Pretexts for Ethnography: On Reading Fieldnotes." In Sanjek, *Fieldnotes*, 71–91.

Liebow, Elliot. 1967. *Tally's Corner: A Study of Negro Streetcorner Men*. Boston: Little, Brown.

Lofland, John, and Lyn H. Lofland. 1995. *Analyzing Social Settings: A Guide to Qualitative Observation and Analysis*. 3rd ed. Belmont, CA: Wadsworth.

Lofland, John, David Snow, Leon Anderson, and Lyn H. Lofland. 2006. *Analyzing Social Settings: A Guide to Qualitative Observation and Analysis*. 4th ed. Belmont CA: Wadsworth/Thomson.

Lofland, Lyn H. 1985. *A World of Strangers: Order and Action in Urban Public Space*. Prospect Heights, IL: Waveland Press.

Lutkehaus, Nancy. 1990. "Refractions of Reality: On the Use of Other Ethnographers' Fieldnotes." In Sanjek, *Fieldnotes*, 303–23.

Lyman, Stanford M., and William A. Douglass. 1973. "Ethnicity: Strategies of Collective and Individual Impression Management." *Social Research* 40:344–65.

Lynch, Michael. 1985. *Art and Artifact in Laboratory Science: A Study of Shop Work and Shop Talk in a Research Laboratory*. London: Routledge and Kegan Paul.

Marcus, George E. 1986. "Afterword: Ethnographic Writing and Anthropological Careers." In Clifford and Marcus, *Writing Culture*, 262–66.

Marcus, George E., and Richard Cushman. 1982. "Ethnographies as Texts." *Annual Review of Anthropology* 11:25–69.

Marcus, George E., and Michael M. Fisher. 1986. *Anthropology as Cultural Critique*. Chicago: University of Chicago Press.

Marger, Martin. 1991. *Race and Ethnic Relations*. Belmont, CA: Wadsworth.

Matza, David. 1969. *Becoming Deviant*. Englewood Cliffs, NJ: Prentice Hall.

Maynard, Douglas W. 2003. *Bad News, Good News: Conversational Order in Everyday Talk and Clinical Settings*. Chicago: University of Chicago Press.

McCall, M., and Howard S. Becker. 1990. "Performance Science." *Social Problems* 32: 117–32.

Mills, Margaret A. 1990. "Critical Theory and the Folklorists: Performance, Interpretive Authority, and Gender." *Southern Folklore* 47:5–15.

Mishler, Elliot G. 1979. "Meaning in Context: Is There Any Other Kind?" *Harvard Education Review* 49:1–19.

Moerman, Michael. 1969. "A Little Knowledge." In *Cognitive Anthropology*, ed. Stephen A. Tyler, 449–69. New York: Holt, Rinehart and Winston.

Morris, Edward W. 2007. "Researching Race: Identifying a Social Construction through Qualitative Methods and an Interactionist Perspective." *Symbolic Interaction* 30:409–25.

Mulkay, M. 1985. *The Word and the World: Explorations in the Form of Sociological Analysis.* London: George Allen & Unwin.

Myerhoff, Barbara. 1978. *Number Our Days.* New York: E. P. Dutton.

Myerhoff, Barbara, and Jay Ruby. 1982. "Introduction." In *A Crack in the Mirror: Reflexive Perspectives in Anthropology,* ed. Jay Ruby, 1–35. Philadelphia: University of Pennsylvania Press.

Nader, Laura. 1969. "Up the Anthropologist—Perspectives Gained from Studying Up." In *Reinventing Anthropology,* ed. D. Hymes, 284–311. New York: Vintage.

Okpewho, Isidore. 1992. *African Oral Literature: Backgrounds, Character, and Community.* Bloomington: Indiana University Press.

Ong, Walter J. 1975. "The Writer's Audience Is Always a Fiction." *PMLA* 90:9–21.

Oring, Elliott. 1986. "Folk Narratives." In *Folk Groups and Folklore Genres: An Introduction,* ed. Elliott Oring, 121–45. Logan: Utah State University Press.

Ottenberg, Simon. 1990. "Thirty Years of Fieldnotes: Changing Relationships to the Text." In Sanjek, *Fieldnotes,* 139–60.

Papadopoulos, Irena, and Shelley Lees. 2002. "Developing Culturally Competent Researchers." *Journal of Advanced Nursing* 37:258–64.

Pollner, Melvin, and Robert M. Emerson. 2001. "Ethnomethodology and Ethnography." Chapter 8 in Atkinson et al., *Handbook of Ethnography.*

Pollner, Melvin, and Lynn McDonald-Wikler. 1985. "The Social Construction of Unreality: A Case Study of a Family's Attribution of Competence to a Severely Retarded Child." *Family Process* 24:241–54.

Prus, Robert. 1996. *Symbolic Interaction and Ethnographic Research: Intersubjectivity and the Study of Human Lived Experience.* Albany, NY: SUNY Press.

Psathas, George, and Timothy Anderson. 1990. "The 'Practices' of Transcription in Conversation Analysis." *Semiotica* 78:75–99.

Richards, T. J., and Lyn Richards. 1994. "Using Computers in Qualitative Research." In Denzin and Lincoln, *Handbook of Qualitative Research,* 445–63.

Richardson, Laurel. 1990. *Writing Strategies: Reaching Diverse Audiences.* Newberry Park, CA: Sage Publications.

———. 1992. "The Consequences of Poetic Representation: Writing the Other, Writing the Self." In *Investigating Subjectivity: Research on Lived Experience,* ed. Carolyn Ellis and Michael G. Flaherty. Newbury Park, CA: Sage.

Richardson, Laurel, and Elizabeth St. Pierre. 2005. "Writing: A Method of Inquiry." In *Handbook of Qualitative Research,* Norman K. Denzin and Yvonna S. Lincoln, 3rd ed. Thousand Oaks, CA: Sage.

Riessman, Catherine Kohler. 1987. "When Gender Is Not Enough: Women Interviewing Women." *Gender and Society* 1:172–207.

Rochford, E. Burke, Jr. 1985. *Hare Krishna in America.* New Brunswick, NJ: Rutgers University Press.

———. 1992. "On the Politics of Member Validation: Taking Findings Back to Hare Krishna." In *Perspectives on Social Problems: A Research Annual,* ed. Gale Miller and James A. Holstein, 3:99–116. Greenwich, CT: JAI Press.

Rock, Paul. 2001. "Symbolic Interactionism and Ethnography." Chapter 2 in Atkinson et al., *Handbook of Ethnography*.

Royce, Anya P. 1982. *Ethnic Identity: Strategies of Diversity*. Bloomington: Indiana University Press.

Sacks, Harvey. 1992. *Lectures on Conversation: Volume 1*. Cambridge MA; Blackwell.

Sanjek, Roger, ed. 1990a. *Fieldnotes: The Making of Anthropology*. Ithaca, NY: Cornell University Press.

———. 1990b. "Preface." In Sanjek, *Fieldnotes*, xi–viii.

———. 1990c. "A Vocabulary for Fieldnotes." In Sanjek, *Fieldnotes*, 92–121.

———. 1990d. "The Secret Life of Fieldnotes." In Sanjek, *Fieldnotes*, 187–270.

Sarat, Austin, and William L. F. Felstiner. 1995. *Divorce Lawyers and Their Clients: Power and Meaning in the Legal Process*. New York: Oxford University Press.

Schatzman, Leonard, and Anselm Strauss. 1973. *Field Research: Strategies for a Natural Sociology*. Englewood Cliffs, NJ: Prentice Hall.

Schegloff, Emanuel A. 1997. "Whose Text? Whose Context?" *Discourse and Society* 8: 165–87.

Schutz, Alfred. 1962. *Collected Papers*. Vol. 1, *The Problem of Social Reality*, ed. M. Natanson. The Hague: Martinus Nijhoff.

———. 1964. *Collected Papers*. Vol. 2, *Studies in Social Theory*, ed. A. Brodersen. The Hague: Martinus Nijhoff.

Schwartz, Barry. 1975. *Queuing and Waiting: Studies in the Social Organization of Access and Delay*. Chicago: University of Chicago Press.

Schwartz, Howard, and Jerry Jacobs. 1979. *Qualitative Sociology: A Method to the Madness*. New York: The Free Press.

Seale, Clive, Giampietro Gobo, Jaber F. Gubrium, and David Silverman, eds. 2004. *Qualitative Research Practice*. London: Sage.

Shaw, Linda L. 1988. "Board and Care: The Everyday Lives of Ex-Mental Patients in the Community." Ph.D. diss., University of California, Los Angeles.

———. 1991. "Stigma and the Moral Careers of Ex-Mental Patients Living in Board and Care." *Journal of Contemporary Ethnography* 20:285–305.

Sherzer, Joel. 1983. *Kuna Ways of Speaking: An Ethnographic Perspective*. Austin: University of Texas Press.

———. 1992. "Ethnography of Speaking." In *Folklore, Cultural Performances, and Popular Entertainments: A Communications Centered Handbook*, ed. Richard Bauman, 76–80. Oxford: Oxford University Press.

Smith, Dorothy E. 2002. "Institutional Ethnography." In *Qualitative Research in Action: An International Guide to Issues in Practice*, ed. Tim May, 150–61. London: Sage.

———. 2005. *Institutional Ethnography: A Sociology for People*. Toronto: Alta Mira Press.

Snow, David A., and Leon Anderson. 1993. *Down on Their Luck: A Study of Homeless Street People*. Berkeley and Los Angeles: University of California Press.

Spradley, James P. 1979. *The Ethnographic Interview*. New York: Holt, Rinehart and Winston.

———. 1980. *Participant Observation*. New York: Holt, Rinehart and Winston.

Srinivas, Lakshmi. 2010. "Cinema Halls, Locality and Urban Life." *Ethnography* 11: 189–205.

Stacey, Judith. 1998. *Brave New Families: Stories of Domestic Upheaval in Late Twentieth Century America.* New York: Basic Books.

Stahl, Sandra Dolby. 1989. *Literary Folkloristics and the Personal Narrative.* Bloomington: Indiana University Press.

Stoddard, Kenneth. 1986. "The Presentation of Everyday Life: Some Textual Strategies for 'Adequate Ethnography.'" *Urban Life* 15:103–21.

Stoller, Paul. 1989. *The Taste of Ethnographic Things: The Senses in Anthropology.* Philadelphia: University of Pennsylvania Press.

Stone, Ruth M., and Verlon L. Stone. 1981. "Event, Feedback, and Analysis: Research Media in the Study of Music Events." *Ethnomusicology* 25:215–25.

Strauss, Anselm L. 1987. *Qualitative Analysis for Social Scientists.* Cambridge: Cambridge University Press.

Strauss, Anselm L., and Juliet Corbin. 1990. *Basics of Qualitative Research: Grounded Theory Procedures and Techniques.* Newbury Park, CA: Sage Publications.

Sudnow, David. 1967. *Passing On: The Social Organization of Dying.* Englewood Cliffs, NJ: Prentice Hall.

Tavory, Iddo, and Stefan Timmermans. 2009. "Two Cases of Ethnography: Grounded Theory and the Extended Case Method." *Ethnography* 10:243–63.

Taylor, Steven J., and Robert Bogdan. 1984. *Introduction to Qualitative Research Methods: The Search for Meanings.* 2nd ed. New York: John Wiley.

Tedlock, Dennis. 1979. "The Analogical Tradition and the Emergence of Dialogical Anthropology." *Journal of Anthropological Research* 35:387–400.

———. 1983. *The Spoken Word and the Work of Interpretation.* Philadelphia: University of Pennsylvania Press.

ten Have, Paul. 2004. "Ethnomethodology." Chapter 9 in Seale et al., *Qualitative Research Practice.*

Thorne, Barrie. 1980. "'You Still Takin' Notes?' Fieldwork and Problems of Informed Consent." *Social Problems* 27:284–97.

———. 1993. *Gender Play: Girls and Boys in School.* New Brunswick, NJ: Rutgers University Press.

Van Damme, Wilfried. 2003. "Western Philosophy and the Study of Aesthetics in African Cultures." *Thamyris/Intersecting* 11:95–106.

Van Maanen, John. 1978. "The Asshole." In *Policing: A View from the Street,* ed. Peter K. Manning and John Van Maanen, 221–38. Santa Monica, CA: Goodyear.

———. 1988. *Tales of the Field: On Writing Ethnography.* Chicago: University of Chicago Press.

Wacquant, Loic. 2002. "Scrutinizing the Street: Poverty, Morality, and the Pitfalls of Urban Ethnography." *American Journal of Sociology* 107:1468–1532.

———. 2004. *Body and Soul: Notebooks of an Apprentice Boxer.* New York: Oxford University Press.

Walker, Anne Graffam. 1986. "The Verbatim Record: The Myth and the Reality." In

Discourse and Institutional Authority: Medicine, Education, and Law, ed. Sue Fisher and Alexandra Dundas Todd, 205–22. Norwood, NJ: Ablex Publishing.

Warren, Carol A. B. 2000. "Writing the Other, Inscribing the Self." *Qualitative Sociology* 23:183–99.

———. 2001. "Gender and Fieldwork Relations." In Emerson, *Contemporary Field Research: Perspectives and Formulations*, 203–23.

Warren, Carol A. B., and Jennifer K. Hackney. 2000. *Gender Issues in Ethnography*. 2nd ed. Thousand Oaks, CA: Sage.

Warren, Carol A. B., and Tracy Xavia Karner. 2010. *Discovering Qualitative Methods: Field Research, Interviews, and Analysis*. 2nd ed. New York: Oxford University Press.

Wax, Murray L. 1980. "Paradoxes of 'Consent' to the Practice of Fieldwork," *Social Problems* 27:272–83.

Weitzman, Eban A., and Mathew B. Miles. 1995. *Computer Programs for Qualitative Data Analysis*. Thousand Oaks, CA: Sage.

West, Candace, and Don H. Zimmerman. 1987. "Doing Gender." *Gender and Society* 1: 125–51.

Whyte, William F. 1955/1993. *Street Corner Society: The Social Structure of an Italian Slum*. Chicago: University of Chicago Press.

Wilson, William A. 1986. "Documenting Folklore." In *Folk Groups and Folklore Genres: An Introduction*, ed. Elliott Oring, 225–54. Logan: Utah State University Press.

Wiseman, Jacqueline P. 1970. *Stations of the Lost: The Treatment of Skid Row Alcoholics*. Englewood Cliffs, NJ: Prentice Hall.

Wolcott, Harry F. 1990. *Writing Up Qualitative Research*. Newbury Park, CA: Sage Publications.

Wolf, Margery. 1992. *A Thrice-Told Tale: Feminism, Postmodernism, and Ethnographic Responsibility*. Stanford, CA: Stanford University Press.

Wolfinger, Nicholas H. 2002. "On Writing Field Notes: Collection Strategies and Background Expectancies." *Qualitative Research* 2:85–95.

Yitah, Helen. 2009. "'Fighting with Proverbs': Kasena Women's (Re)Definition of Female Personhood through Proverbial Jesting." *Research in African Literatures* 40(3): 74–95.

Yocom, Margaret R. 1990. "Fieldwork, Gender, and Transformation: The Second Way of Knowing." *Southern Folklore* 47:33–44.

Yoder, P. Stanley, ed. 1982. *African Health and Healing Systems: Proceedings of a Symposium*. Los Angeles: Crossroads Press.

Young, Alford A., Jr. 2008. "White Ethnographers on the Experiences of African American Men: Then and Now." In *White Logic, White Methods*, ed. Tukufu Zuberi and Eduardo Bonilla-Silva, 179–200. New York: Rowman & Littlefield.

Young, Jane M. 1988. *Signs from the Ancestors: Zuni Cultural Symbolism and Perceptions of Rock Art*. Albuquerque: University of New Mexico Press.

Zavella, Patricia. 1996. "Feminist Insider Dilemmas: Constructing Ethnic Identity with 'Chicana' Informants." In *Feminist Dilemmas in Fieldwork*, ed. Diane L. Wolfe, 138–69. Boulder, CO: Westview.

Index